SINISTER
TWILIGHT

ALSO BY NOEL BARBER

Black Hole of Calcutta

The Daughters of the Prince

The Fall of Shanghai

A Farewell to France

Lords of the Golden Horn

The Other Side of Paradise

Sakkara

Seven Days of Freedom

The Singapore Story

The Sultans

Tanamera

The War of the Running Dogs

The Week France Fell

The Weeping and the Laughter

A Woman of Cairo

SINISTER TWILIGHT

THE FALL OF SINGAPORE

NOEL BARBER

CASSELL

Cassell Military Paperbacks

Cassell
Wellington House, 125 Strand
London WC2R 0BB

First published by Collins 1968
This Cassell Military Paperbacks edition 2002

British Library Cataloguing-in-Publication Data
A catalogue record for this book is available from the
British Library

ISBN 0-304-36437-1

Printed and bound in Great Britain by
Cox & Wyman Ltd., Reading, Berks.

CONTENTS

ILLUSTRATIONS

Lt.-Gen. A. E. Percival (*Imperial War Museum*)

Lt.-Gen. H. Gordon Bennett (*Imperial War Museum*)

Marjorie Hudson (*Catherine Bell*)

Tim Hudson (*Catherine Bell*)

Gen. Sir Archibald Wavell inspects Singapore's defences (*Imperial War Museum*)

Key men from England, Australia, China, Thailand, Malaya and the Far East Command meet in conference at Singapore (*Imperial War Museum*)

Elgin Bridge, Singapore (*Paul Popper*)

"Lease and Lend" material from the U.S.A. arrives at Singapore Docks (*Imperial War Museum*)

"Transit Camp" among the rubber trees (*Imperial War Museum*)

Malayan rescue workers in Raffles Place (*Associated Press*)

The last days at Singapore—the evacuation of women and children (*Imperial War Museum*)

Native houses reduced to smouldering ruins after the Japanese bombers have passed over (*Imperial War Museum*)

General Percival on his way to surrender the British stronghold to Japanese General Yamashita (*Paul Popper*)

British prisoners in the hands of the Japanese after the surrender (*Paul Popper*)

For 'Jamie'

The one and only James Kinross, the novelist—remembering all the happy times we spent together and all the encouragement he gave me.

Japanese thrusts and routes with dates of occupation
Railways
Roads

SIMULTANEOUS JAPANESE LANDINGS
8th Dec. 1941; 0025 hrs.

Singora
Patani
Sadao
Jitra
Alor Star (13 Dec.)
Kota Bahru
Gurun
Sungei Patani
Kroh
Gong Kedah
Georgetown
PENANG
(Evacuated 16/17 Dec.)
Butterworth (16 Dec.)
(14 Dec.)
Grik (16 Dec.)
Kuala Krai
Selama (20 Dec.)
K. Trengganu (18 Dec.)
Port Weld
Taiping
Kuala Kangsar
K. Dungun
Ipoh (28 Dec.)
Kuala Lipis
Telok Anson (1 Jan.)
Jerantut
(1 Jan.)
Slim River (7 Jan.)
Amphibious Japanese landings (3/4 Jan.)
(9 Jan.) K. Kubu
Kuantan (31 Dec.)
Selangor
Bentong
Temerloh
Maran
Approximate position of sinking of Prince of Wales and 'Repulse'
Port Swettenham
Kuala Lumpur (13 Jan.)
Seremban
Gemas (15 Jan.)
Endau
Port Dickson
Labis
Mersing (26 Jan.)
Malacca
Yong Peng
Kluang
Muar (16 Jan.)
Batu Pahat
Kota Tinggi
(31 Jan.) Johore Bahru
SINGAPORE (15 Feb. 1942)

0   20   40   60   80   100 Miles
0   40   80   120   160 Kilometres

CAST OF PRINCIPAL CHARACTERS

The Civilians

FREDDY RETZ, a young American widow
PHILIP BLOOM, a doctor whom she married during the siege
THE REV. JACK BENNITT, of Singapore Cathedral
GEORGE HAMMONDS, a journalist
KAREN, his half-Siamese wife
'BUCK' BUCKERIDGE, of the Singapore Fire Brigade
LUCY, his wife
LESLIE HOFFMAN, a journalist
TIM HUDSON, of Dunlop Rubber Co. Ltd. and a Divisional
    Commander of Air Raid Precautions
MARJORIE, his wife
MEI LING, the Hudsons' amah
'WEE-WEE', a Chinese ARP warden working with Hudson
JIMMY GLOVER, Managing Director of the *Malaya Tribune*
JULIENNE, his French wife
M. C. HAY, Inspector of Mines
MARJORIE, his wife
DR. CICELY WILLIAMS, an English doctor

The Government

SIR SHENTON THOMAS, The Governor
LADY THOMAS, his wife
STANLEY JONES, Colonial Secretary
ROB SCOTT, a member of the War Council
A. H. DICKINSON, Inspector-General of Police
RT. HON. SIR ALFRED DUFF COOPER, Churchill's special envoy
GROUP CAPTAIN R. L. NUNN, Head of the Public Works
    Department
HUGH FRASER, Acting Colonial Secretary

The Military

AIR CHIEF MARSHAL SIR ROBERT BROOKE-POPHAM, Commander-in-
    Chief Far East
GENERAL SIR ARCHIBALD WAVELL, Commander-in-Chief, ABDA
    (American, British, Dutch, Australian) Command
REAR-ADMIRAL E. J. SPOONER, Senior Naval Officer

LT.-GENERAL A. E. PERCIVAL, General Officer Commanding, Malaya

AIR VICE-MARSHAL C. W. H. PULFORD, Senior RAF Officer

BRIGADIER IVAN SIMSON, Chief Engineer and Director-General of Civil Defence

LT.-GENERAL H. GORDON BENNETT, General Officer Commanding all Australian troops

The Opposite Camp

GENERAL TOMOYUKI YAMASHITA, Commander-in-Chief of all Japanese forces in Malaya

COLONEL MASANOBU TSUJI, Chief of Planning Staff in Malaya

ACKNOWLEDGEMENTS

My grateful thanks are due to the many people who made this book possible: Lady Thomas, widow of Sir Shenton Thomas, the Governor during the war, arranged for the embargo on her husband's unpublished private papers and diary extracts to be lifted for the first time. Brigadier Ivan Simson, the Chief Engineer and Director of Civil Defence in Singapore in 1942, made available to me his lengthy, detailed, unpublished reports. He also gave me many hours of his time. Mr. A. H. Dickinson, Inspector-General of Police, lent me police reports, papers, letters and gave me much of his time. Sir Robert Scott, Director of the Far Eastern Section of the Ministry of Information, and a member of the War Council in Singapore, gave me permission to use his unpublished notes, and also spent much time reading the manuscript for me. Mr. Hugh Bryson, Secretary of the British Association of Malaysia, was directly responsible for leading me to an extraordinary cache of several deed boxes containing invaluable accounts of particular aspects of the war, by authors who ranged from business men to the Acting Colonial Secretary. Many had been compiled during the first months of internment, concealed from the Japanese, and had hardly seen the light of day since.

I am also indebted to Dr. W. McGregor Watt, Director of Civil Medical Services in Singapore during the war, who corrected passages referring to the civilian nurses; and to Mr. James Leasor who made available to me a lengthy tape recording of General Percival's views just before the General died.

I am also indebted to the following (in alphabetical order) who lent me their diaries or notes, compiled at the time: The Rev. A. J. Bennitt; Mrs. Freddy Bloom; Mr. & Mrs. B. C. J. Buckeridge; Mr. & Mrs. 'Tim' Hudson; Mr. & Mrs. M. C. Hay; Mr. George Hammonds; Mr. Leslie Hoffman; Mr. C. T. Kitching (for the loan of his late father's diaries); Mr. 'Willie' Watt; Dr. Cicely Williams.

Mr. L. Newsom Davis, who worked closely with the late Governor, and Mr. C. W. Dawson, Minister of Defence at the time, both helped me considerably and made many invaluable suggestions after reading the manuscript, though I should make it clear that the opinions expressed by me are not necessarily shared by them, nor for that matter, by the many others who read the manuscript.

I should also like to thank Mr. John J. Tawney, Director of the Oxford University Colonial Records Project, for his help; the Superintendent of the Rhodes House Library, Oxford, for searching out important documents; the staff of the London Library for their unflagging zeal, and lastly, Donald Dinsley, for the many patient months he spent helping me with research.

An alphabetical bibliography of the books consulted, including those whose authors and publishers have kindly permitted me to use extracts, appear at the end of this volume.

Noel Barber
London & Singapore,
November 1965-October 1967

PART ONE

BEFORE

CHAPTER ONE

THE LAST DAY OF PEACE

Sunday, December 7, 1941

In the last uneasy days before its decades of peaceful, unhurried existence were to be shattered, there was no city in the world quite like Singapore. With the outbreak of war in Europe, the leisurely ways of a steaming, opulent Eastern city had been transformed overnight into a life of almost unseemly frenzy. A Europe in turmoil, a re-arming America, urgently clamoured for raw materials—and Malaya had over three million acres of rubber under cultivation, and produced half the world's tin. To the rubber planters and the tin miners, one thing only mattered—the desperate race to fill the holds of vessels impatiently lining the quays of Keppel Harbour.

Singapore was the focal point for this vast, expanding trade, for it was to this teeming, frenetic, humid port, 90 miles north of the equator, that the wagons rolled down the peninsula's ancient single-line railway, bearing their cargoes of crude rubber tapped by Tamils in lonely plantations sometimes 400 miles to the north near the Siamese border, or of tin dug by the Chinese from the mines that impinged like vast ant heaps on the jungles of central Malaya. First the railway reached the island—diamond shaped, measuring 26 miles across, 14 from north to south—which lay at the southern tip of Malaya, and was connected to the mainland by a causeway across the narrow Straits of Johore. From there the railway straddled the verdant island until it ended at the docks of the great sprawling city itself. The docks were at the southern tip of the island, but the southern boundary of the city stretched four miles along the sea, sometimes palm-fringed, sometimes an ugly span of docks, warehouses, cranes and shunting yards.

The sea was everywhere. Each street seemed to lead to a lapping water's edge, to ships shimmering on the fiery horizon, to the glimpse of a passenger liner in the outer roads attended by a flurry of sampans, to the square patched brown sails of junks, to a hardworked, battered, rusted freighter being loaded by an endless human conveyor belt of chanting coolies. Or if the streets did not lead to the sea, then they led to the Singapore River, the hub of the metropolis, which twisted through the heart of the city. Not a large river, but one alive with sampans on which entire families were born, lived and died; sampans packed so close to each other that one could see agile Chinese boatmen using them as stepping stones, hopping across the water without ever wetting a foot.

Down by the docks and the river—and the narrow streets clustering around them—a potent smell assailed the nostrils; the smell of the tropics, compounded of drains, swampland, of dried fish and a score of sweet spices that lay waiting to be unloaded from the junks which had sailed north from Bali, Java and the spice islands. Curiously, it was not ---pleasant; once smelled, it was never forgotten. To the planter or miner coming from up-country for a week-end in the city, the first whiff told him he had arrived as clearly as the big lettered sign on Singapore railway station. It was the smell of Singapore—the smell of an exciting, polyglot city built on swamp, where the heat and humidity pressed down day after day like a blanket; where half a million Malays, Chinese and Indians jostled in the gaudy, narrow streets while the European tuans drove past in their cars.

It was a city of extravagant contrasts. In Chinatown whole families pecked at their lunches with chop-sticks by the roadside. Lacquered ducks as flat as pancakes, birds' nests, sharks' fins, hung from shops that were little more than holes in the walls. Chinese hawkers cried their wares, loping along with the heavy containers of food dangling at both ends of the bending bamboo poles arched across bony shoulders. In every garish street coloured washing on poles jutted out like flags from the windows of the tall, flimsy buildings. This was China. A few blocks away the poles of washing vanished. The noise and bustle seemed to belong to another world, in streets filled with languid Indians in flapping shirt tails and women in vivid saris. The hectic frenzy of Chinese life had gone. The men squatted on their haunches or walked gently, almost indolently, often holding hands; the women sauntered by with their dressed-up children. Every pavement was daubed with the scarlet stains of betel nut, expertly spat out by incessant chewers. The smells had changed—

18

to peppers and curry and tropical fruits. Round the corner, the road became an Indian market, alive with shoppers in front of mounds of fruit spilling over into the street—mangoes, papayas, star fruit, lichees, pomelos, chillies.

Yet if there seemed to be no end to the colour and jumbled confusion of houses, fragile but swarming, the government and business sections of the city were entirely different, with the space and orderliness of a typical Colonial city. The narrow streets were replaced by spotless wide avenues with trim grass verges and sensuous flowers, or exotic flame or frangipani trees. Traffic policemen at every corner still wore basketwork 'wings' strapped across their backs, so they did not need to wave their arms in the incessant heat, but leisurely turned their feet to direct the cars. The slim spire of St. Andrews Cathedral rose from its island of cropped green, near the dome of the Supreme Court, and the ostentatious, soulless but gentlemanly government offices, white and clean and slightly forbidding, clustered together as though for protection. Raffles Hotel was a block away facing the sea, as the road turned along the waterfront, past the green padang of the Cricket Club, with its football and cricket pitches, tennis courts and bowling greens.

'White' Singapore was above all a beautiful city. Not only did the sea beckon at each corner, there were patches of green everywhere—sports grounds, golf courses, parks, gardens between straight streets leading out of the city to the island villages, where the gentle Malays lived on the edge of rubber or coconut plantations or by the sandy beaches with their fishing traps. It was as though the early planners had (with all their faults) striven to build some tangible copy of the life they had left behind in England, something to compensate for the wet heat from which nobody could escape. And somehow they had succeeded. Men sweated and cursed at the Colonial shibboleths which demanded collars and ties and limp white suits for office wear, dinner jackets or short white mess jackets (known as 'bum freezers') in the evenings, yet everyone loved the city with its tang of adventure, its noises, its smells, its leisurely life—and its opportunity of making a fortune. A man-made sentinel dominating the narrow waters between the China Seas and the Indian Ocean—and thus between east and west, between Asia and Europe—Singapore in those carefree days was irresistible.

With new wealth, with money to burn, new trade had

boomed. The skeleton-like rickshaw wallahs, each with a twist of dirty cloth round its taut neck, the veins showing, bobbed along Orchard Road carrying passengers to the Asian markets. The tiny eight-horsepower yellow Ford taxies buzzed past them, setting down men and women at the Cold Storage, a grand white building selling everything from 'French' bread freshly-baked each morning to Sydney Rock oysters flown in daily from Australia; to say nothing of row after row of tinned foods evoking nostalgia for England, for the next leave; sausages, baked beans, Irish stew, and for the children English ice cream which had the supreme quality of being 'safe'.

The heart of the city was Raffles Place and here, or in the adjoining Battery Road, you could buy the latest books at Kelly and Walsh, get an Elizabeth Arden 'facial' (very popular with Chinese ladies) at Maynards the chemists, or if you were bored, wait for friends in Robinson's new air-conditioned restaurant.

Everyone knew Robinson's, whose big new building dominated Raffles Place. Robinson's would sell a bottle of aspirin over the counter or send a motor lawn mower to a lonely planter up by the Siamese frontier. 'I'll meet you for coffee in Robinson's' was a catch phrase. In short, the place was an institution.

For the white man, life consisted of regular activities taken at a gentle pace. Nobody could hurry in a country where the temperature stayed around the nineties for most of the year. Work started early, finished around five o'clock. There were sports at the clubs before the sun set around 6.30 every day of the year. And after that, men would go home, past Government House in its grounds of a hundred acres, often to a big, old-fashioned bungalow in the outskirts; not pretentious, but big so as to give room for the hot air to circulate, and surrounded by a compound with its glimpses of attap huts, palms, broad green banana leaves, all giving the impression of up-country jungle far removed from any city. One of the peculiar charms of Singapore in those days was that the city never seemed to encroach on the outskirts. The dripping jungle foliage seemed to hang almost over the city, and at night the bellow of bullfrogs in the mangrove swamps kept some people awake. Even on the Bukit Timah Road, with its canal running down to the sea, you could pick orchids by the roadside. At the Tanglin

Club the occasional monkey would lope off beyond the tennis courts as members on the verandah gratefully downed their stengahs or Singapore gin slings after a day's work.

Money was plentiful but—long before the vogue of credit cards—nobody carried any cash, for under the 'chit' system everyone signed for anything from a tin of cigarettes to a new car. In one's own house, life was assisted by an array of Chinese boys and amahs, so that after tennis or 'volunteer' snooker at the Cricket Club, it was easy to phone home and order dinner for a dozen friends, secure in the knowledge that it would be ready in an hour, and that if there were not enough plates to go round, they would have been borrowed from neighbouring boys. (Guests often found themselves eating with their own knives and forks when invited out.)

Whisky, gin, cigarettes were cheap in a duty-free port. Strawberries and fresh roses arrived daily from the hills at up-country Cameron Highlands, smoked and fresh salmon from Australia. In those happy days Singapore was the last resort of yesterday in the world of tomorrow.

And this was especially true because the white man, the tuan, not only lived a life which the tropics of necessity made more than usually comfortable, he was also cocooned in a myth of utter security. It was not smugness, nor was it complacency. It went much deeper than that; it was an absolute conviction, carefully fostered by authority at home, even after Munich, even after September 1939, that nothing —nothing on earth—could ever disturb the peace of Britain's 'arsenal of democracy'. A mother might send her sons to fight in Europe, they might die in that distant war with Germany, but meanwhile life would go on in Singapore as it had done since Raffles snatched the magic island from under the noses of the Dutch in 1819 in order, as he said, 'to secure to the British flag the maritime superiority of the Eastern seas'.

Certainly, the Japanese were behaving belligerently, but after all, the evidence of security was there for all to see —and it was indisputable. The *Prince of Wales* and the *Repulse* had been rushed out to the empire's mightiest naval base (though without a carrier escort). The R.A.F. flew overhead. And across the length and breadth of the peninsula and island the troops stood to arms, thousands and thousands of men, all spoiling for a fight, and only disgruntled because they were convinced there would never be one.

People prepared for the worst, of course—'just in case'—for, however remote, Singapore still was a limb of a Britain at war. Volunteer nurses, air raid wardens, auxiliary firemen, local defence volunteers had trained for months. There had been practice brown-outs and sessions of bandage rolling. Men and women had volunteered for blood transfusions. Food for six months had been stored, medical supplies for two years. It had all been done with a will, yet it had sometimes been difficult for civilians to realise it was not just an exaggerated make-believe, for there were few visible signs of impending war. No one could be whipped into a state of anxiety when there were hardly any shelters in the streets. Despite the war raging in Europe, there was virtually no rationing. The clubs and hotels dispensed unlimited drink. There was dancing every evening, bathing every Sunday, either at the Tanglin or Swimming Clubs, or on the beaches facing Johore less than a mile across the Straits—a shore to be defended, but as yet unmarked by a single pill box or roll of barbed wire. True, one saw large numbers of troops, but to the civilians it seemed they had no sense of urgency. The officers dressed for dinner in their best blues; the 'other ranks' went dancing, souvenir-hunting, or queued up at Mr. Mimatsu's, the Japanese photographer behind Raffles Hotel, who with eager hisses offered cut-rate photos of groups of soldiers to be sent home to wives or sweethearts. To the European civilians it was like living in a big garrison town during peace-time manœuvres.

This mood had spread throughout Malaya. It touched not only the 18,000 Europeans—half of them women and children—in Malaya, but also the Asians who had been caught up in the 'fortune fever'. For the polyglot population included 2,000,000 Malays, almost as many Chinese—who concentrated on trade, many at that time having no real roots in the country—and 1,000,000 Indians and Tamils, who worked on the rubber estates and the railways, plus Armenians, Arabs, Javanese, Burmese. Malaya absorbed them all tolerantly. But to them war was not only unlikely, it was an event they did not even comprehend. Britain had never conquered Malaya, it had bought its first footholds—and for over a century it had taught the once-warlike Malays the arts of peace. War to the people of Malaya was a phenomenon that was completely mystifying, for there had never been a military governor, no occupying army (apart from a small garrison in Singapore) and the whole country was 'ruled' by a police force which employed less than 200 British officers.

And just to make doubly sure that nobody became apprehensive, politicians and military leaders reiterated almost daily—and with the same insistence displayed by Chamberlain after Munich—that there would be no war with Japan. It was all very confusing. And it was even more difficult to forget iat next morning there was rubber to be tapped, tin to be m.ied, ships to be loaded—and money to be made.

This was Singapore on December 7, 1941. No wonder that for those who lived there, it was a city on the edge of paradise; and no wonder that with their blinkered eyes, they could not realise that it was a city on the brink of war.

On this Sunday morning, Jimmy Glover, the shrewd Yorkshire-born managing director and editor of the *Malaya Tribune*, was on the balcony of Dulverton, his house at Holland Park outside the city, when his phone rang. Glover had worked his way to the top during fifteen years in Malaya. In his forties, he was a man who, through the *Tribune*, championed the cause of the Chinese, and he was a man unafraid of authority. He was, however, afraid of the future, as the Sunday edition of his newspaper showed, for across its front page in black type stared the ominous headline '27 Japanese transports sighted off Cambodia Point'. Cambodia Point was at the southern tip of Indo-China, and the ships were, according to the details that followed, steaming west —towards the east coast of Malaya or southern Siam. Glover had hesitated before printing the story, for he had no wish to spread alarm, but this news was too significant to be suppressed, particularly when read in conjunction with an official announcement telling people not to travel, and urging those on holiday to return home. Glover wondered 'how long the peace and serenity which I had come to regard as my right in Malaya would last.' The telephone stammered again and Julienne, his French wife, called to him, 'For you, Jimmy.'

To Glover's astonishment Air Chief Marshal Sir Robert Brooke-Popham, Commander-in-Chief of the Far East, was on the other end of the line—in person, and very angry. Before Glover could edge a word in, he complained bitterly about the *Tribune*'s 'pessimistic view of the Far East situation',

'I consider it most improper to print such alarmist views at a time like the present,' he snorted. 'The position isn't half so serious as the *Tribune makes out*.'

'That's not fair,' retorted Glover. 'The news was released by Reuter's and passed by the censor. To me,' he added, 'the presence of those Japanese transports off Cambodia Point means war.'

Glover managed to keep his temper until Brooke-Popham had rung off. Then he and Julienne got out the car and drove to play their part in what had become almost a weekly rite—Sunday morning drinks at the Sea View Hotel.

Not far from Glover's house, in a bungalow requisitioned for four British officers, another man was reading the significant headline—and he, too, was filled with foreboding. Brigadier Ivan Simson, Chief Engineer, Malaya Command, was destined to become deeply involved in the siege of Singapore, not only as a leading military figure, but ironically as a civilian too. Simson had been posted to Malaya only four months previously with instructions from the War Office to improve and add to the fixed defences in the area—only to find himself blocked by military minds which seemed uninterested in everything he proposed. At 52 Simson was a professional soldier of long standing with a distinguished record. He was handsome, straight-backed, with a trim military moustache —and a restlessness that always urged him to be doing something. He had travelled 6,000 miles across the length and breadth of Malaya by plane, by car, even at times on horseback. He knew more of the country and terrain than any other soldier—and more about the lack of defences.

Only a few days previously he had received the shock of his life. When visiting formations up-country he had been struck by the ignorance of troops on the best methods of dealing with enemy tanks. Yet he knew that large quantities of official War Office pamphlets giving non-technical advice had been sent from London before he took over his job.

He had found the pamphlets. Hundreds and hundreds of pamphlets, still lying, neatly tied in bundles, in the cupboards at military headquarters. They had been there for months, since the day they arrived.

Simson had been so appalled that he had sought out General Percival and asked for permission to compile quickly a new condensed leaflet on the subject. Percival had agreed—though like most military leaders in Malaya, he did not think the

Japanese would use tanks. Simson was convinced they would and had gone ahead. But only just in time, for the last leaflets had been printed only twenty-four hours previously.

Now it was Sunday morning—and there was no time to linger over the black type of the *Tribune*. Nor would there be any swimming for him this Sunday. Simson drove down to his office at Fort Canning. It would take the best part of Sunday to organise a Malaya-wide distribution of the only instructions Allied troops were ever likely to get on the best way of dealing with the tanks Simson was certain would soon be rumbling down the peninsula.

By far the most popular place for drinks on Sunday morning was the Sea View Hotel, a couple of miles or so out of Singapore on the east coast road. It not only faced directly on to the sea, laced with the long, spidery lines of Malay fishing traps and the low, hot green islands beyond; but in the curious way that a place will catch on—and so be popular one day, but shunned the next—this unlikely venue, with its pillared terrace and lofty dome in the centre, had become identified in the minds of Singaporeans with Sunday morning drinks at the local pub back home in England. Home always tugged the emotions in Singapore, but never more than on Sunday mornings, when one had time to think (and inevitably drink) while bridging the mental as well as physical void between breakfast and a large curry tiffin.

It was a fine hot day by the time the Glovers got there. The violins of the orchestra struggled through 'palm court' selections from Ivor Novello and Disney's *Snow White*. As Jimmy glanced round, the Chinese boys, balancing trays of gimlets, stengahs or Tiger beer, slithered from table to table. It was stiflingly hot before the monsoon. The sun penetrated everywhere, and one could hardly touch the wooden tables. The men—in their Sunday 'uniform' of open-necked shirts and shorts—wiped away the sweat appearing at their necks every time they gulped a drink or made the physical effort of grabbing for the chit to sign (the worst insult in Singapore was to describe a man as 'pencil shy'). The women— many also in shorts—fanned themselves as they gasped for air and with minute handkerchiefs dabbed at the beads of moisture on their foreheads as they leaned across to talk to their neighbours, their fretting children left behind with amahs at home or at the Swimming Club.

Every table was occupied and everyone seemed to know everyone else. There was a great deal of waving and beckoning and invitations to share the small, round, crowded tables facing the sea. Glover waved to Freddy Retz (Freddy being short for Elfrieda), a New Yorker of 27 and a widow, whose husband had died a year or so previously in Penang and who had drifted down to Singapore to escape painful memories. She was not a 'typical' American, though she had the good figure, the long elegant legs and even white teeth that are the hallmark of her race. Beside her sat a major in the Royal Army Medical Corps, a South African called Philip Bloom, a gentle, intelligent man with a crinkly smile, who was obviously more than normally 'interested' in Freddy. Leaning across from the next table to talk to her was George Hammonds, assistant editor of the *Tribune*, with his beautiful Eurasian wife. Tall but not gangling, with serious eyes behind spectacles, and forever clutching a round fifty tin of Players, George was one of those characters every polyglot city produces. A man everybody knew, part of the middle stream of the city, the sort of man who could get you a room at Raffles when there was no room to be had. Policemen, parsons, pimps—everybody knew George, with his slightly hesitant voice, and everybody was envious of him when they first saw Karen, his wife.

She sipped an orange juice, uncomfortably aware that most of the young officers lounging round the nearby tables were greedily eyeing her—for her Danish father and Siamese mother had produced a startling mixture of two handsome races, a firm Danish chin with wide, enormous soft pools of eyes framed by high cheekbones; the tall figure of the Viking with the slow effortless movement of the Asian. She was stunningly beautiful. George Hammonds, now 35, had fallen madly in love with her when he arrived in Singapore ten years previously, had married her right away and cheerfully resigned from the Tanglin Club, an all-white stronghold where her presence was unwanted.

By now the Sea View was packed. Latecomers were being turned away, for the moment had arrived when the orchestra on its stage struck up the resounding chord for which all had been waiting. As the starling-like chatter ceased abruptly, everyone picked up small, rectangular cards placed on the tables each Sunday and bearing the verses and chorus of 'There'll always be an England'.

26

This Sunday sing-song before lunch had become a ritual among the British inhabitants, and as silence fell, another chord gave the drinkers their final cue. Then the orchestra, almost with the reverence of an organist in church, started the first verse. By the time the chorus had been reached every single man and woman was lustily singing the cheap, sentimental words,

> There'll always be an England,
> And England will be free,
> If England means as much to you,
> As England means to me.

It was as if the throaty, out-of-tune voices united everyone briefly in a burst of shared loneliness; not only the civilians, but the soldiers sprinkled among them, all of them 8,000 miles or more away from the last raid on London, the fighting in North Africa, the Russians defending the gates of Moscow. George Hammonds was not sentimental but 'the syrupy song brought a lump to the throat' as everybody sang so far away from a war which distance had made incomprehensible; and on this Sunday unknowingly, unwittingly, 'There'll always be an England', was more; it was a swan song to peace and a way of life, though hardly anyone seemed to realise it, for a curious light plays on this last Sunday. The diaries and papers that were later to be filled with emotion and opinion, with frustration and bitterness, give no real clue to how people felt, except to make it abundantly clear by omission that all sense of apprehension was absent.

A mile or so away, near St. Andrews Cathedral, the Rev. Jack Bennitt summed it up in his diary as 'another hot fine day', and apart from noting that 'I did a terrible thing this morning—slept till twenty to seven when I was supposed to celebrate at the Cathedral at ten to'—little else was worth recording. To everybody it was an 'ordinary day'. 'I suppose I went for a swim.' 'We must have had a curry tiffin—we always did on Sunday.' 'I think we went to the flicks.' Nobody remembers doing anything special, though the Governor noted in his diary, 'Up at 4 a.m. for urgent cable from Colonial Office. Worked all a.m.' Now he was preparing for a luncheon party for eight. George Hammonds was looking forward to a game of snooker at the Cricket Club, Jimmy and Julienne

Glover to a swim at Tanglin Club. It was, in fact, one Sunday like a hundred others, and with the monsoon ready to break, the lucky chance of a fine day stuck in people's memories more than any other single fact.

None realised this was a Sunday nobody in Singapore would ever forget; for this was not only the last day of peace but of an era of history.

'Come on!' cried George Hammonds to Freddy Retz, 'let the second chorus rip!' and hundreds of lusty voices swelled out as they reached the words they knew by heart,

> There'll always be an England,
> And England will be free.

CHAPTER TWO

THE FIRST DAY OF WAR

Monday, December 8

At 1.15 a.m. precisely, while Singapore slept, a telephone call awoke the Governor, Sir Shenton Thomas, and banished all thoughts of sleep. General A. E. Percival, General Officer Commanding, Malaya, speaking from military headquarters at Fort Canning with agitation and urgency in his voice, informed the Governor that the Japanese had begun landing operations at Kota Bahru, a coastal town on the east coast near the Siamese border.

'Well,' replied Shenton Thomas, 'I suppose you'll shove the little men off!' Then, still in his pyjamas, the Governor picked up the receiver of his direct 'green' telephone and told the police to begin the long-planned rounding up of all Japanese males. Awakening his wife and the servants, Thomas ordered coffee, and despatched a message to his Colonial Secretary warning him to stand by. Only when he had phoned several other departmental heads did the Governor scramble into a pair of slacks and an open-necked shirt, while his wife poured out a much-needed cup of coffee which they sipped on the large first-floor balcony of Government House where they normally breakfasted.

Here, for a few moments, they enjoyed their last glimpse

of Singapore at peace. Because Government House is built on a rise, the balcony offers a magnificent view, and as they sat there in the bright moonlight, the great glowing port and city were spread out before them, looking like one of those old-fashioned, slightly indistinct ᵍ·ey etchings. The lights of the streets blinked in the hot air, and towards the centre it was possible to distinguish the silhouettes of the Cathay Building (Singapóre's only skyscraper) and the white Municipal Buildings in a ring of brighter light. Beyond, the moon played on the still harbour crowded with dozens of vessels of all sizes.

On this tropical night it was very beautiful, and if either had any fears, they said nothing; and, the coffee finished, the Governor told his wife to go back to bed. Tomorrow would be a busy day, but there was nothing anybody could do now, for the war was still 400 miles away.

Shenton Thomas had at this time been Governor for seven years after an honourable, if unexciting, career in the Colonial Service, and he was now approaching the time of retirement. Of average height, he was beginning to put on a little weight, but in a way this suited him, especially in his starched drill uniform with its white cockaded topee. He rather prided himself on 'being easy to get on with'. He liked being liked. He had always believed that it was the duty of the white man to look after the interests of 'the natives', and though he appreciated the trappings of high office (which included a yacht), he was not pompous. If he had a fault, it was a tendency to be over-optimistic.

He had inherited many administration headaches in the matter of civil government, for, as Governor, Shenton Thomas ruled one of the most complicated constitutions in the British Empire. In 1941 Malaya comprised the Straits Settlements of Singapore, Malacca, Penang (with Province Wellesley on the mainland opposite) which formed a British colony. But Shenton Thomas was also concerned with the Federated States of Malaya—Perak, Selangor, Negri Sembilan and Pahang. A Federal government at Kuala Lumpur administered their general policy, but in many respects each was self-governing. If this were not enough, there were also the Unfederated States of Johore, Trengganu, Kelantan, Kedah and Perlis—each governed by its own autocratic Sultan with a British adviser, and incorporated in the Empire by separate treaties. As Governor of the Straits Settlements and High

29

Commissioner for both the Federated and Unfederated States, Shenton Thomas often had to deal with eleven separate governments before an agreement affecting Malaya as a whole could be reached.

As Singapore slept on, there was nothing else the Governor could really do at that time of night. He could hardly rouse the city and alarm his people, for after all the Japanese at Kota Bahru were 400 miles away and might well have been driven back into the sea before dawn. And his position was somewhat anomalous. For though he bore the courtesy rank of Commander-in-Chief, he had no more military authority than his King, who enjoyed a similar title. He might have become highly unpopular with the military, who had at this moment become the real masters, had he acted without consulting them.

Below the verandah the grass, bathed in moonlight, looked so inviting that Shenton Thomas descended the broad staircase (so magnificent that 'descended' is about the only appropriate word) and strolled out through an equally pretentious porch on to the lawns in front of Government House. He was still pacing between the flower beds when at four in the morning the telephone rang again. Air Vice-Marshal C. W. H. Pulford, who commanded the RAF, wanted to speak to the Governor. He had news as terse and frightening as Percival's. Hostile aircraft were approaching Singapore. They were already within 25 miles of the city. The Governor had barely time to telephone the Harbour Board and the Air Raid Precautions before the first bombs came crashing down at exactly 4.15 a.m.

It took Jimmy Glover less than five minutes to get his car out of the garage and set off with Julienne for the *Malaya Tribune*, in Anson Road near the docks. The journey presented no difficulty for the street lamps were on. Orchard Road was a blaze of light. So was military headquarters at Fort Canning. As they approached the centre of the city, the arc lamps picking out the new law courts and the Municipal buildings shone even more brightly; so did the illuminated clock tower of the Victoria Memorial Hall. By the time they reached the Cricket Club padang, the waterfront had become crowded with people, mostly Chinese, watching the flashes of gunfire. By Fullerton Building an ambulance swerved past them into Battery Road; a fire engine clanged
30

along Collyer Quay to the dock area, chasing the red glow of a fire.

The raid, by seventeen planes, was not big and, possibly because the street lights remained on, thousands of bewildered Chinese, Tamils, Malays—together with hundreds of Europeans—refused to believe this was anything but another practice alert. An Englishwoman who lived above her dress shop near Raffles Place had been hurled out of bed by the blast from a bomb, but when she phoned the police and cried, 'There's a raid on!' the officer soothed her by saying it must be a practice; at which she retorted, 'If it is, they're overdoing it—Robinson's has just been hit!'

The Reverend Bennitt was convinced for most of the night that it was 'not the real thing'. He was an ARP warden, and when the guns started he had dressed quickly ('leaving off the dog collar for this sort of job') and reported to his post at Yoch Eng school near Kallang airfield, where he and his fellow wardens decided, as he noted in his diary, that 'it was a good idea to give us an unrehearsed practice as realistic as possible. The only thing that spoilt the realism was the lack of black-out.'

Long before dawn, the raid was over. Sixty-one people had been killed and 133 injured. Most of the bombs had fallen in Chinatown, though one had scored a direct hit on Robinson's new air-conditioned restaurant in Raffles Place, and another had shaken the police headquarters in New Bridge Road, where 'Dickie' Dickinson, Inspector-General of Police, was going about his methodical task of seizing 45 suspicious Japanese fighting vessels and rounding up every one of the 1,200 Japanese on whom he could lay his hands—(including Mr. Mimatsu, the 'official' photographer to the forces, who it transpired was a World War One colonel seconded to Singapore to photograph troops).

Dickinson 'called it a night' around seven a.m. and drove home for a shower and breakfast. So did George Hammonds, who with Glover had worked without a break through the night. At least it had been worth it for the *Tribune* had beaten the *Straits Times* by two hours with its special edition.

So it had. But the *Tribune* had not included one item of news which had not yet been released—news of such staggering and world-shattering significance that it was, by a strange twist of irony, to relegate the coming struggle in

Malaya to secondary importance in the global strategy of the war.

As Singapore prepared for its first breakfast at war, Churchill had gone into the dining-room at Chequers for dinner. Mrs. Churchill had not been feeling too well, and did not come down for the meal, but sitting with the Prime Minister were Averell Harriman and John Winant from Washington. Churchill 'looked very grim and sat in complete silence'. Though news of the attack on Malaya had not reached him, he was certainly aware of the imminent dangers and was possibly depressed because he could see no clear hope that any such attack would automatically bring in the United States.

Just before nine o'clock, Churchill told Sawyers, the butler at Chequers, to bring in the portable radio (a $15 set which Harry Hopkins had given him). There was a moment or two of music—and then an anonymous voice warned listeners to stand by for important news.

One can picture the scene at Chequers as the three men, unsuspecting, sat in silence, waiting. And then it came—the news that was to change the fortunes of war and assure ultimate victory beyond all doubt. In a calm, grave voice, the BBC announcer told them that the Japanese had attacked Pearl Harbour. There were no details. That was all. But it was enough.

Incredibly, none of the three men had had the remotest idea of what to expect. The BBC had beaten Churchill's own intelligence service by hours, with news that came as a profound—and to Churchill an almost exhilarating—shock.

No wonder Churchill's first emotions bordered on something akin to elation. After months of cajoling, begging, bargaining with Roosevelt, the Japanese had brought the United States into the war.

And no wonder that when later that night news of the attack on Malaya came in over the air, it was dwarfed by the magnitude of what had happened at Pearl Harbour, by the profound implications of a disaster that had without warning changed the whole concept of the war.

Almost at the time Churchill was dining, the radio announced the same news—around breakfast time in Singapore. For George Hammonds, breakfast was not eaten that morning —at least, not while it was warm—for 'just as I was about to spear an egg' the radio murmuring by his side told him the news. He dropped his knife and fork, and 'the tiredness seemed to drop off me too'. It was the same with everyone. Freddy Retz was driving down to Raffles Place to look at the bomb damage when she was startled to see a friend run straight out in front of her car and shout, 'Hi! You're in the war!' Within moments the Japanese raid on Singapore and its implications had been forgotten, save by the curious Chinese who blocked Raffles Place and Battery Road. The electrifying news of Pearl Harbour dwarfed everything else —even the prospect of another raid that night, even the Japanese landings on the east coast of Malaya.

Singapore had its fair share of Americans, and by mid-morning, when work had started again, when the dust and debris had been cleared away, there was visible evidence of the new partnership in arms. Driving up Orchard Road on her way home, Freddy Retz espied one or two small American flags which had suddenly appeared as though out of nowhere, blossoming mysteriously from the windows of Chinese shops. By lunch-time George Hammonds and his friends were toasting their 'new allies' at the long bar at the Cricket Club. More than one bemused American had a hazy afternoon siesta without ever having been permitted to sign for a single drink. The entry of the United States into the war was received with profound relief, and the feeling of elation was doubtless reinforced by the first war communiqué issued from General Headquarters in Singapore. Briefly this announced that the first Japanese attempt to land at Kota Bahru had been repelled. A few hours later a second communiqué spread the story that only a few bombs had been dropped on an airfield outside the town without causing casualties. Crowding round the briefing officer for his copy of the communiqué, George Hammonds read the reassuring words: 'All surface craft are retiring at high speed, and the few troops left on the beach are being heavily machine-gunned.'

Hammonds had already been tipped off that military operations in the north were not going as well as had been hoped, so he read the words with a certain scepticism, but to an uninformed community of mingled races the official news of the repulse of the first Japanese attack did nothing but inspire confidence.

After all, the long, narrow Malay peninsula stretched 400

miles from the Siamese border to the Straits of Johore and Singapore Island; a backbone of granite mountains rising to 7,000 feet zig-zagged down its centre. Four-fifths of the country was covered with dense, tropical jungle—the rain forests.

The Japanese had landed on the east coast, with its silvery beaches, but with poor roads leading due south from Kota Bahru. With the first monsoon rains already drenching the countryside no troops could hope to advance southwards through this impassable terrain. Nor did it seem possible to armchair critics that the Japanese could strike westwards on the single road from Kota Bahru across the neck of the peninsula where they knew they could find better roads and railways in the west. For northern Malaya was crowded with troops, and RAF fighters and bombers ready to pick out enemy troop concentrations and slaughter them. For months they had been eagerly awaiting just such an opportunity as this; a moment to demonstrate the superiority in battle of the white man over the Asian. How often had it been drummed into them—and the civilians too—that it was one thing for the Japanese to fight the Chinese, but wait till they came in contact with British steel! It would be vastly different for the Japanese who (despite World War One) had hardly come face to face with white forces since the Battle of Port Arthur in 1905, when they had only been matched against a demoralised, corrupt force of Czarist Russians.

And now, what had happened? A tiny enemy force had attacked an isolated British outpost—well, that sort of thing was bound to happen, but they would pay the inevitable price for such rash folly.

Indeed, so graphic was the wording of the communiqué that a visual picture sprang immediately to mind, particularly among the Asians. It was not difficult for them to imagine the moonlit beach, with a few khaki-clad Japanese left bewildered to their fate by cowardly comrades who were bolting 'at high speed' in their boats. And since this came direct from military sources it presumably was what they wished the civil population to believe. Why otherwise should they issue a communiqué which was so manifestly misleading? Of course the surface craft were retiring 'at high speed' (a phrase which would give the simple Asian the impression they were running away); why should they dawdle? The Japanese had landed their troops successfully, and were naturally returning to their base as quickly as possible.

The truth was significantly different. The beaches at Kota Bahru had been bathed in bright moonlight when shortly after midnight three transports anchored two miles offshore. Almost immediately the sparsely held defences were being shelled by the attacking warships. Within the hour the first Japanese landing craft—which had proved difficult to launch in a heavy swell—were making for the shore. The defenders fought magnificently and though the Japanese captured two strong points before dawn after heavy hand-to-hand fighting, this first and crucial battle in the Malayan campaign was by no means lost until everything was changed by a sudden disaster. British forces were still holding the vital airfield outside the town when a rumour swept the lines that the Japanese had broken through and were at the perimeter. It was quite untrue, though 'the passage of stray bullets probably gave credence to it'. Within a few minutes, some unauthorised person—never to this day identified—gave instructions to evacuate the airfield. Though two senior officers made a rapid reconnaissance and proved the rumour false, it was too late. Everybody bolted by any vehicle they could grab. In their terror they did not even destroy the stocks of bombs, the petrol, or make the runways unusable. Within a matter of hours Kota Bahru was in enemy hands. It was an ominous preface to the panic and disorder to come.

The bare bones of the situation were that the High Command had been caught on the hop, just as thousands of miles away the Americans had suffered a similar fate at Pearl Harbour, and the High Command naturally enough was doing its utmost to cover up in the hope of better news to come.[1]

But then, in these early days, even the High Command did not realise that the Japanese invasion of Kota Bahru, under the over-all direction of General Yamashita—the man destined to conquer Singapore—was only one of the four prongs of a carefully timed attack, which had been decided upon in Tokyo as far back as November 7. So vast is the Pacific

[1] This was borne out by General Wavell, who in 1948 admitted to Shenton Thomas that 'the original sin' for the lack of preparation must be placed on the heads of the military, who, Wavell was convinced, never really expected a Japanese invasion or prepared properly for it.

that differing local time zones tend to make nonsense of comparisons, but by the clocks in Tokyo the Japanese attacked Pearl Harbour, Malaya, Singora (in Siam) and Hong Kong within a few hours of each other in the early hours of December 8—Malaya at 2.15 a.m., Pearl Harbour at 3.25 a.m., Singora at 4 a.m., and Hong Kong at 8.30 a.m. When translated into local Pacific times, however, Pearl Harbour was attacked at 7.55 a.m. on the 7th and Malaya at 12.45 a.m. on the 8th—despite the fact that there was only an hour and ten minutes between the two. The timing of the attack on Kota Bahru was ironically determined only because it was Sunday in Pearl Harbour, when the Japanese expected most of the U.S. Fleet to be in harbour.

Of all this the civilians in Singapore knew nothing—in fact, after they had read the communiqués the news looked good on the first Monday of war, even though a number of uneasy questions were already being asked. What for instance had happened to the street lights during the raid? Why had they not been put out? And why hadn't the British night-fighters gone into action? Since the High Command must obviously have known about the Japanese landings shortly after one o'clock, and had been presumably on the alert, how had it been possible for Japanese bombers to penetrate to within 25 miles of Singapore without any advance warnings?

These questions could hardly have been answered at the time without seriously undermining public confidence, and even to this day they have never been properly answered, though what had actually happened was so simple (and in its way understandable) that official reticence at the time is a little hard to understand.

The actual situation had been as follows: Pulford of the RAF had warned the Governor at four a.m. that hostile aircraft were approaching Singapore, which gave Shenton Thomas only 15 minutes to alert the city. Yet Air Vice-Marshal Maltby, Pulford's 'number two', later admitted that the RAF had had 30 minutes' warning of the raid. Nobody has ever explained the mystery of the last 15 minutes. With only 15 minutes' warning it would have been impossible to order a crash black-out in Singapore. Part of the city was lit by gas lamps operated by the men with old-fashioned poles. Some districts had their own electric installations. There was no central switch, and in any event, the ARP was not on a

36

war footing. Its leaders were in bed asleep—as on any other night of peace. And it also was true that all the 'top brass' —the Commander-in-Chief, the Commanders of the three services, the Governor, the Colonial Secretary, all spent hours after one a.m. discussing the landings at Kota Bahru—and not one of them thought of ordering a black-out, because not one of them thought a raid was remotely possible, since the nearest Japanese airfields were 600 miles distant in Indo-China.[2]

Since the raid was made by 17 Japanese planes, many people in Singapore felt that a few night fighters taking off from the main airfield of Seletar could have quickly broken up the attack. Unknown to them, three Buffalos of the Royal Australian Air Force actually had been alerted and warmed up. The pilots had been eager to take on what one of them was later to describe as 'the most perfect night-fighter target which I have ever seen'. Permission to take off was, however, refused at the last moment by RAF headquarters, apparently because the RAF did not trust the AA gunners, some not yet blooded in warfare, and feared they might in their enthusiasm have shot at our planes. So night fighters did not go up.

The main question, however, which lingered deeply on this first day of war was the distressingly obvious lack of shelters. Most of Singapore had been built so close to sea level, and on such marshy ground, that deep shelters were held to be virtually impossible. Even the most shallow slit trenches filled rapidly with water and provided breeding grounds for mosquitoes. In happier days it had almost been a joke that when a cricket match was about to begin on the Cricket Club padang, the captain who had won the toss invariably elected to bat if it was low tide, but chose to bowl if the tide was lapping against the high water mark.

Several government committees had debated the shelter question thoroughly, but it is hard to escape the feeling that the very real problems had served in the 12 months preceding war as excuses for misguided policies. Swampy ground, said the government, made deep shelters impossible;[3] slit

[2] On his way to police headquarters, Dickinson, the Inspector-General of Police, had noticed that even Fort Canning, the Military headquarters, was a blaze of light.
[3] This is a fallacy. There is today a large underground car park in 'swampy' Raffles Place.

trenches were breeding grounds for mosquitoes. But there were many who were thoroughly disgusted by the official government attitude, who felt that in a raid it was better to dive into a trench at the risk of catching malaria; who felt that even if deep shelters might be impossible, at least the government could have put up blast walls in the streets. Instead there were virtually no shelters for the ordinary people, especially in Chinatown. And this was to result in thousands of deaths.

But that was in January, the month of the bombs.

CHAPTER THREE

THE WEEK OF DISASTER

Tuesday, December 9—Tuesday, December 16

George Hammonds was not a man given to swearing, but as he read the communiqué which the Tamil messenger had just handed to him in the *Tribune* office he let it flutter down on his desk and said blankly, 'What a pack of bloody lies!'

It was shortly after ten o'clock on the Tuesday morning. Leslie Hoffman, who worked in the *Tribune* newsroom, was sitting opposite. He smiled faintly, for it took a great deal to make George Hammonds angry.

'It's an Order of the Day,' explained George bitterly. 'I can't believe it—I can't believe anybody could deliberately tell so many lies. Here! Read it.'

Hoffman read over the more important passages: 'We are ready. We have had plenty of warning and our preparations are made and tested. . . . We are confident. Our defences are strong and our weapons efficient. Whatever our race, and whether we are now in our native land or have come thousands of miles, we have one aim and one only. It is to defend these shores, to destroy such of our enemies as may set foot on our soil. . . . What of the enemy? We see before us a Japan drained for years by the exhausting claims of her wanton onslaught on China. . . Let us all remember that we here in the Far East form part of the great campaign for the preservation in the world of truth and justice and freedom.'

George wiped the sweat from his neck and poured out

two glasses of the ice-cold, fresh lime juice he always kept in a Thermos on his desk. Both he and Hoffman knew much more of the truth than the average civilians—including the incredible fact that this grandiose proclamation had actually been prepared six months previously.

'They say it was to give them time for translations,' said George. 'We could have done the whole job in the office in a couple of days.'

Hoffman was a slim, handsome young man of 26, who was to have a big future in Malaya. Perhaps aided by his mixed blood—his father had come from Ceylon—he had an instructive intuition where British officialdom was concerned, and though the authors of this document still remain obscure, Hoffman immediately put his finger on one salient point. Its condescending note, its patent obliviousness of the true situation, could only mean that it had come from the 'Whitehall wallahs'. It bore their 'trademark'. Official spokesmen had made it abundantly clear to men like Hoffman or Hammonds at off-the-record briefings that their policy had been to avert war with Japan by treating the Japanese with 'kid gloves', while at the same time deliberately exaggerating our military strength to make them hesitate in case the first line of policy failed. Even Brooke-Popham, the Commander-in-Chief, had been forced to endorse this 'line of attack'. Hammonds had toured the island and Malaya time after time. He had seen for himself that Whitehall's boast of an impregnable fortress, a powerful fleet, highly trained troops, modern aircraft, was nothing but a myth.

Barely a week previously the Navy had been on show when the *Prince of Wales* and the *Repulse* had arrived, with not a carrier to guard them. Indeed, all that could be mustered were three cruisers, four destroyers, and some smaller craft. Few people on the island realised that these two great warships had been ordered to Singapore by Churchill against the express advice of the Admiralty, who had urged him to despatch instead a larger fleet of older battleships. Churchill, however, had insisted on sending the new ships because of 'the tremendous political effect of a really modern ship in the Far East'. He had at least agreed that they should have air support and the carrier *Indomitable* had been detailed to attend them. Unfortunately she had run aground just as she was about to sail for Far Eastern waters. Notwithstanding this setback to his plans, Churchill had insisted that the *Prince of*

Wales and *Repulse* should sail for Singapore—without air cover.

Hammonds had also seen a good deal of the soldiers who constituted the garrison. There were over 88,000 of them, who crowded the Singapore dance halls when on leave. On several tours up-country he had found only a few who were 'jungle trained' among the 19,600 British, 15,200 Australians, 37,000 Indians and 16,000 locally enlisted Asians. And there was not a single tank on the island.

Yet few people in Singapore knew this. Only that morning Hammonds had overheard Karen telling their eight-year-old daughter, Barbara, the war would be over in a couple of weeks. She probably felt—as thousands did—that since the jungle was 'impassable', the Japanese would have to launch a seaborne assault against Singapore, and could never survive against the great 15-inch guns that faced out to sea. In fact some of these guns (contrary to popular misconception) did have a limited traverse, but they were still totally ineffective against land targets as their only ammunition consisted of armour-piercing shells. Even worse, the supporting 9.2-inch guns had only 30 rounds each. Since Whitehall reckoned that—if invested—Singapore would have to hold out for six months before naval relief could arrive, this meant that in the event of a siege the gunners would be in the ludicrous position of being able to fire only one shell each six days.

And as for the communiqué's boast that 'our defences are ready', George had actually taken the children bathing a couple of weeks previously, choosing a spot they loved on the north shore—and they hadn't seen so much as a strand of barbed wire, a pill-box, or a single trench. Just Johore, opposite.

Had Hammonds known of the desperate plight of the RAF, he would have been even more shocked; he had had his doubts when watching the ancient Wildebeeste planes with their old-fashioned open cockpits; he had wondered why members of the Singapore Flying Club had dubbed the Buffalos the 'peanut specials'. Yet, after all, Brooke-Popham had only a week previously told Hammonds at a conference that, 'We can get on all right with the Buffalos here. They are quite good enough for Malaya.' And after all, Brooke-Popham was an RAF type. He should know.

In fact, instead of the 366 first-line aircraft which Whitehall had promised Malaya 'by the end of 1941', the RAF could only call on a shop-soiled, bedraggled assortment of 141 operational aircraft, mostly obsolete or obsolescent.[1] Of its 22 airfields on the peninsula, 15 had only grass runways. Of the four airfields on Singapore Island, Tengah had only been completed the day war broke out, when officers and men laid 400 yards of metal paving in 24 hours.

But of this, even George Hammonds—who was trained to keep his eyes open and was frequently trusted with 'off-the-record' information—knew very little.

He had, however, made it his business to study the history of vacillation, inter-service quarrels, stupidity throughout the years from 1925 when service chiefs in London had met to discuss the best ways of protecting Singapore's growing new naval base. It had all started then—with the Navy and Army wanting heavy fixed armaments to repel an attack from the sea, and the Air Force proposing the use of aircraft, which they claimed could attack an enemy before it came within range of the big guns.

The Navy and Army had won— and this had precipitated an inter-service quarrel so bitter that by 1929, when Hammonds attended military conferences, he had to travel five miles between the Army and RAF headquarters while, incredibly, the Navy headquarters were fifteen miles distant by road from the city. There was virtually no co-operation between the services. The Army had insisted that no enemy could ever advance by land down the Malay peninsula. The RAF had a totally different conception, and as early as 1936 had started constructing airfields up-country, without properly consulting the Army, which would have to defend them. The Army was furious. George remembered one angry brigadier shouting that 'Some of the bloody airfields can't even be defended. The damn fools have built them in the wrong places.'

This bitter quarrel was no doubt one reason why officially British Army chiefs stubbornly refused to admit that any Japanese force could ever advance down the Malay Peninsula. 'Officially'—for more than one British general in pre-war Malaya had sent reports back to Whitehall warning that such a course was possible. They had been quietly pigeon-

[1] This force was composed of 17 Hudsons, 34 Blenheim bombers, 27 Wildebeeste torpedo bombers, 41 Buffalos, 10 Blenheim night fighters, three Catalina flying boats, four Swordfish, five Sharks.

holed, not only 'to teach the RAF a lesson', but because the Navy threw its weight behind the Army. Right from the start the Navy had staked its reputation on the premise that any Japanese assault must come from the sea, and now it stuck to its useless guns—so much so that no one ever gave any serious thought even to defending the north shores of Singapore Island.

As the quarrelling continued, the picture to George Hammonds was one of 'unrelieved stupidity'. Even when war broke out in Europe, the services were still involved in inter-service disputes[2] or were in disagreement with the civil government.

The quarrel with the civil government had erupted into the open at one bitter conference where Hammonds had listened to the military demand conscription of civil labour, only to be told by the Governor that the Foreign Office insisted on priority for tin and rubber production. The 'FO' view was that Japan had been at war with China for over three years and was in no position to attack. 'The threat to Singapore should be regarded as remote, and nothing should interfere with Malaya's economic effort,' said the Foreign Office. As a result, strained relations between the services were to spread rapidly to a point where they also deteriorated into sharp antagonism between the military and the civilians.

In June 1940, the picture underwent a startling change with the collapse of France. Until this moment Britain had always relied on a French fleet in the Mediterranean to contain the Italian Navy, allowing British warships to patrol Far Eastern waters. Now Britain was dramatically faced with the need to keep her fleet in the Mediterranean, leaving the defence of Malaya to land and air forces.

At long last Whitehall turned to the RAF—they had no other choice—and gave a promise that 366 first-line aircraft would be available in Malaya by the end of 1941. They also decided—in October 1940—to do something about the 'mutual jealousy and mutual determination to avoid co-operation'[3] between the services, by appointing Air Chief Marshal Sir Robert Brooke-Popham Commander-in-Chief Far East.

Brooke-Popham was 63. He had served with the RAF in

---

[2] Even as late as 1939, there was, according to the official history *The War Against Japan,* 'insufficient consultation between the services in Singapore'.

[3] From *The War Against Japan.*

42

World War One, and in 1937 had become Governor of Kenya, only to be reinstated on the active list in 1939. The news of his appointment reached Singapore editors before his terms of reference were made public, and consequently the first brief announcement did much to cheer up those 'in the know', for the bitterness between the services was an open secret. This was exactly what was needed—a man of seniority to dominate the other personalities and heal the wounds between the services.

George Hammonds would never forget his sense of dismay, even stupefaction, at Fort Canning when he was told that Brooke-Popham, far from being overall commander, would have no control over the Navy; so that, with Britain fighting a desperate war for survival in Europe, Singapore discovered itself in the ludicrous position of having two Commanders-in-Chief, each responsible to a different authority in London, while the Combined Intelligence Bureau, on which each of the three services relied for information on Japanese intentions, troop movements and so on (and which should obviously have been under the jurisdiction of the C-in-C) remained under the control of the Navy.

Brooke-Popham, in fact, was nothing more than a buffer —the unkind might say an old butter.

By November 1940, Brooke-Popham had succeeded in setting up a GHQ with a principal staff of seven officers, with headquarters at the Naval Base. This certainly enabled him to keep in touch with his opposite number in the Navy and with the Combined Intelligence Bureau, but on the other hand, it meant that he was fifteen miles from the Army and RAF—and the very forces of which he was in command.

These headquarters were served by an intelligence service which hardly lived up to its name. Just before the Japanese attack George Hammonds had gone with several spare-time ARP wardens to a lecture, where an RAF officer had insisted that there was no need to man ARP stations at night as the Japanese pilots could not fly in the dark. On another occasion a Colonel Ward had given a lecture stressing the magnificent fighting qualities and the intensive jungle training of Japanese troops. He was not invited back to air his 'defeatist' views. Another instance of the intelligence service's abysmal talent for misinformation came six months before war broke out in Malaya, when the Navy had asked the Chiefs of Staff for some Hurricane fighters, and the

Vice-Chief of the Air Staff (on their advice) had retorted that Buffalo fighters 'would be more than a match for the Japanese aircraft, which were not of the latest type'.

This unfortunate appraisal was made only a month before a Japanese Zero had made a forced landing in China and details of its armaments, tankage, performance were passed to Whitehall. But 'this valuable report remained unsifted', with the consequence that when the first Buffalo planes found themselves facing Zeros in combat, the British pilots were still under the delusion they were flying the better machine.

Now war had come to Malaya. None of the promises had been fulfilled. Nor could they be now. Ships that should have routed the Japanese, bombers that could have devastated their convoys of troops, Hurricanes that could have blasted the Zeros out of the skies, tanks that could have matched Japanese tanks—all these had been sent to meet the enemy on other fronts.

No wonder that later, when the official history came to be written, *The War Against Japan* remarked gloomily, that 'the Naval Base at the Western Gateway of the Pacific, the keystone of British strategy in the Far East, was doomed before the war started.'

The first thing Freddy Retz did when America entered the war was to join the Medical Auxiliary Service (the MAS) and arrange to start work at the General Hospital; the second was to fix up a black-out in her flat in Chatsworth Road, between Tanglin and the Alexandra Hospital.

It was an old-fashioned flat consisting of half the ground floor of a converted house; it had a big living-room, dressing-room, bedroom, and a garden with a tennis court. A Chinese amah with the unromantic name of Marsha was Freddy's slave, and a small green Morris car, with the romantic name of 'Green Spot', was Freddy's pride and joy. With the flat she had inherited a massive pedestal desk seven feet long and four feet wide with a knee-hole big enough for her and Philip Bloom, on his occasional visits, to shelter under during the raids which came later. It was a typical, agreeable, airy flat—'and practically impossible to black-out'.

But a constant black-out was virtually impossible in a humid country where people sweltered the moment a window was closed, where women like Freddy virtually lived on their balconies; where indeed to most people the balcony was the main 'living-room' of the house. So except during actual raids, Singapore compromised with a brown-out—which allowed the inhabitants to show a little light behind the balcony.

On this morning Freddy drove down to Robinson's. Because of the bomb damage in Raffles Place, she had to park the Green Spot in Collyer Quay, and once inside the emporium with its crowd of shoppers, it took her an hour to get near the counter. All around her frenzied women were begging for black-out material. Fortunately there was plenty—the trouble was a lack of assistants. Some were clearing up the bomb debris; others collected the remnants of the furniture from the bombed restaurant on the top floor. This had to be taken down to a basement, where Robinson's planned to set up a temporary restaurant so the ladies could still meet for morning coffee.

People solved their black-out problems in different ways. In her flat at Amber Mansions, Karen Hammonds blacked-out the dining-room by covering the windows and openings with brocaded Indian shawls which George had planned to take as gifts on his next leave in Europe.

Above all, in the first days of war, people tried, almost desperately, to emulate London's motto of 'Business as usual'. It became a point of honour not to let the Japanese interfere more than necessary with work—and for that matter, play.

On the very first night, George and Karen Hammonds went dancing at Raffles Hotel. In those days this was Singapore's ultimate in luxury hotels; a rambling, ornate building, world-famous, with a vast roofed-over verandah for dancing, flanked by lawns where dinner was sometimes served in front of a majestic line of tall, fan-like travellers' palms. Normally an expensive evening out at Raffles was 'an event', and the Hammonds had been invited, but all day Karen had hated the idea of leaving her daughter and baby son; George, however, felt that now, in this crisis, it was supremely important for the white man to show the Asian that he was not afraid, though he realised that this was something that Karen with her mixed blood perhaps couldn't quite understand. In fact George felt 'even more scared than Karen, but I had to insist—I knew the people were watching us and would take their lead from the way we behaved.'

They almost had a row, but what finally won Karen over was the Order of the Day. George felt that in the circumstances it was better not to disabuse her.

Raffles was a dreary flop. Few preparations had been made to brown-out the vast, barn-like verandah where Dan Hopkins's orchestra on its raised dais was playing old-fashioned dance music. The lights were so dim that the only illumination seemed to be provided by the moonlight. A few couples struggled gallantly through a series of slow fox-trots (dance music was invariably played at a slow tempo as a deterrent to excessive sweating) and there was a certain amount of forced humour as couples bumped into each other ('Oh! I *knew* it would be you with those big feet!') and the men with the aid of pencil torches tried to distinguish which chit they had to sign.

Relief—and an excuse to go home—came only when the sirens sounded. Every waiter bolted (allowing more than one shadowy figure a swig from the whisky bottles left on the table) and Karen began to feel terrified about the children at home. As they drove down Stamford Road, however, the all-clear sounded—it had been a false alarm—and when they reached Amber Mansions, it was to find the children asleep, and the amah sitting on the floor in the dark, wearing George's tin helmet.

Living in a flat, George could do nothing about making an improvised shelter, so he decided that the next morning he would buy a dozen mattresses and pile them around the dining-room table as splinter protection. Those who lived in houses were more fortunate. Though the government still insisted that rain-filled slit trenches were breeding grounds for malaria, Jimmy Glover realised that even the smallest rise of ground would allow water to seep away. He dug a zig-zag trench; boring partly into the grassy bank leading from his house to the garden below. This he planked over, and covered the planks with earth from the trench. Then he dug a narrow ditch to carry the rain away.

'Buck' Buckeridge of the Auxiliary Fire Service—the AFS —had a different kind of problem. He was short of helmets. Every demand had been refused. Two requisitions had been put in months ago to the Colonial Office; no helmets had arrived. So Buckeridge decided on more unorthodox tactics.

Tugging on his bristling goatee beard, as he always did when worried, Buckeridge waited for the all-clear, then

46

confessed his problems to a Swiss friend who ran an import business, and who had a week previously told Buckeridge, with typical Swiss caution, that he *might* be able to lay his hands on a small shipment of helmets if war came.

Buckeridge told him that war had definitely come—and discovered that the helmets had been there all the time, awaiting shipment to Siam, now under the control of Japan. With some pride, the Swiss businessman produced one—and for a moment Buckeridge was taken aback. It was exactly like a German helmet. But of course it couldn't matter less. The only thing that did matter was getting helmets for his men. He sent a lorry to collect them.

To other people, the problems were more personal; for Maynards the chemists, it meant getting wood to board up their shattered windows against possible looters in the event of another raid. To Jimmy Glover, whose printing plant was near the docks and therefore highly vulnerable, it meant installing an emergency printing plant in the large compound at Dulverton, his home. It seems incredible that he encountered no serious problems. Without any hindrance he was able to start building an attap-covered print shop. He went out and quite easily bought a new linotype machine, a range of hand-set type, then transferred a flat-bed printing press and twenty tons of newsprint from Anson Road to Dulverton. A hundred coolies from the electricity company worked in relays for 36 hours laying an underground cable to run the machines. The Singapore Telephone Company installed a special line.

Though it seems strange that the Governor had not long ago conscripted every one of these coolies to erect blast walls in Chinatown, at least Glover knew what he wanted and set about getting it with typical Yorkshire determination; a quality that seems to have been sadly lacking in the more rarefied atmosphere of the War Council.

For already in the initial days of war there was the first inkling of the bitterness and pettiness that was doomed to break up any coherent action, and in which Mr. Duff Cooper, Chancellor of the Duchy of Lancaster, who had arrived in Singapore on September 9, was to figure prominently. He had been sent out originally to study ways of improving co-ordination in the vast territories—ranging from India to New Zealand—under the British flag in the Far East.

Already he had unearthed some absurd situations. In

Singapore he had discovered two important officials—each with his own staff—doing exactly the same job for two different Whitehall departments, the Ministry of Economic Warfare and the Ministry of Information. The two men lived in the same house, happily pooling all their information. Their only grouse was that they were not allowed access to any Naval information, as this was under the control of an ex-Naval officer who had spent twenty years in the Fiji Islands 'and whose conception of his duties,' as Duff Cooper dryly noted, 'was to prevent anybody, especially the Americans, from obtaining any information whatever.'

Duff Cooper was a short man of remarkable ability who might have gone far in politics had he not been disposed to treat dull routine work as something to be despised. He enjoyed making excellent speeches, he was a brilliant writer, with a remarkable sense of history, and he had a shrewd brain.—But he loathed anything that smacked of routine. He had hardly been a conspicuous success in London as Minister of Information, possibly for this reason; but he was a close friend of Churchill's, and it is difficult to escape the conclusion that when he resigned the Ministry, he was sent to the Far East so that he could be found the sort of a job which hardly called for an exacting role, in an area where the Prime Minister had repeatedly emphasised that he did not expect an extension of the war.

The outbreak of war had changed the picture completely, and on the Wednesday—three days after the first Japanese landings (and when the civilian population had little inkling of the disastrous news about to descend on them) Churchill sent Duff Cooper a personal telegram which elevated him to Resident Minister for Far Eastern Affairs with cabinet rank. His task was to include settling emergency matters on the spot when (in Churchill's words) 'time does not permit of reference home': but his terms of reference warned him that he was in no way to 'impair the existing responsibilities' of the Commanders-in-Chief or government representatives, who would still deal directly with their departments in Whitehall.

Apparently Duff Cooper had other ideas. He now found himself President of a War Council which met daily, and he presided over the first meeting that Wednesday evening. Duff Cooper had an aggressive personality that he sometimes found difficult to contain; and like many highly intelligent

48

men, an ability to see quickly to the heart of a problem that made all the 'ifs' and 'buts' a source of great irritation to him. It is not difficult to understand his impatience at the often endless discussions over a problem to which he felt he had the simple answer; but in this highly individualistic War Council he found himself dealing, not only with the Governor (to whom he referred scathingly amongst his friends as 'the little man'), but with the Commander-in-Chief and commanders of the three services who instinctively distrusted the idea of a political figure telling them how to run their war.

There was trouble at the very first meeting. Duff Cooper was soon claiming that his instructions included 'the development of a clearing house for the prompt settlement of minor routine matters' and made it clear that the War Council should have strong powers. Sitting across the table from him, Shenton Thomas made no bones about the fact that he did not agree. In his view, Duff Cooper's appointment certainly didn't mean a War Council with executive powers to run the war.

Duff Cooper retorted that if the War Council had no real powers, then he would be nothing more than political adviser. Duff Cooper had a special 'stony stare' and now, leaning across, he fixed it on the Governor, and added in a steely voice, 'As far as I'm concerned, the duty of the War Council is to wage war.'

At this point Brooke-Popham, the C.-in-C., opened his eyes and spoke up. Brooke-Popham had an unfortunate habit of falling asleep on the slightest pretext, particularly at social functions—a trait which may have been due to the onerous duties imposed on his advanced years. It was a habit that enraged Duff Cooper, who had an alert, uncompromising brain. And he made no secret of the fact that he didn't like Brooke-Popham. This did not deter Brooke-Popham. In the council meeting at Duff Cooper's home in Dunearn Road there was dead silence among the members as the Air Chief Marshal said politely, but with ominous determination, that he took his orders from the Chiefs of Staff in Whitehall and not from Duff Cooper—and he didn't propose to change.

Duff Cooper could hardly control himself. 'You've produced the worst example of the old school tie I have ever met,' he cried.

Brooke-Popham 'smiled sweetly' and merely drawled, 'That's not fair!'

Shenton Thomas supported Brooke-Popham—which meant that from that moment Duff Cooper and the Governor were sworn enemies—so much so that Shenton Thomas privately summed up to a friend their relations with the words, 'From the time of his arrival to the time of his appointment as Chairman of the War Council, he was as pleasant as could be; thereafter he was exactly the reverse.' Perhaps the impatient Duff Cooper had forgotten one sentence buried in Churchill's personal telegram to him: 'The successful establishment of this machinery depends largely on your handling of it in these early critical days.'

Dramatically enough, this unseemly wrangling took place at almost the same time on that Wednesday evening as the people of Singapore were to receive the first of two major shocks from which civilian morale was destined never fully to recover.

Unaware of the wrangling in high quarters which was to exert such a devastating influence on his own life, George Hammonds had just walked out of the long bar at the Cricket Club to the verandah overlooking the padang. It had been a suffocating day but dusk was falling. The Tamils were taking down the tennis backstop nets so they could mark out courts in fresh places the following morning—a simple expedient (providing the labour was cheap) to prevent brown worn patches at the base lines.

In the hot, stifling evening, the lazy fans turning in the big open room with its array of silver cups hardly stirred the enervating air. Music blared from a radio, but nobody paid any attention as the showered tennis players emerged from the locker rooms boisterously demanding long, cool drinks. Hammonds remembers that he was in a 'long chair', the sort always popular in the East, with swivelling extensions on which one could rest one's legs, and George was tired after long journeys between the *Tribune* and Dulverton helping to organise the *Tribune*'s relief printing works. He hardly realised the music had stopped, that a voice was speaking out of the radio. It was more the sudden stop in the loud talk at the bar that brought him out of his chair, for now the room was utterly still except for one voice, announcing impersonally that the *Prince of Wales* and the *Repulse* had been sunk.

The silence continued for perhaps thirty seconds—until one old member dropped his glass; like a starting pistol,
50

the sudden shattering noise began a pandemonium of bewildered conversation. George 'literally ran out of the club', got into his car, which was parked in the members' enclosure, and raced past Fullerton Building to the *Tribune* office, forgetting Karen, forgetting everything.

All who were in Singapore on that evening and who remember this moment, felt like Churchill, who 'In all the war . . . never received a more direct shock. . . . As I turned over and twisted in bed the full horror of the news sank in upon me.'

'Dickie' Dickinson's wife, who worked at the Blood Transfusion, had just finished her day shift when a doctor came running down the passage and told her the news, adding in a rasping, brusque voice, possibly to hide his emotion, 'You'd better stay on for the night. The casualties may start coming in soon.'

Freddy Retz was in her flat waiting for Philip—who, being at the General Hospital, never turned up. But there was a knock on the door, and her neighbour Mr. Jim Henry, who lived in the flat above, came to offer advice. He was going to buy a stock of food and whisky and bury it under the tennis court in the garden. 'It's the beginning of the end,' he said gloomily. Could he get some supplies for Freddy at the same time?

When the news reached Raffles Hotel, the famous verandah emptied 'as though the last waltz had just been played', and Leslie Hoffman who had been meeting someone there 'had a feeling that everybody suddenly felt terribly guilty—caught out drinking'.

After the first shock, Jimmy Glover turned to a friend whom he had invited up to Dulverton for drinks and gave voice to the first bitter thoughts entering his head: 'Within 48 hours the Japanese have bombed Singapore, landed troops, captured an airfield and sunk two battleships. It looks like bad unified control on our part.'

The disaster had a profound effect on Singapore. Only a matter of hours before, the two great ships—pride of the British Navy—had secretly slid out of the harbour and up the east coast. Their very presence there—the cheers as they had berthed at the Naval Base, the publicity that had greeted their arrival—had somehow seemed an augury, a proof—if proof were needed—that the Naval Base after all these years meant something tangible and real.

Now they had gone, and it seemed to George Hammonds, waiting at the *Tribune* office to make up a new page one, as though 'not only the ships had gone to the bottom, but the bottom had fallen out of everything else as well'.

What had happened? Despite a warning that he could not be guaranteed air cover from land-based planes, Admiral Sir Tom Phillips had decided that the two battleships with four destroyers should sail up the east coast 'looking for trouble.' He had *hoped* for air cover, plus an element of surprise because of the monsoon weather. On the 9th—Tuesday—he received a cable that 'fighter protection . . . will not, repeat not, be possible.' Yet, while the heavy rain and grey skies hid the British warships they steamed on. Then the sky suddenly cleared—and immediately Phillips radioed Singapore that he had decided to return to the Naval Base. They were on their way back when Phillips received a report that the Japanese were invading the township of Kuantan, on the east coast, barely 140 miles north of Singapore. He decided to 'go in and help'. Unfortunately two unaccountable things happened. For some extraordinary reason, Phillips did not trouble to notify Singapore of his change of plans. And the report of the invasion of Kuantan was false. The result was that the Japanese pilots were offered a sitting target after their reconnaissance planes had identified the warships. Thirty-four high-level bombers and fifty-one torpedo bombers went in to the attack, sinking both ships with a total loss of 840 officers and men.

By now—though the civilian population did not know the worst—the tactical advantage had been lost forever. On land, British troops in Northern Malaya were falling back as the Japanese thrust inland from Kota Bahru. It did not matter how valiantly the defenders fought, this was a kind of war for which even the few seasoned troops were totally unprepared. While the British staggered under a burden of heavy equipment in blinding rain, swarms of Japanese commandeered bicycles and rode pell-mell through the rubber plantations. Ofter they wore nothing but shorts and singlets. They resembled the Malays so closely that to many of the British it was impossible to tell whether they were friend or foe. The Japanese by-passed the 'impenetrable jungle', moving swiftly through dripping rubber plantations or the narrow roads that linked one to another, often so silently that the British knew nothing until they were attacked from the rear

52

or cut off. To the Japanese, the jungle or the rubber plantation presented no fears. To the British it was an unknown world of elephants, tigers, snakes, flying foxes—of unearthly noises, of buzzing insects, dripping vegetation, of humid rubber plantations, now hissing with torrential monsoon rain, which bred a damp, isolated gloom. In there the enemy could be anywhere—or everywhere.

This was bad enough, but due to faulty strategy at headquarters British troops were falling into a trap which was to have disastrous consequences. It was a trap of which Churchill, almost immediately after the first Japanese assault, had gravely warned the commanders in Malaya, in a cable which ran, 'Beware lest troops required for ultimate defence of Singapore Island and fortress are not used up or cut off in Malay peninsula. Nothing compares in importance with the fortress.' But already the Japanese, by moving rapidly over all kinds of country, by using enveloping tactics rather than head-on assault, were accomplishing just what Churchill had feared. Added to this, indecision and hesitancy at GHQ were so disastrous that, as *The War Against Japan* put it, 'It is possible that he [Brooke-Popham] did not fully realise the importance of speed. . . . The need for a quick decision was not apparently realised at headquarters, Malaya Command.'

And by this Wednesday, December 10, when command of the seas had been lost, the RAF was falling back too. After systematic Japanese attacks on RAF planes—many of them refuelling on the ground—the RAF had only 50 planes fit for operations and most of these were being withdrawn from Malaya to Singapore Island. The Japanese had 530 aircraft—all of better quality. Daylight bombing of Japanese troops was stopped because our bombers could no longer be given sufficient fighter protection. As a result of this decision, Dutch air reinforcements flown in from Java were already being flown back again because they had not been trained for night bombing.

Now it was the turn of the civilians to have a taste of catastrophe. Although the disaster occurred far from Singapore, it nevertheless had a profound effect on all the people of the capital.

The *Malaya Tribune* printed a local edition at George Town, the only city in Penang, the beautiful hilly island off the west coast of Malaya, nearly 400 miles north of Singapore. On

53

Wednesday evening Glover put through a routine call to Paterson, the local editor, who assured him that all was well; the island was calm. Japanese aircraft had been 'buzzing around all day' without dropping any bombs, though they had attacked the RAF airfield at Butterworth on the mainland opposite. The raid had been clearly visible from Penang, said Paterson, and wardens and police had found it impossible to stop crowds of Asians lining the sea front for a grandstand view of Butterworth being blitzed.

About 11 o'clock the next morning—Thusday, December 11—a formation of 27 Japanese bombers again flew over George Town, and again thousands of people rushed out to see the 'free show'. They looked up, watching the planes in perfect formation. There was not a British fighter in the sky, nor the bark of a single AA gun, when the bombs fell. 'At first it sounded as if every bomb had fallen simultaneously; then for some minutes there was an earthquake-like rumble of explosions.' In a second, the hot, steamy morning had been transformed into chaos. One of the first bombs demolished the fire station. Another hit a main police station. Hundreds were killed instantly, thousands more were badly injured, and left writhing in the streets. There were virtually no shelters. There was no defence, and altogether over a thousand people were killed.

This was the first terror raid on Malaya—and though it was perhaps hard for the people of Singapore 400 miles to the south to visualise the chilling catastrophe in terms of human beings killed and maimed, the long-term effects were to prove even more disastrous than the raid itself, for even when the first shock was over, the more penetrating shocks still remained to come.

Before the attack the colourful streets of George Town had been plastered with the boldly printed Order of the Day, 'We are ready; our preparations have been made and tested; our defences are strong and our weapons efficient'. In stark truth the main 'weapons' allotted to the defence of the island against attack consisted of nothing more than two six-pounders.

This realisation, which soon reached Singapore on the Asian grapevine, provided the first shock. The second was to have even deeper implications and exert a calamitous effect on Asian morale throughout Malaya. Unknown to the civil government in Singapore, which had firmly guaranteed

54

that no discrimination between whites and Asians should be shown in the event of any evacuation, the military commander of Penang now took it upon himself to order the secret evacuation of all European women and children.

Without warning, European women who had played a magnificent role, working alongside Asian women who looked to them for leadership, were told to prepare to leave by night. It was a military order 'which could not be disobeyed'. The strictest secrecy was enjoined, for this was 'a military operation'. And so the next morning the Asians in Penang awoke to discover that the invincible tuan had deserted them.

Worse still, when the few troops were evacuated with the European men, their ineffective scorched earth policy was so palpably clumsy that the Japanese were left at least one oil installation, large quantities of tin ingots, and oil and petrol in warehouses, scores of launches, sampans and junks —including 24 self-propelled craft—which they were using within a few days to infiltrate behind British lines, and, worst of all, Penang radio station from which they were soon transmitting propaganda to the people of Singapore.

Unaccountably, news of the loss of Penang was not released until three days after the disaster, and when it reached London there was little reaction, despite the earlier report of the sinking of the two great warships. Penang was remote. To those at home—immersed in the great issues at stake and the entry of the United States into the war—an air raid on Penang must have seemed insignificant and a long way away.

In Singapore, however, the fall of Penang had a far more stinging effect even than the loss of the *Prince of Wales* and the *Repulse*. The delay in the official announcement of the news had resulted in the wildest rumours from refugees reaching Singapore. Suddenly, instead of being treacherous and cunning, the Japanese had become monstrous and inhuman. Penang in a dramatic sort of way crystallised to ordinary people in Singapore a new and terrifying picture of the Japanese. It was as though the enemy had been invested in the eyes of both civilians and soldiers with superhuman qualities.

Infinitely worse, Duff Cooper chose this moment to go on the air and give a totally distorted picture of what had happened. 'It has been necessary to evacuate many of the civilian population,' he said. 'We can only be thankful so many people have been safely removed.' He was of course thinking only of the Europeans, and the Asians realised this, for every listener knew that virtually only the Europeans had been evacuated.

An incensed Shenton Thomas summoned a meeting of the leading Chinese, Indian and Malay representatives in order to apologise. In a dramatic confrontation he told them bluntly that the civilian evacuation of Penang had been carried out without his knowledge or that of the Colonial Secretary, but though this was undisputed it was too late. The damage was done, and a wave of defeatism swept down to Singapore, to white and coloured alike.

Duff Cooper had opened his broadcast with the homely words, 'I consider that one of my duties should be to keep in close and constant touch with the people of Singapore by speaking to them on the radio from time to time.'

It was perhaps as well for the tattered remnants of civilian morale that he never broadcast again.

CHAPTER FOUR

THE MONTH OF INACTION

Up to New Year's Eve, 1941

After the first terrible week, the raids ceased, leaving the people of Singapore in a state of unreal calm. Though the news from up-country was increasingly depressing, its implications were so carefully masked that the people of the island continued to exist in a kind of dream world. They were in the war but not a part of it. Gasping with heat, drifting uneasily from one day to the next (in much the same way as the people of Britain had done during the 'phoney war') they existed on rumours. This was all too understandable. The newspapers were compelled to fill their columns with long despatches from the North African and Russian fronts since almost all local news was rigidly censored. Only the official communiqués, studded with meaningless phrases like 'falling back to prepared positions' and 'strategic withdrawals', attempted to conceal a multitude of disasters. George Hammonds, however, was able to follow the progress of Japanese advances throughout December by studying the Hong Kong and Shanghai Bank advertisements which gave a daily list of branches 'closed until further notice'.

Despite the generals, the red tabs, the staff cars, the troops dancing and sweating in the barn-like halls known as the 'Great World' and the 'Happy World', there was no realisation of war in the air. Up-country Malaya was as remote from Singapore as France had been from England in 1940, and possibly the fact that each was separated by a strip of water helped to heighten the illusion of security. And then too, the stifling, humid heat—accompanied now by spells of drenching monsoon rain—seemed to have drained away all energy, to have robbed the leaders, military and civilian alike, of all drive, even the ability to face up to facts.

Up-country, however, the hard-pressed troops were falling back on one ill-prepared position after another, worn out, hungry, tired, in the unceasing rain. It was a different world from Singapore, where many foods were still unrationed; where milk was still delivered promptly each morning by the Cold Storage vans. People could buy two tins of food a day for each member of the family, and even the butter and meat rations were three times as large as in Britain. Eating out presented no problems, for though Raffles, the Sea View and other hotels scrupulously observed·two meatless days a week, this made little difference as poultry and game 'did not count'.

There was still plenty of petrol, for almost everybody drew the extra allowance allotted to civil defence workers, and since many people had two cars, it was a simple matter to lay up the large one and use its generous ration for the Morris Minor.

Schools went on as usual, and one which had had to be hastily evacuated from up-country now advertised that it had 're-opened in Tanglin for the benefit of anyone wanting to further the education of their children'.

On the last day of the autumn term, Karen Hammonds went to pick up her daughter Barbara after the annual nativity play (in which Barbara played one of the wise men). The Reverend Bennitt's wife had spent Friday the 19th mixing her Christmas pudding; the next day her husband led his annual carol concert which raised a gratifying profit of $47; and no doubt the Bennitt family felt they had earned the dip they took at the Swimming Club afterwards.

For some there were terrifying echoes of the enemy guns

that could not be heard and the enemy aircraft that could not be seen. The wounded started arriving in Singapore in ever-increasing numbers. One morning, Freddy Retz was phoned at two o'clock, and from that day onwards she never returned to the easy-going day routine where there had always been time to talk or to slip out to Robinson's for tiffin.

Now every room, every corridor of the General Hospital was crowded with the wounded. Day after day a queue of ambulances waited by Singapore's railway station for the trainloads to arrive from the north. Suddenly the hospital was over-flowing, and Freddy was giving morphia injections, cutting badly burned clothing from open wounds, changing dressings every hour. For over a month she had to go round the wards night after night with a torch, a pair of forceps and a kidney basin, and take the maggots out of open wounds—maggots that had come from the eggs of the ever-present flies.

Confusion seemed rife throughout the city. Mr. Gilmore, the Deputy Municipal Engineer, was asked to dig trenches six feet wide and three feet deep on the many sports grounds in Singapore in order to prevent Japanese aircraft from landing. He managed to round up several hundred coolies, but when the work was half finished another official insisted that the trenches must be re-dug. If people crowded into them during a raid, Gilmore was solemnly warned, straight trenches would be easy targets for machine-gunning. The coolies filled in parts of the trenches which they had laboriously dug and staggered the others; Mr. Gilmore asked what to do with the displaced earth piled up on each side. He was told, 'Leave it there'. Along came another officious busybody, who pointed out in horrified tones that soft earth made ideal landing grounds for parachutists. With a sigh, Gilmore made arrangements to cart the earth away. His coolies had just finished this back-breaking task, when along came the Health Authorities. Trenches in low-lying ground were breeding grounds for mosquitoes, they insisted. At first they demanded that every trench should be filled in, but after some argument, agreed they should be half-filled. Most of the dispersed earth was carted back, and the bottom two feet of each trench filled in.

In the docks confusion was just as bad. Vital rubber stocks lay awaiting shipment because incoming ships could not always be unloaded. Yet the same vessels often contained equipment desperately needed by troops up-country. Whitehall, however, was unable to agree on rates of pay for coolie labour, and so frequently there were not enough coolies to unload the ships. They were working for rubber or tin firms, and there was nothing the military could do about it. Even though they wanted conscription of labour, Shenton Thomas received a cable from Whitehall instructing him that 'the ultimate criterion for exemption (from military service) should be not what the GOC considers practicable, but what you consider essential to maintain the necessary production and efficient labour management.' Such a vague instruction could apply to anybody.—from a coolie tapping rubber on a plantation to a broker sitting in his Singapore office.

In some cases the civilian reaction was arrogant. 'We're producing all the rubber—but the army seems to be mucking things up.' The secretary of the golf club refused the army permission to turn it into a strong point until he had called a special committee meeting; another officer was refused permission to cut down a row of trees on the outskirts of the city to improve his line of fire until he had produced written authority.

Up-country, similar confusion existed in relations between military and civilians. During December the British Resident at Tanjong Malim (on the west coast of Malaya) received a letter from General Sir Lewis Heath, commander of the 3rd Indian Corps, saying 'the army no longer requires civil assistance north of the line Cameron Highlands Tapah-Telok Anson-Bagan-Datch and this is an indication that you have authority to warn any such persons as you consider may wish to withdraw etc. etc.' Naturally enough, the British Resident warned all civilians to leave. Four days later he received an insolent wire from another officer (not Heath) saying 'No civil authority Ipoh. Send authorities to run security police . . . ensure that in future civil authorities do not run away from their duty.'

Ipoh was of course well north of the line General Heath had drawn.

In the small settlement of Port Dickson on the west coast, Jack Masefield, in charge of the police, was suddenly presented with 20 women and children evacuated by order from Singapore. Port Dickson was a tiny township with perhaps 50 Europeans. They housed, fed—and in some cases even clothed—the evacuees, and had just got them nicely settled in when an official ordered them back to Singapore—at the same time as Shenton Thomas was warning evacuees from the north that Singapore was too crowded to receive any more.

As December dragged on, the news got gloomier and gloomier. The whole of Kelantan and Province Wellesley was falling into Japanese hands together with the greater part of Perak. Within three weeks of the first clash of arms, the Japanese were in control of over 100 miles of territory down the west coast, while on the east they had made deep penetrations from the coastal areas as far south as Kuantan less than 150 miles from Singapore. Everywhere the tale was one of unrelieved defeat. Jitra had been a disastrous loss four days after the outbreak of war; so had been the decision to abandon the defensive line above Penang on December 17. Yet it was hard for the average civilian to make geographical sense of the wordy communiqués for, as Jimmy Glover said, 'The constant references to town and villages behind positions previously mentioned—without frank explanations of retreats—was exasperating'.

It is equally hard to understand the thinking of some generals at this time. When Brigadier Simson, the Chief Engineer, went to see Major-General Gordon Bennett (commanding the 8th Australian Division) he found it impossible to make him realise that there was an urgent need for anti-tank defences. 'At first he did not wish to discuss the matter at all,' Simson noted after the meeting. Simson was horrified. Couldn't the Australian general understand that 'there was nothing on the long road to prevent the enemy racing to Johore'?

Apparently Gordon Bennett could not, for in his diary that night he wrote, 'Malaya Command sent Brigadier Simson to discuss with me the creation of anti-tank obstacles for use on the road. . . . Personally, I have little time for these obstacles . . . preferring to stop and destroy tanks with anti-tank weapons.'

No wonder that the Japanese never slowed down, no wonder that time after time British, Australian or Indian troops were annihilated by skilful Japanese enveloping tactics. On the British side wrong decisions were made. Communications broke down. Orders went astray. Whole pockets of troops were cut off. The first Japanese tanks appeared and 'came as a great surprise' to the British who had not one single tank in Malaya. In a jungle country where the British had insisted that tanks could never operate, the Japanese tanks moved easily between the spacious rows of rubber trees. And while the Japanese rested their crack troops, relieving them with other forces, British 'troops who had been fighting or on the move for a week' could only fight 'like automata and often could not grasp the simplest order'. And with the occupation of Penang, the Japanese had been presented with a considerable fleet of boats, junks and barges which the army had 'forgotten' to destroy, and in which they now shipped their men down the west coast, landing behind our lines, then going straight into the attack against inadequately trained troops who had never been warned of the prowess of this speedy, mobile enemy. As confusion spread, panic often set in amongst men who had not slept for a week, men sluggish and nervous and weary with constant retreat.

By Christmas half of Malaya's tin mines and a sixth of the rubber plantations were in enemy hands. The 'arsenal of democracy' was going bankrupt.

One senses that about this time the tug-of-war for power in the War Council was rapidly coming to a head. Even in the official papers a note of glee creeps in as one rival scores a minor victory over another in a free-for-all that was utterly divorced from the realities of a war rapidly engulfing them.

There could be little doubt that Duff Cooper was winning. The Governor was being increasingly relegated to being a figurehead stripped of any power. So was his Colonial Secretary, Stanley Jones, to whom Duff Cooper had taken a violent dislike. This was understandable, for though Stanley Jones was conscientious and hard-working, even his close friends hardly troubled to dispel the picture of a man who, despite some excellent qualities, could be arrogant, and at times intolerably rude, even though to his close friends he might have been charming, considerate and witty. He was a strange mixture. He was an excellent musician, he collected with discrimination, and he had turned his house in the grounds of Government House into a warm and personal place. But his abrupt manner, his 'cussedness' as Hammonds described it, made him many enemies.

Now Shenton Thomas and Stanley Jones came up against Duff Cooper again, this time over the question of evacuation. Duff Cooper wanted priority for Europeans. Shenton Thomas was rigidly opposed to it. The argument in the War Council became little more than an acrimonious wrangle, but before it could be resolved Shenton Thomas received a cable from the Colonial Office stating that there was to be no discrimination in any evacuation. It was one of those odd coincidences—and it was a coincidence—which almost cost Shenton Thomas his job, for Duff Cooper was convinced the Governor had asked for the cable to be sent, whereas in fact it had arrived without request and Thomas never did discover what had prompted its despatch. 'Anyway,' he admitted gloomily to Dickinson, of the Police, 'Duff Cooper never believed it was a coincidence, and I was in the mud.'

Dickinson was to have startling confirmation of this state of affairs, and from no less a person than Duff Cooper himself, who had several times invited him round to his house in Dunearn Road for an evening stengah. Dickinson, a handsome man with a penchant for 'spit and polish', is one of the few men against whom no subsequent historians have ever uttered a word of criticism. He combined iron discipline with a charm and kindness that had earned him the nickname of 'the gentle policeman'. For some time Dickinson had sensed that Duff Cooper was anxious to ask him something. On the night that Duff Cooper finally got round to the question, the two men were sitting alone on the verandah, each with a whisky and soda. Duff Cooper, tired and hot and with his shirt sticking to his back, waited for the boy to depart before telling Dickinson that he was extremely dissatisfied with the civil administration over their prosecution of the war effort. Their abysmal effort could not, he said, stand up to any severe test. Looking Dickinson straight in the eye, he asked him what would happen if he, Duff Cooper, could persuade Whitehall to recall the Governor.

Dickinson was completely taken aback. It was unthinkable, he retorted. To millions of people in Malaya, the Governor —weak or strong—was as much a symbol as the King was in Britain. 'It was just not on,' and would be a fearful blow to civilian morale.

Duff Cooper did not seem put out, and changed the subject by suggesting that the civil government might be improved if Stanley Jones, the Colonial Secretary, went instead. Again Dickinson said that it should not be done, though he had to admit that Stanley Jones had an unfortunate manner.

It is an extraordinary feature of these semi-secret meetings between Duff Cooper and Dickinson (and several others) that a man of Duff Cooper's political experience should have exhibited such an astonishing lack of caution in canvassing men in the Governor's service behind his back, but it must be remembered that, for all his power, Duff Cooper remained an uneasy stranger in the midst of an establishment which instinctively regarded him with suspicion. Nor did he know the country, or its problems. (One of his favourite grumbles was 'Why don't we burn down the gum trees before the Japs get them?' without the local knowledge that with an average of 80 rubber trees to the acre, there were over 300 million rubber trees in Malaya.) Above all, what Duff Cooper failed to realise was that, though Shenton Thomas was not a dynamic personality, he was greatly liked by the leaders of the various racial communities. He was 'for them'. He was, in fact, approachable, helpful and understanding, and even if it took a great deal of time for suggestions to go through the cumbersome mill of civil government, the country was used to this leisurely tempo, and its Chinese, Malay and Indian dealers trusted him.

After his unsatisfactory meeting with Dickinson, Duff Cooper sent an airmail letter to Churchill suggesting that 'some senior civilian officials' could not cope with war conditions and that other changes might later be necessary.

One of these was already *en train*. Duff Cooper was quietly hastening the recall of Brooke-Popham. Even before war broke out in the Far East, it had been agreed that General Pownall (who had been Chief of Staff to the Commander of the British Expeditionary Force in France) should succeed Brooke-Popham. He was a young man, and had practical experience of modern war. No fixed date had been decided for the take-over, and when the Japanese attacked, the Chiefs of Staff in Whitehall had decided that it would be unwise to change horses in mid-stream. They pointed out to Churchill that in any event Brooke-Popham had no authority to control or interfere with the actual military operations which lay in the hands of the three service commanders. This decision was relayed to Duff Cooper who found it so unsatisfactory (and disliked Brooke-Popham so intensely) that he took the unorthodox step of bringing pressure to bear on Churchill through his War Cabinet secretary. This ruse proved effective, with the result that the Chiefs of Staff found themselves the recipients of political directives which forced them into taking an action they thoroughly disapproved. General Pownall was instructed to leave for Singapore as soon as possible. He arrived on December 23 and took over from Brooke-Popham four days later.

We now come to one of the most extraordinary secret meetings of the war in Malaya, and it was perhaps as well for Pownall's peace of mind that he did not know of this, for it took place on the day he assumed command. It was between General Percival, the Commanding Officer, and Brigadier Ivan Simson, his Chief Engineer—the man who had discovered the bundles of anti-tank leaflets.

Simson's attempts to improve and add to the defences had been balked at every turn, largely by General Percival, who seemed to have a fixation against such measures. Above everything else, Simson was most concerned about the complete lack of any defences on the north shores of Singapore Island, facing Johore, and now becoming increasingly vital as the Japanese advanced southwards. Nothing had been done, nothing was being done, despite many previous pleas. Simson had felt for a long time that his only chance of ever persuading Percival to let him throw up any defences on the north shores lay in getting the General alone, so that he could talk to him as man to man, and not before other senior officers.

At last the opportunity arrived—at 11.30 p.m. on Boxing Day. Simson was on his way back from the front and General Heath had given him an urgent message for Percival. During the long journey down the peninsula there had been two air raids. The brigadier was dead-tired, grimy and unwashed, but Heath's message gave him the excuse he had longed for, and he made his way directly to Flagstaff House, Percival's residence.

Percival was just about to go to bed and looked with some astonishment at this late visitor. When, however, Simson announced that he bore an important message, Percival invited him in. Simson took off his Sam Browne and revolver and Percival politely offered him a whisky and soda, which Simson gratefully accepted. The Brigadier gave Percival the message—and then instead of leaving, drew a deep breath and announced that he would like to take this opportunity of a heart-to-heart-talk on the subject of defences. Percival looked 'a trifle startled' but sat down with a tired expression and listened. The General was a difficult man to 'warm up'. Tall, thin, with two protruding teeth, he was a completely negative personality, and his first instinct when faced with a problem was that it couldn't be done—in direct contrast to Simson, whose first thought was always 'Well—let's try'. This was why Simson had elected to stay and risk all at this strange meeting in the dead of night, and now he spoke with the passionate eloquence of the professional. Defences were his main job. He believed implicitly in their value which history had repeatedly proved in modern war. And he had all the materials to hand. Indeed they had reached Malaya long before the Japanese attacked. He had the staff and materials, he said to Percival, to throw up fixed and semi-permanent defences, anti-tank defences, under-water obstacles, fire traps, mines, anchored but floating barbed wire, methods of illuminating the water at night. And since it now seemed inevitable that the Japanese would soon reach Johore and attack the island across the narrow straits, the matter was one of extreme urgency. But it could be done, said Simson. He could throw up defences on the north shore, covering the Johore Straits, 'and the water surface and shore line would be the main killing area'. To the Brigadier's dismay, Percival refused his pleas, but Simson—'knowing I must not give way as the situation was so critical'—put down his whisky glass, leaned forward and said intently, 'Sir—I must emphasise the urgency of doing everything to help our troops. They're often only partially trained, they're tired and dispirited. They've been retreating for hundreds of miles. And please remember, sir, the Japanese are better trained, better equipped, and they're inspired by an unbroken run of victories.'

It had been a powerful plea. At first Simson had tried to speak as dispassionately as possible, but as the clock moved round to one in the morning and he seemed to be making no impression, Simson found it hard to control his anger.

'And it has to be done now, sir,' he pleaded. 'Once the area comes under fire, civilian labour will vanish. But if we start now we can do it.'

Incredibly, Percival still refused to change his mind.

The two men were alone in the room and at last in desperation Simson cried, 'Look here, General—I've raised this question time after time. You've always refused. What's more, you've always refused to give me any *reasons*. At least tell me one thing—why on earth *are* you taking this stand?"

It was at this point that Percival gave his answer. 'I believe that defences of the sort you want to throw up are bad for the morale of troops and civilians.'

This was the commanding officer speaking, and Simson was 'frankly horrified' and remembers standing there in the room, suddenly feeling quite cold, and realising that, except for a miracle, Singapore was as good as lost.

One can understand Simson's horror, and wonder, too, why Percival had found it necessary to make such an illogical excuse. For Percival must have been well aware that, long before he had taken over command of Malaya, defence lines in Johore and on the north shore of the island had been the frequent subject of discussion. The reason they had never been built before the war (when there would have been no labour shortage) was simple; every department in Whitehall had refused to foot the bill for a war that might never take place. Now at least, in war, it could and should have been done.

As he put on his Sam Browne, Simson could not forbear to make one last remark.

'Sir,' he said, 'it's going to be much worse for morale if the Japanese start running all over the island.'

Then he closed the door behind him. It was just two o'clock on the morning of December 27.[1]

By one of those astonishing coincidences that would hardly be permitted in a work of fiction, Brigadier Simson was the central character in another equally astonishing scene three days later, when, by pure chance, he became involved in the struggle for power between the Governor and Duff Cooper. It had nothing to do with the secret meeting that had taken place between Percival and Simson. Not a soul knew about

---

[1] Why was General Percival so biased about defence works? Simson believes that, like some other Commanders in Malaya who were indifferent, 'somewhere in their military education such a dictum on morale had been impressed upon them or they possibly misunderstood the value of defences in the circumstances such as now existed'. It is interesting to note that when Hore-Belisha was Secretary for War he visited the BEF in 1939 and was aghast at the lack of defence works, and plainly showed his annoyance, with the result that, according to his diary of December 2, 1939, 'Ironside (CIGS) after his visit to BEF, came to see me and with great emphasis told me that the officers were most upset at the criticisms made about lack of defences. . . . He said Gort was threatening to resign.'

this. Nor had Simson ever met Duff Cooper, while he had only a nodding acquaintance with the Governor.

Nevertheless it seems that Duff Cooper had heard good reports about Simson, whom he described as 'a sensible and resolute officer', for on December 30 the Brigadier received an urgent summons to attend that morning's meeting of the War Council. Unknown to Simson, Duff Cooper had decided that an 'overlord' was needed to handle and control the various branches of civil defence which came under Shenton Thomas, and while Simson was making his way to Dunearn Road, Duff Cooper announced to the startled War Council that the civil defence organisation was unsound, and that he had detected 'a certain lack of confidence' among the civilian population. He proposed that one man should be appointed to run all civil defence—and the man should be Brigadier Simson. Duff Cooper had timed this dramatic announcement with political acumen, choosing a day when the Governor was absent from the War Council, for the appointment he had in mind was, of course, the official prerogative of the Governor. In fact Thomas was, as Duff Cooper well knew, on an up-country tour, and Stanley Jones was deputising for him. Duff Cooper hoped that in the Governor's absence he could bull-doze the appointment through the Council.

Simson had arrived and was waiting in an ante-room, completely mystified by a summons from a man he had never met. He was called in, offered a chair, and Duff Cooper said he had heard he was an expert on civil defence and had given some lectures on the subject in Malaya. Would he care to give the War Council a brief résumé of his lecture?

Simson was as startled as the others. He *had* given a series of lectures, but they were based only on a modest acquaintance with civil defence in London during the blitz.

'I'm sorry to disappoint you,' he replied. 'But I'm *not* an expert. I suppose as a regular officer in the Royal Engineers, I have the necessary background and training, but that's all.' Nevertheless he described as best he could the civil defence organisation in London, gave details of its equipment, and was asked as retire.

A few minutes later he was called back and Duff Cooper told him, 'The Council has unanimously agreed to offer you the post of Director General of Civil Defence—subject of course to the approval of General Percival'. (Duff Cooper had no qualms on this score. He had already sounded out Percival, who had agreed that Simson could take the post while also retaining his military position of Chief Engineer.)

'I'm extremely sorry,' said Simson speaking straight from the heart, 'but I can't possibly accept it.'

Duff Cooper's 'voice sharpened' as he asked brusquely, 'Why on earth not?'

Simson told him that he believed Singapore would shortly be invested, and during a siege the Chief Engineer became a key man, often second in importance only to the GOC.

In an almost comical fashion Simson was now asked to retire once again. A few minutes later he was recalled, and Duff Cooper, fixing him with his special stony stare, said firmly, 'I'm sorry, Brigadier, but the War Council has decided that you *must* take over Civil Defence.' He indicated that the subject was now closed. Simson had been ordered into this job.

The Governor, of course, was away, but Duff Cooper pooh-poohed all Simson's questions of possible opposition, and then and there gave him in writing plenary powers to cover both Singapore Island and Johore. He also made certain that the text of Simson's commission was published in the *Straits Times* before the Governor returned.

Shenton Thomas reached Singapore before breakfast the following morning. Jones had already advised him of what had happened, and by the time the Governor reached Government House, ready for coffee on his favourite balcony, he was fuming at what he considered 'a despicable trick' by Duff Cooper. His ADC remembers that he had rarely seen Thomas in such a rage. What particularly angered him was to learn that Duff Cooper had already told several of his friends how he had 'put one over on the little man'.

Stanley Jones was waiting for him. He poured out two cups of coffee and quietly advised Thomas to accept the situation without demur. The Governor, however, showed more spirit and flatly refused. *He* was the one who should have made an appointment, not 'the Chancellor', as he called Duff Cooper. He would cancel it. After some discussion, Jones warned him bluntly that if he cancelled the appointment —especially as it had already been officially announced in the Press—it could lead to an open rift and that 'anything could happen'. And he emphasised that Duff Cooper did after all hold Cabinet rank.

Shenton Thomas calmed down a little. Then he thought of a compromise. He sent for Brigadier Simson—by now in an intolerable position—and promptly substituted for Duff Cooper's plenary powers others of a more moderate character. He offered Simson no explanation.

'You can have full powers for civil defence on Singapore Island only,' he said, adding coldly a warning, 'but they'll be subject to the existing law, and if any one of your activities is challenged, you must refer the matter to the Malayan legal department.' Johore, he added, was 'out'.

As patiently as he could Simson pointed out that if he had to refer questions to the legal department, it completely stultified the whole object of speed in Duff Cooper's plenary powers. Simson then begged the Governor to allow him to retain his powers in Johore. It was vital, he said, for there was a large untapped labour force of evacuees from up-country remaining there to avoid working in the danger areas of Singapore.

'That's impossible,' replied the Governor. 'We have no legal rights to do such a thing. If we did, the Sultan would blow up.'

Johore was an unfederated state—and the Sultan was a powerful, fabulously wealthy old man, who dined off gold plate, and who had already crossed swords with Shenton Thomas, who, on the advice of the Colonial Office (which had heard some unseemly rumours from Johore) had at one stage virtually barred the Sultan from entering Singapore. Yet the Sultan had power in his own state of Johore. Shenton Thomas thought he *could* have been awkward. On the other hand, the Sultan was a staunch British patriot (he had, indeed, presented Britain with a warship) and Simson made the obvious suggestion: 'Well,' he said, 'let's go and talk to him. He seems a reasonable sort of chap.' Shenton Thomas refused to abandon his stand.

There was only one consolation for Simson. Fortunately, the Governor's substitute orders were never printed in the local Press—and Simson spent the rest of the war with the Governor's restricted orders in one pocket and Duff Cooper's plenary powers in the other. Duff Cooper knew and accepted the situation, but as General Percival admitted privately to Dickinson, 'The situation created by (Duff Cooper's) appointment of the DG of Civil Defence was made over the

Governor's head who was, I think justifiably rather incensed at the proceeding'.[2]

New Year's Eve came and the weekly *Straits Budget* celebrated it by asking 'Who are our leaders?' and answering in its leading article—rather sweepingly, one must admit—'If instant dismissal had been the unavoidable consequence of proved incompetence, the ranks of the Malayan Civil Service would have been seriously depleted since 8th December'.

The article appeared on the first day of the New Year, when, as though awakened from a drugged sleep, the people of Singapore were suddenly plunged into a chilling awareness of reality. For this was the month of the bombs. Now the civilians were to discover themselves thrown brutally upon their own untried resources.

CHAPTER FIVE

THE MONTH OF THE BOMBS

January, 1942

Even to this day no historian has come near an accurate computation of the number of civilian deaths in Singapore between January 1 and the day on which the island capitulated.

In England during the heavy periods of bombing it had been a very different story; the whole population had been provided with documents. Ration and identity cards had made it comparatively simple to trace those who had vanished in the course of a raid. No such aids to identification existed in Singapore, however—particularly in Chinatown, whose influx of refugees from up-country was daily increasing the

2 *The War Against Japan* put it more bluntly: 'The selection of the senior Royal Engineer Officer in Malaya for the appointment of DGCD at a time when it was possible that Singapore might be invested . . . seems in retrospect to have been a mistake . . . Brigadier Simson . . . accepted the appointment only under pressure. Not only did he consider his task as Chief Engineer to be the more important, but in his opinion it was too late to reorganise effectively the civil defence. . . . Nevertheless he did what he could and it was largely due to his efforts and to the devotion to duty of the members of the various units that, when put to the test, the civil defence services functioned as well as they did.'

city's normal population of half a million. After a raid it was discovered that scores of men, women and children had simply vanished—and more often than not the officials had little or no idea as to their identity. In some of the heaviest attacks whole sections of Chinatown were obliterated and hundreds of bodies were never dug out. The hospitals and aid posts did try to keep some records, but even most of these were lost in the confusion following surrender.

From now on, hardly a day was to pass without its quota of raids. Overnight Singapore became a city of bewildering contrasts. Houseboys and amahs stayed stolidly with their masters, insisting on serving 'formal' meals. Before men went to work each day, however, those who had no modern plumbing had, because of the coolie shortage, to dig a hole at the bottom of the garden and bury the nightsoil (as it was politely called). In the residential Tanglin area, with its up-to-date houses, a friend with a modern lavatory was a friend indeed.

Down at the docks the labour force was dwindling under the incessant strain of sirens and falling bombs. Hundreds of workers had fled with their families to villages inland. No shelters meant no labour. British troops were soon forced to unload their gear under a hot tropical sun. As for the vital raw materials so urgently needed at home, huge stocks of rubber remained piled high on the wharves without a single man to load them into the waiting ships.

The raids were almost always in daylight, and made by formations of 27, 54 or 81 planes. They rarely needed any fighter escort, and their method of bombing was simple. The formation was led by one marksman who, when he felt he was on target, signalled to the accompanying pilots. All then dropped their load of bombs at the same moment. The method had devastating results, and Brigadier Simson reckons that throughout January at least 150 people a day were buried in the cemeteries, though obviously many more were killed and never traced.

Despite Duff Cooper's gloomy forebodings, the civil defence behaved magnificently, the Chinese volunteers in particular working under constant bombing with a fortitude many Europeans might have envied. Despite a shortage of hoses and helmets, the ARP and the AFS coped with hundreds of incidents and fires. Often there were no canteens, no food for hours on end as one raid was telescoped into another.

Most Tamil native burial squads disappeared after two out

of three Tamil camps had been bombed. In the hot and humid city bodies began to decompose quickly. After a raid they were laid out for a brief period so that relatives could identify them and arrange (at first). for decent burials. But if a corpse remained unclaimed, it was carted away to a mass grave. In severe raids men could not always reach the bodies under the mountains of smashed-up houses, and when the stench of putrefying flesh became noisome, nobody would collect them. Within a week the danger of typhus was so great that the government ordered free injections.

Though the communiqués were still non-committal, even embarrassingly hopeful, everyone knew now that the Japanese were advancing towards Johore, so that it was no surprise to the inhabitants when steel pylons sprouted on the beautifully kept padang of the Cricket Club as a deterrent to gliders (though the club bar remained open). The Golf Club was finally turned into a military strong point, with anti-aircraft guns and troops in the club house. The Coconut Grove, Singapore's most fashionable nightclub, closed down, together with two of the three 'Worlds'. Though the dance band at the Swimming Club had packed up and departed (leaving a notice by the stage 'We'll be back!') the club remained a popular centre for swimming, and lunch was still served on its broad verandah overlooking the pool. Indeed there was an added, if macabre, 'attraction'. As lunch was served, one could sometimes watch a raid on the docks as impersonally as if one were watching a war film.

At Raffles Hotel the management had by now perfected a satisfactory black-out for its large dance room, and the orchestra still played from eight to midnight, though transport soon became a major problem, as most taxis vanished after dusk.

By day it was better, though more and more bewildered evacuees, often with children, crowded the streets, passing endlessly in dejected little groups through Raffles Place as they made for Robinson's, whose cellar had been turned into a makeshift restaurant—hot, but at least a shelter in itself —now frequently packed with women searching for friends evacuated from up-country. For the price of a coffee, they would wait for hours, and sure enough the friend always seemed to turn up. If one waited long enough, 'everybody' turned up at Robinson's, especially those who had fled on military orders with no money, and who now, as though turning to an old friend, went to Robinson's which had been a part of their lives since the day they had first landed in Malaya.

Lucy Buckeridge—the wife of 'Buck' Buckeridge, the AFS chief who had acquired the German-style helmets—worked in the accounts department at Robinson's, and solved their problem. With the agreement of the manager, she opened a private 'bank' which made loans of a hundred dollars or so[1] to those in urgent need of 'petty cash'. (All the loans were entered in the ledgers, which were kept open until the day before surrender, when they were locked in Robinson's strongroom which was never opened by the Japanese. Not a single survivor failed to repay his or her debts.)

As soon as the sirens wailed, everything closed—banks, post offices, shops, private firms—but the moment the all clear sounded it was 'business as usual' with a sort of added frenzy, as though to make up for lost time. The centre of Singapore was, oddly enough, comparatively safe, for the bombers were aiming mainly for the docks and airfields. But it was a crazy sort of existence. The big shops calmly sold their wares during raid-free periods, but a woman setting off for Raffles Place could never be sure whether the shop would be open. Things worked—but they worked in different ways, and the result was often bewildering.

Freddy Retz, on her way to the hospital one morning, was driving her 'Green Spot' near the Municipal Buildings when the planes came over. She ran into the Supreme Court building and sheltered inside the open doorway in front of the roadway where Tamil labourers (at a moment when dock labour was desperately needed) were diligently scything the grass verges.

Karen Hammonds rushed home for lunch after picking up Barbara at school and noticed that her amah somehow looked different. It took her a couple of minutes to realise that instead of wearing the traditional white blouse, the amah had changed into a black one. And when Karen asked her why (for such a liberty was unheard of) the amah replied stolidly that it was so the Japanese pilots would not see her.

The schools had started their spring term, as Buckeridge discovered once, after he had received an urgent instruction to take over a girls' school in Tanglin for an extra AFS post —and arrived to discover the girls in the middle of an exam.

[1] The Straits' dollar is worth 2s. 4d.

Mundane chores were still the order of the day. Hammonds remembered that evening to pay the fifteenth instalment on his refrigerator—'only seven payments to go'.

As the *Straits Times* gloomily remarked, 'Everybody in this country seems to have been lulled into a false sense of security by confident statements regarding continuous additions to our armed might. The only people who have not been bluffed by them are the Japanese'.

It was on this evening that Leslie Hoffman, Hammonds's colleague on the *Tribune*, invited George and Karen Hammonds to Raffles for a farewell dinner party for his wife who had promised to leave for Australia before the end of the month. Hoffman had been married less than a year, and his wife was pregnant. Convinced that Singapore would be invested, he had insisted that she should leave.

Raffles was crowded. The orchestra was in great form— even if the tempo was slow—and the boys in their starched white uniforms bustled from table to table taking orders. There was a sprinkling of officers, one of whom sat goggling at Karen for fully ten minutes before coming across to their table, bowing politely, and announcing simply, 'You're the most beautiful woman I have ever seen,' and left. It put them all in a good mood and George, after his second whisky-water—he never touched soda—decided to stop trying to persuade Karen to leave, at any rate for that evening.

Karen was looking stunningly beautiful. She was more relaxed, she was not as afraid as usual, for the simple reason that the children were in the safe hands of two sergeants whom she had invited to share her Christmas turkey, and who had offered to baby-sit when off duty.

Two drinks stretched into three or four. The fish course of fried ikan merah had been excellent. The steaks were almost due when the sirens sounded. Fifteen seconds later a near miss shook the cavernous room. The effect was electrical. George was still dancing with Karen when a Chinese boy, bolting for the door, almost knocked her down, slithered across the crowded floor and disappeared. By the time that George had fought his way back to their table with Karen, every boy had vanished.

As Karen sat down, Leslie Hoffman (one of those engaging, imperturbable characters who always seem capable of a smile in moments of stress) calmly announced that as their steaks seemed destined to be delayed, he had better go

74

and cast an eye over the kitchen front. He had a languid way of moving and he uncoiled his slim body from his chair, strolled across the empty room and pushed his way through the doors leading to the kitchen. In less than a quarter of an hour Leslie, who was an excellent cook, had returned bearing a tray with four steaks and four cold Tiger beers.

While the civilians did their best to obey the Governor's exhortations to 'carry on as usual' Brigadier Simson was finding it much more difficult than he had imagined to put the civil defence organisation on a more realistic basis. His concern was not with the bravery of individuals—that was beyond dispute—but with making their work easier, providing them with better facilities, and thus helping to save lives. For though Simson had told Duff Cooper it was too late in the day to make radical changes in the civil defence system, he was no defeatist. He had been given a job. Now he set about doing what he could to improve the defences against air attack.

Before anything else, he had decided to spend two or three days watching the volunteers of civil defence at work during raids. There was no point, however, in appearing in uniform; it would have put the men on their 'best behaviour'. So he took off his red tabs, and in the drenching rain put on his old macintosh and became part of the crowds. He gave assistance whenever he could—but always as an unknown civilian.

His disguise resulted in at least one unusual experience. He was helping to carry the wounded out of a small hotel in Macpherson Road which had been hit, when the sound of screeching horns and car sirens heralded an approaching VIP, complete with a convoy of outriders. It was the Governor. Shenton Thomas stepped out of his car with his wife, mixed with the ARP workers ('he showed great sympathy and understanding') while Simson shrank into the anonymity of the crowd.

The following evening Shenton Thomas asked Simson round for a drink to see how he was getting on. (It says much for Simson's ability to handle men that he and the Governor still remained on good terms.) As they sat on the verandah, with the last rays of the sun glinting on the windows of the Cathay Building, Shenton Thomas suggested, 'You know, Simson, if I were in your shoes, I'd get around and

75

see things for myself. I was out yesterday watching the men at work.'

'I know, sir,' replied Simson, 'I was there and I saw you.'

At first the Governor refused to believe him, but Simson described the scene with such a wealth of detail that finally Thomas said, 'But I didn't see *you*, Simson!'

'No sir,' replied the Brigadier, 'I was working as a stretcher bearer.'

Simson had hoped to make some rapid changes, but he quickly discovered it was not going to be easy. Part of the trouble stemmed from the fact that he had not been permitted to choose his second-in-command. Duff Cooper had picked his own man, Mr. F. D. Bisseker, chairman of the Eastern Smelting Company, one of the biggest men in 'tin'. Unfortunately for Simson, Bisseker had long been one of the sternest critics of 'government apathy', with the result that he was heartily disliked by many members of the Malayan Civil Service.

Simson met Bisseker for the first time early in January—and liked him on sight (a first impression that he never changed). Before getting down to work, they had to find an office and a small staff, and in all innocence, Simson drove with Bisseker up to the grounds of Government House to see Stanley Jones and ask him to provide the necessary accommodation. To Simson's astonishment the Colonial Secretary refused to help in any way. This attitude seems incredible, considering that Simson was trying to save some of the 150 or more civilians a day who were being killed in raids. Yet Stanley Jones refused point-blank even to find a small office, and, according to Simson's notes, 'his refusal was couched in very rude terms'. It was Simson's first inkling of the bitterness that existed between many officials and businessmen.

'I was soon to discover,' Simson noted, 'that no civil servant would help Mr. Bisseker or anyone associated with him.' In point of fact Shenton Thomas on several occasions pressed Simson to get rid of Bisseker, but Simson always gave the same reply: 'I'll do so immediately if he fails at his job. But until then, I'm not prepared to challenge Duff Cooper's choice.'

The first thing Bisseker did after leaving Jones was to rent an office in Tanglin Road, staff and furnish it—and pay for it out of his own pocket. Here the two of them made their modest headquarters until later in the month when Duff Cooper left, and they took over his office.

Simson and his assistants did a magnificent job against odds that were almost—but not quite, at that time—overwhelming. They concentrated on finding men and transport. They organised pools of labour, commandeered vehicles right and left, so that when the services asked for men to work at given spots, they could often oblige. Simson, of course, had his military duties as Chief Engineer as well as Head of Civil Defence. 'By working 19 hours a day, I was able to do both.' As far as civil defence was concerned, Simson managed to persuade the Governor to sack the chief of the ARP, and replace him with a more vigorous leader. He tightened up the volunteer force, re-arranged duties, produced more mobile canteens, so that, although there were never enough men to deal with the increasingly heavy raids, the volunteers at least got some spells of rest, and a few creature comforts, during the long hours of digging out bodies or fighting fires.

Every day Simson reported progress to Duff Cooper, usually after lunch and again each evening. Soon the evening meetings became more informal, taking place after a quiet dinner at Duff Cooper's house in Dunearn Road. Duff Cooper liked the modest, efficient soldier, and appreciated the fact that, despite his problems with the civil government, he still managed to keep on speaking terms with the Governor. Usually they dined quietly with Lady Diana, the toast of London and New York, the two men taking their coffee into Duff Cooper's study after the 'scratch meal' was over.

Naturally, Simson reported his brush with Stanley Jones to Duff Cooper, and after the fourth or fifth dinner together, the two men talked far into the night. It was on this occasion that Duff Cooper asked Simson why he had first refused the job of tackling civil defence. Simson told him of the urgent need for defences facing Johore. For the first time in Duff Cooper's presence he unburdened his soul, telling him every detail of the dramatic midnight meeting with General Percival—and of the General's obtuseness. Duff Cooper asked Simson, 'I'd take it as a favour if you'd prepare me a list of the ten most important things—both military and civilian—which you think should have been done in the past months.' This 'list' was to have a curious sequel, for Duff Cooper despatched a copy to Churchill.

Duff Cooper also broached his favourite topic. 'Can you suggest someone,' he asked the Brigadier, 'who could take

77

over as Governor and Commander-in-Chief? He would need some sort of military experience of course.' Simson suffered from none of the loyalties that had affected Dickinson when Duff Cooper had posed a similar question to him. He hesitated for another reason, and Duff Cooper, thinking he was embarrassed, added, 'It would be very distasteful to me to depose the King's representative. On the other hand I won't hesitate to do so if we can find the right man.'

Simson had only hesitated because he could not think of 'the right man'. 'Like you, sir,' he explained, 'I'm a newcomer to the country. And I've been so busy I've refused all social engagements.'

This conversation took place a few days after General Sir Archibald Wavell had been appointed—at the suggestion of President Roosevelt—Supreme Commander of a newly-formed ABDA (American, British, Dutch, Australian) Command, comprising forces in the various war theatres in the Far East (as apart from the Pacific). The British Chiefs of Staff had disliked the idea of having Wavell (who had up to that time been Commander-in-Chief, India), taking over this new command, no doubt fearing the effect on American public opinion of having U.S. troops under a British commander if there were to be more bad news from Malaya. Nor did Wavell relish the new post, for his first wry comment was, 'I have heard of men having to hold the baby, this is twins.' Churchill, on the other hand, possibly flattered by Roosevelt's confidence, urged Wavell not to shirk this 'unenviable command'.

Within a matter of days Wavell flew into Singapore from his new headquarters in Java. At nine in the morning, after a meeting with Duff Cooper, who had showed him Simson's 'list', he sent for Simson, and cross-questioned the Brigadier for an hour, demanding details of every obstacle that had been placed in his way. Then Wavell sent for Percival. It seems that Wavell still could not believe that Percival had really deliberately ignored the north shore defences and the advice of his Chief Engineer. Perhaps Wavell might have wondered if Simson, as an engineer, had been exaggerating, or was biased. At any rate, he said nothing to Percival at first, but reached for his cap and asked the General to accompany him on an inspection of the island's defences.

The two generals drove up to the north shore, and of this historic moment when Wavell first realised the shattering

78

truth, we have only the sketchiest account from a letter Wavell later wrote. But we do know that as they got out of their car and stood facing the Straits of Johore, with the mainland a bare thousand yards away, Wavell, in his own words, was 'very much shaken that nothing had been done'. He turned to Percival, and speaking 'with some asperity' demanded why no defences had been started, and asked for some explanation 'for his neglect'.

The GOC's answer must have taken Wavell aback, for Percival made precisely the same reply he had made to Simson—that the construction of defence works would have had a bad effect on morale. Wavell retorted sharply that the effect on morale would be infinitely worse were the troops on the peninsula to be driven back into the island. And, he warned Percival, the danger now seemed quite near.

One can sympathise with Wavell's 'asperity' for, quite apart from the danger to the island, British negligence of this sort was hardly calculated to inspire the Americans under his new command. Wavell's new job was a big one—and it had one immediate consequence, even as the shaken general drove back with Percival to Fort Canning. There did not appear to be a place in the new hierarchy for Duff Cooper, who at this very moment had received a telegram. It was from Churchill, and Duff Cooper—who naturally already knew of the ABDA command—had been half expecting it. In it the Prime Minister told his old friend that his mission was now at an end. The Prime Minister's cable instructed him to return home 'by the safest and most suitable route'.

Duff Cooper and Wavell were to have a final meeting that evening, when Duff Cooper invited him to Dunearn Road for a farewell dinner. The situation was discussed at length, and Wavell made no bones about the fact that he would like Duff Cooper to remain. They both knew that since America had generously agreed to allow her forces in the area to serve under a British commander, any political adviser would have to be an American. Yet Wavell felt that Duff Cooper could still perform a useful function even if he were restricted to Malaya. (It should be remembered that though events had forced Duff Cooper to remain in Singapore, his original terms of reference had covered a vast area of Asia.)

Duff Cooper didn't like the idea at all. He had, he said, been sent to do a job. Events had overtaken it. The dinner party broke up at midnight after Duff Cooper had given a firm 'no'. Duff Cooper went straight to bed, but he had hardly fallen asleep before a servant awoke him. An urgent message had arrived by hand. Sleepily Duff Cooper tore open the envelope. It contained a note from Wavell, together with a draft of a telegram which he proposed to send to Churchill requesting that Duff Cooper's orders to return be cancelled and that he be retained in Singapore. Duff Cooper jumped out of bed hastily, managed to telephone Wavell and begged him not to send the cable. He stressed the fact that, in view of Wavell's new job and the ABDA Command, he would have no position, nor any authority. In fact he was not even needed, and could probably do much more useful work elsewhere. Wavell tried in vain to persuade him to change his mind, but Duff Cooper was adamant. In any event, there was little time for discussion as Wavell flew back to Java the next day.

So, on January 3, Duff Cooper left with 'an uncomfortable feeling that I was running away' but with the knowledge, which was true, that despite the pleas for him to stay, he could not do so because 'if I stayed I should be without any power or significance.'

Before leaving he sent a final cable to Whitehall expressing once again his conviction 'that there existed a widespread and profound lack of confidence in the administration and that, as a breakdown might well paralyse the fighting services, changes were desirable.' This was to have significant repercussions. Within a week, a cable brought the revelation that Stanley Jones had been ignominiously dismissed, and it happens that we have a fascinating picture of Stanley Jones's dismissal, because just before this time an old friend of his had arrived out of the blue. She was Marjorie Hay, wife of M. C. Hay, Government Inspector of Mines, who had joined the volunteers as a corporal. Marjorie was well read and intelligent—and she kept an excellent daily diary.

Late at night Marjorie, accompanied by Ah Lit, her houseboy, drove over the causeway from Johore and made straight for the Colonial Secretary's house, for she had cabled Stanley Jones (whose wife was in England) asking for a bed. The telegram had never arrived but Jones came to the door in his dressing gown and found a 'bed' for her.

Life in the Colonial Secretary's official residence in Government House grounds had changed a great deal since her last visit. Half a dozen other evacuees, including Hugh Fraser, the Federal Secretary, were now all 'doubled up', some sleeping under the piano in the corner of the living-room, others under the big table in the 'L' part of the dining-room overlooking the grounds. Yet despite this influx, Stanley Jones had managed to keep up some pretence at normality, and though he scrupulously refused to buy any food which was not available through normal sources (for a black market was already springing up in the city) dinner was served each evening with beautiful silver and glass and lace mats, and the vases were filled with fresh flowers. Only the clothes of the diners seemed a trifle bizarre. Instead of black ties the men wore open-necked shirts, and Marorie Hay remembers that on the first evening, just after a raid, she was dressed in a blue shirt, shorts and red slippers.

The devastating news of the dismissal overwhelmed the Colonial Secretary four days later. There had been a heavy raid at four a.m. and Marjorie, together with Stanley Jones and the other evacuees, had made for the shelter, leaving Hugh Fraser, who said 'he couldn't be bothered' to sleep peacefully in a deep armchair throughout the raid and afterwards, despite the strident tones of the all clear.

Whilst the sirens were announcing the end of the raid Sir Shenton Thomas was returning with his wife from the shelter through the spacious grounds of Government House when a secretary handed him an urgent cable. Since it was franked 'Top Secret' nobody except the Governor possessed the key to the code and he hastened to his study at the far end of the big downstairs reception room. Before he had decoded the first line he became aware that in Whitehall orders had gone out that somebody should be sacked. But who? As he afterwards confided to a friend, the cable was worded in such a devious manner that until he had reached the very last line, the Governor was convinced that he was decoding news of his own dismissal, for 'I knew that Duff Cooper wanted to get rid of me.'

His name, however, was not the vital one on the last line of the cable. But Stanley Jones's most certainly was. There was nothing for the Governor to do but pen a personal note and send the cable down to the other big house in the grounds, where Marjorie Hay, after an early breakfast, was on the verandah when Stanley Jones walked out after reading it. Immaculate in freshly starched white drill trousers and a buff coloured 'palm beach' jacket, Jones's face was grim as he carried the cable in his hand. Without a word he handed it to her, waited until she had read it and then announced that Hugh Fraser would be taking over. Even at that moment the natural courtesy of this strange, mixed-up man did not desert him and he told her, 'I'm sure Hugh will let you stay on.' But his control was only surface deep. He went to see the Governor, and in tears begged to be allowed to stay in Singapore. He even offered to become an ARP warden, but Shenton Thomas was unable to help his old friend. Fearing that his presence might encourage divided loyalties, Whitehall had insisted that he must be flown out on the first available aircraft.

The dismissal broke Stanley Jones. During the next few days he said his few private farewells, including a special 'thank you' to Jimmy Glover, whose *Tribune* announced bluntly that the wrong man had been sacked and that Stanley Jones had been made a scapegoat.

Jones had much to answer for. He could be awkward and obstructive, as Simson had discovered. Yet those who had pierced his aggressive and unpleasant exterior liked him, and Jones's last hours in Singapore left a lasting impression on other members of his circle. Over farewell drinks with Tommy Kitching, the Chief Government Surveyor, he confided that the reason Whitehall had advanced for his recall was that of lack of co-ordination between the services and the civil administration. And though Jones's manner towards friendly, well-mannered men like Simson had been appalling when they met for the first and only time in their lives, many senior civil servants like Kitching still felt that this was the grossest slur of all. They were ready to admit that Jones had an unfortunate manner, but lack of co-ordination, many felt, was not his fault and lay fairly and squarely on the short-comings of the military.

Although a question was to be asked later in the House of Commons, the news of Stanley Jones's recall made little stir in England. The *Economist* commented,

'No clear report has come out, but quarrelling and re-criminations are obviously going on, with past maladminis-tration as the background with the Governor, the Colonial Secretary, the Military Command, the Civil Servants, the non-official community and the journalists as protagonists.

82

Through the haze of partial information, it is not a pleasing picture; and it does not seem easy for some Britons in Malaya to regard Chinese or Malays as allies instead of coolies.'

Desperately the Governor tried to restore confidence. In a circular to the Malaya Civil Service he declared:

'The day of minute papers has gone. There must be no more passing of files from one department to another, and from one officer in a department to another.'

'The announcement is about two and a half years too late,' commented the *Straits Times* acidly.

Indeed it was, for by mid-January, after a ferocious battle around the Muar river on the west coast, 80 miles north of Singapore (in which out of 4,000 Indian troops only 800 returned), British forces had been pressed back to a 90-mile line stretching across the southern tip of the Malay peninsula from Mersing to Batu Pahat. It was barely 50 miles from Singapore Island.

It seems incredible, but even when the news filtered through to Singapore—as it was bound to do—that the Japanese were over-running Johore, the civilian population did not seem able to grasp its implications. Even now, many preferred to believe that British troops had deliberately retreated to Johore where (so it was said in the clubs) the terrain would be 'more favourable to us'. Despite the evidence before their eyes—streams of dispirited, wounded troops in the streets of the city, the incessant bombing, the lack of any serious defences against air attacks—people did not see these latest enemy advances as Japanese victories, but more as a skilful Allied delaying action leading up to the moment where the tide of war would turn in Johore, the battlefield of our choosing.

The Chinese, however, were far more realistic. They had no doubts about what had happened at Muar. The news travelled swiftly along the Asian grapevine, with the result that suddenly, overnight, as though a secret order had gone out, an event occurred which was to shake the fortitude of white Singapore more profoundly than any raid.

Every Chinese shopkeeper abruptly terminated the age-old chit system. Except in the clubs and some of the big stores, cash down was now the startling order of the day—and this could only mean one thing. As George Hammonds put it, 'It was the Chinese way of telling us we'd had it.'

In a city which had lived on credit since the days of Raffles, a community in which even the humblest clerks paid their bills monthly, thousands of men now literally found themselves without sufficient loose cash to buy food. The situation became so acute that the government was forced to start paying many of its employees twice a month; as an added incentive to stability, it also offered advances of up to $30 to anyone who wanted to buy food stocks.

Inevitably there was a run on food by those still in possession of substantial funds. Indeed, the government unwittingly exacerbated the situation by urging people to lay in stocks. Buckeridge bought five lbs. of tea, five lbs. of coffee, 20 lbs. each of sugar and flour, a case of condensed milk and a bag of rice. His wife Lucy insisted that goods like tea and coffee should be stored in tins, but everybody seemed to have conceived the same idea and there was a sudden shortage of containers. Finally Buck got hold of some four-gallon kerosene tins, washed them out and eventually got rid of the smell of kerosene by repeatedly swilling whisky in them, round and round. Glover, with the aid of a *Tribune* van, was able to stock his 'shop' in the compound at Dulverton with provisions, and even acquired special uniforms for Hammonds and himself who had now been appointed heads of a small private police force to guard against theft. Freddy Retz bought some tinned salmon, corned beef and rice and packed it in old bread tins, sealing them up with sticking plaster, after which she dug a hole in the tennis court, lined it with sacking, and buried the lot.

But while it remained possible to lay in tinned stocks, there was a sudden shortage of fresh food. Japanese troops were already fighting less than seventy miles from Singapore in northern Johore with its lush market gardens which since time immemorial had been Singapore's kitchen garden. Supplies of fresh food like chickens, fruit and vegetables began to dwindle noticeably. In the old days the Chinese cookboys had fetched these each morning from villages on the island. Now they had to travel still farther afield, often during raids; inevitably, women relied more and more on the food from the Cold Storage. Here strange figures in uniform were now in evidence strolling around the stores like military shop-walkers; volunteers who not only had to keep an eye on distracted Asian assistants who often did not know the prices but were also charged with discreetly making sure that no customers got more than their fair share.

Yet, though the shoppers could no longer pick and choose the food they wanted, most of the big stores still carried vast stocks of luxury goods. Freddy Retz, walking down Battery Road, found a choice of a dozen makes of refrigerators. Kelly and Walsh had just received a new shipment of the latest books from England; gas cookers and electrical appliances were featured 'at reduced prices' in one store; and with a grim irony, Robinson's had an extensive display of the 'latest fashions' for women and children; garments at which the penniless evacuees could only stare longingly.

Many women evacuees and their children were reduced to living out of one suitcase. They had little or no money, apart from the small amounts lent to them by friends, who in some cases offered the lucky ones a bed. But the more unfortunate were billeted in hastily prepared dormitories in Raffles College or schools, where families and their fretting babies, who had been used to half a dozen servants, had no privacy and often nowhere to cook even simple baby foods. Few had the faintest idea what had happened to their husbands. The only way to pass their time was to go out—but now the hot streets were often cut off by swift downpours of drenching rain, sometimes so fierce that even cars were forced to stop. And though the heat in itself was almost unbearable, it was the humidity that made it really intolerable. Everything was dripping wet to the touch—clothes, mildewed books, salt, walls and floors. Never, so it seemed, had the north-east monsoon been so fierce. Some resourceful women who hardly possessed a change of clothing did the only thing ˇpossible—they took a taxi or begged a lift to the Swimming Club, changed into bathing suits, and while it rained washed their clothes in the ladies' changing rooms, then when the sun came out, they swam after laying out their clothes on the lawns to dry.

This crazy, unfamiliar pattern which now dominated the lives of the civilians in Singapore was complicated and made more alarming by a fifth column scare shortly after the introduction of Martial Law in January. Martial Law in itself hardly affected the civilian population. It was a precautionary move, and the Governor felt that he should go to the microphone and reassure the population that they need not entertain any fears on account of it. Unfortunately, though Malaya had virtually no fifth columnists, he linked the two subjects together, by saying that 'there is no need for anyone to worry . . . I signed the proclamation because it was necessary to make certain that evil-doers against the state shall be punished quickly . . . I know you will agree that men who conspire against the state . . . should be dealt with properly and quickly.' This was an unfortunate choice of words. Although Sir Shenton Thomas's intention had merely been to reassure the public that Martial Law would make comparatively little difference to their day-to-day lives, his reference to evil-doers and conspirators aroused an uneasy suspicion that the existence of a large fifth column was the sole reason for imposing Martial Law, and soon hundreds of people were looking nervously over their shoulders.

One morning soon after this announcement Hammonds arrived at the *Tribune*, called for a cup of tea and discovered that one of the messengers had been arrested—suspected, of all things of being a German spy. Angry at this ridiculous news, Hammonds drove to a sub-police station in River Valley Road. He discovered that although the Chinese boy had not been officially arrested he had been seized by a group of angry Chinese, 'because he was wearing an enemy helmet'. It was one of the German-type helmets which Buckeridge had acquired, and given to Hammonds for 'office use'. Only a couple of days later the same misfortune was to happen to one of Buck's men, with the result that Buckeridge had no alternative but to withdraw every one of the suspect helmets, leaving his men unprotected against falling shrapnel.

On another occasion, a messenger reported for duty at the *Tribune* wringing his hands and crying that the police were seizing all the bicycles they could lay their hands on. He begged for a chit to prevent the police seizing his precious machine, the only piece of property he possessed in the world. Hammonds phoned the police. The story was well founded. The military had demanded over a thousand bicycles, and the police had been given power to seize any machine in good condition unless the owner could produce on-the-spot evidence that he could be exempted. Why were the bicycles needed? asked Hammonds. Nobody apparently knew. George gave the Chinese a chit, but also advised him that the simplest way to save his bike was to remove all the air from the tyres.

Within 24 hours the great bicycle fiasco came to an abrupt end—when the army, which had originally demanded 1,200 'found they had made a mistake' and required only 100. So nine out of ten bicycle owners could now (in theory, but in theory only) have their machines back—if they could ever find them.

By now virtually every able-bodied European man and woman was doing some sort of war work. All Europeans reaching Singapore from up-country had to register at a Manpower Bureau where Marjorie Hay 'had to confide crudely my exact age to a beauteous young Chinese maiden, at which she gave me a vague though charming smile. I doubt if she could count up that far'. No man was allowed to leave without special permission, while for the women who wanted to leave, there was an evacuation committee with priority to those with the most children. But many women could not make up their minds whether to go or stay.

Some would have gone immediately—and Karen Hammonds was one of them—except that in some curious manner the word had gone around that it would be like running away. A woman like Karen with a family would have found no difficulty in obtaining a passage. But she and many others felt that they could not *ask* to go. What they wanted in their hearts was to be *ordered* to go; what they needed was an official lead from the government, implementing a demand by Churchill that all 'useless mouths' should be evacuated. No such lead ever came. It was left to the individual—and in mid-January the *Narkunda* sailed from Singapore for Australia half empty.

Some were being pressed to go, including Freddy Retz, who was working full-time at the hospital. Philip Bloom of the RAMC—who also worked at the General Hospital—had made it plain that he wished to marry her and that he wanted her to go. But Freddy refused, even though as an American citizen it would have been easier for her to get a passage. For she—like others who worked with her—was haunted not so much by the hundreds of wounded overflowing into every nook of the hospital, but by the wide eyes of the Eurasian and Chinese volunteers; eyes which somehow seemed to say that everything would be all right in the end if the memsahibs elected to stay.

On Tuesday, January 20, the Japanese stepped up the intensity of their raids, and 81 aircraft in three waves of 27 flew leisurely over the heart of the city—with not a British plane in the air—so high that they were undisturbed by the AA guns. For the first time Orchard Road was badly damaged.

Tim Hudson, manager of the Dunlop Rubber Purchasing Company (and a divisional ARP commander), was driving his wife Marjorie to the General Hospital where she worked in the MAS, and was opposite Wearne's garage when the first bombers appeared, looking to Hudson 'like silver fish floating in a blue sea'. He jammed on the brakes of his Hillman and both dived for the nearest drain. But there was barely room for Marjorie in the smelly concrete ditch so Tim ran for the shelter of a doorway 20 yards away. The bombs seemed to straddle them. One obliterated the shop-house next to Tim, who was lifted across the pavement into the road. He had a vague impression of a body flying through the air, but almost simultaneously two bombs landed either on or near the drain. A third tore a hole at the side of the road, uprooting a lamp-post and hurling a car through the broken plate-glass front of a shop. Hudson groped his way through the fog of dust to look for Marjorie. Three blazing cars all but stopped him—and next to them was a petrol tanker. A European with his right arm blown off, the stump bleeding, yelled, 'Get the bloody tanker away!' Somewhere behind that dust Marjorie must be lying. Tim *had* to discover her and drag her out of the bombed drain.

'For Christ's sake get a move on—it'll blow up at any moment,' yelled the man; an instant later he had flopped in the road, dead or unconscious. Tim had never driven anything like this monster before. Somehow he climbed into the high cab, discovered the switch and crashed a gear in— he never knew which one it was—and the tanker lurched forward in a series of jumps. Something now went wrong, he suddenly discovered that he couldn't change gears. He jerked across the wide stretch of Orchard Road, now alive with figures, hit an uprooted tree, and came to a halt with his front off-side wheel in the ditch on the opposite side. Only then did he scramble out and run back for Marjorie.

The all clear sounded as he reached the drain and started to dig with his hands, dragging out three dead Indians who were lying on top of her; with a tremendous effort he managed to pull them aside and discovered Marjorie, covered with dirt and debris. Before he even saw her, his hands, scrabbling in the dirt, felt soft invisible flesh, and his first sickening thought was that she was dead. He tore the debris away, uncovered her ashen face, and leaning down, tried to pull out the body from which most of the clothes had been ripped off. She did not move. Filthy water lined the bottom of the deep trench, but Tim clambered in to reach it, cupped his hands and threw some in her face. After what seemed like an age her eyes suddenly flickered and opened. She owed her life to one thing—the blast that killed the Indians had thrown them on top of her and protected her when the second bomb fell.

A few yards away the Cold Storage had had a 'near miss'. Jimmy Glover was outside, waiting for his wife Julienne who had gone in to do some shopping. As Jimmy watched, the entire store seemed to shake; unknown to him something terrible had happened inside; without warning the whole store started to cloud with gas, and as the horrified yet strangely fascinated shoppers watched the visible wraiths creeping towards them, one screamed 'Gas bombs!'

It was not gas. The bombs had damaged the pipes leading to the refrigerator room, causing a leak of ammonia, but no one knew this, and in a pandemonium every woman ran for the doors which were always kept closed because of the air-conditioning. Screaming, coughing, spluttering women fought with assistants to wrench the doors open. Julienne covered her face with a handkerchief and, in acute danger of being trampled underfoot, somehow managed to crawl to a side door, forced her way out and ran stumbling across the road where she found Jimmy. Still choking and gasping she promised him, 'From now on, I'll do my shopping at six in the morning'.

Some distance away in the garden of Cathedral House two bombs had fallen killing Archdeacon Graham-White's secretary but leaving Mrs. Graham-White, who was knitting beside him, untouched. In the grounds of Government House twenty-six bombs had fallen, killing only a tawny cat and some chickens. Nine alone had exploded in the Colonial Secretary's compound. Marjorie Hay, who had been alone in the living-room, had had no time to reach the shelter, but dived under the piano as the blast blew all the doors off their hinges, tore a gaping hole in the ceiling, showering the room in plaster and debris. A second bomb landed just outside the

89

verandah. Its blast sliced off the top of the piano under which she was sheltering. The phone installation was smashed, the water system was damaged, and Marjorie's silk pyjamas, which were drying on a verandah rail, 'were reduced by blast to a network of slits'. One bomb demolished the driver's quarters and set several cars alight. Another unexploded bomb embedded itself in a corner of the verandah of Government House, and the grounds between the two houses were pitted with scars and craters and littered with torn-up trees.

Just as Hugh Fraser, the new Colonial Secretary, and his staff were returning for lunch, the bombers struck again. Fraser pushed Marjorie under the long dining table; the others managed to squeeze in, crowding her uncomfortably. There they waited for half an hour—watching a pair of brown feet belonging to Ah Lit, Marjorie Hay's boy, who was calmly setting the table for lunch.

Soon the raiders had left them in peace and were concentrating on the docks. At Raffles the boys returned to duty and, dressed in spotless white uniforms, started to serve tiffin. Round the corner, by the synagogue off Beng Swee Place, the dead were being laid out on the pavement for identification.

There were three raids that day and in the evening Shenton Thomas and his wife visited Hugh Fraser to inspect the damage. Marjorie Hay found them 'pleasant, ordinarily devoid of pomposity, but if now they are just a trifle puffed up over their unexploded bomb, it must be forgiven them.' Stanley Jones was still waiting for the plane due to take him away from Singapore to South Africa on Friday; all he growled was, 'I'm damned if I'm going on that Friday plane as if I'm running away.' Darkness brought relief if not peace, and Leslie Hoffman spent the night in the *Tribune* building, after coping with a linotype operator who had arrived at 5.30 with the news that his wife had been killed and there was nobody to look after the children. By this time Hoffman was used to such disturbing reports and refused to believe him. 'I'd heard about the office boy and his grandmother's funeral.' Putting on a stern front, he explained that it was too late to get a substitute and the man went on night duty 'quite happily'.

Next morning the Japanese bombers returned and this proved the heaviest raid the city had yet experienced. At least 383 people were killed and over 700 wounded, most

90

casualties being in Chinatown. Over 100 aircraft attacked the Asiatic quarter of Beach Road where 47 shophouses were destroyed. Another bomb scored a direct hit on Clyde Terrace market. Scores of people were burned to death when a third hit Havelock Road market.

George Hammonds was in the Cricket Club at the time. A friend had just asked him if he would like a game of 'volunteer' snooker (at which George professed some skill) but he had refused and the man went moodily off to the billiard room to knock a few balls around.

The first bomb blew a crater on the padang. The second hit the members' car park by the main entrance, lifting one car like a toy and hurling it through the side of the building into the billiard room, where the man who only a minute or two ago had asked George to play was killed instantly.

Many people had miraculous escapes. At the time when the second wave had been on the way, Buckeridge's fire engine had been en route, its bell clanging, to a fire behind the Supreme Court. He had left Lucy to spend the morning with a friend in Malcolm Road on the outskirts of the city. Hours later he returned to fetch her, racing past Dickinson's big house on Mount Pleasant, then crossing Whitley Road to reach the winding, hilly lane on which the house had stood. There was nothing—nothing but a pile of smouldering debris. The house had received a direct hit and his own AFS men told him everybody inside had been killed. At that very moment Lucy ran towards him. 'I thought she was a ghost,' recalled Buckeridge. She told him that she had been trying to phone but couldn't get through. Just before the bomb fell she had walked down the road to a small Chinese shop to buy a bar of chocolate.

It was in this raid that the godown by the docks in Keppel Road, which Tim Hudson rented for Dunlop's, suffered its first bomb; however, thanks to his foresight, it was hardly damaged, for after the very first raid on Singapore, Hudson had constructed an enormous shelter for 200 inside the godown by stacking up scores of squat, tightly-packed bales of rubber, supporting a rubber roof six feet thick with planking. Now, dozens of pieces of shrapnel tore the roof into ' a piece of lace', and in the next godown 11 coolies were killed outright. But not one piece of shrapnel penetrated more than a few inches into his own rubber shelter.

Hudson—a spare-time Divisional ARP commander—was

a remarkable man who throughout these perilous days some-how managed to do three jobs. In addition to buying rubber for Dunlop's, and controlling his ARP station with 300 wardens at Tiong Bahru in Chinatown, he also broadcast regularly on ARP matters. Indeed, he was becoming something of a local radio hero for his talks were factual, down to earth and uncompromising, in direct contrast to the official plati-tudes so often handed out.

In his early forties, Hudson was still trim and slim enough to look well in his khaki ARP bush jacket. Of average height, with a thatch of thick, dark brown hair, he sported a tuft of brown beard which stuck out at an aggressive angle so that he looked not unlike Captain Kettle. One feels he would have been pleased with the allusion for he could be aggres-sive, short-tempered with fools, and astute; three qualities badly needed in his job, which entailed buying 4,000 tons of crude rubber a month from a variety of Chinese (not all of them honest) and running an office staff of 20, together with 500 coolies who handled the heavy bales.

That night Hudson was broadcasting and he dispensed with his normally censored script. Throughout the day he had worked alongside Asiatic AFS and ARP men who toiled with-out helmets, without food, without drink, and now he spoke passionately and movingly of the Chinese—describing the heroic work they were doing, the example they were setting; and painting a word picture of the fatalistic attitude to life and death that made them carry on impassively. He described how after the first big raid he had driven down to Beach Road where bodies lay untended in the streets, the flies crawling everywhere, as friends and relatives waited for the burial squads. Etched in his mind were two pictures he would never forget. The first was of Chinese children nonchalantly playing ball while lorries unceremoniously loaded up a grisly assortment of corpses, and a little boy, running too fast as he chased the ball, fell over a man's headless body, and as he got up, looked at his bloody hands, then—perhaps un-comprehendingly—smelled the blood on them before wiping them on his smock. And the other picture was of fire hoses playing on a burning shophouse—while four grave old Chinese ladies were carefully throwing cigarette tins of water on the flames in an effort to help.

Hudson had been in the thick of it, but on others this big raid had hardly made an impact. Freddy Retz dived into a shelter to find it occupied by several elderly ladies, each with her own cushion, and all occupied with needlework or knitting. Leslie Hoffman and his old father were in their shelter when a polite Chinese arrived and announced that he had come to read the gas meter. George Hammonds was at the Singapore Golf Club, with the two sergeants who occasionally used to baby-sit for Karen. They had asked him time and again if he could arrange a visit to this temple of the Singapore tuan. He had obtained special passes—and on his arrival had been astounded to find a dozen golfers putting out on the greens, and could hardly believe that he himself was sitting there, peacefully drinking a gimlet in front of the lake, with the war so close.

There were other strangely peaceful interludes. The next evening George Hammonds visited the New World with its Chinese taxi girls, only to find that he couldn't get in because of the crowd of waiting soldiers—possibly because the New World was advertising in the *Tribune*, 'Non-stop dancing and cabaret and the usual tiffin dance on Sunday'. This was only one of the bizarre advertisements now appearing in the *Tribune*, and as the staff which normally handled these advertisements had shrunk, George often had to help out—and was staggered when one came in: '*For sale—European Guest house in select non-military area. Good business proposition. Reply with bank references.*' The Goodwood Park Hotel still advertised itself as '*Charmingly situated. Ideal for visitors and tourists.*' The Alhambra cinema offered Greta Garbo and Ramon Navarro in *Mata Hari*. The Cathay advised readers to '*fling away your troubles and have a fling at love and laughter*' by watching their latest comedy.

But the Personal Column of the *Tribune* now began to fill with heartrending advertisements:

'Mrs. J. Norman Milne of Lower Perak and her two children are staying at 27 Newton Road, Singapore, and anxious for any news of her husband, Sergeant J. N. Milne.'

'Can anybody please give news of her husband to Mrs. Wong Ah Chan, c/o Maynards, Battery Road.'

'Will Mrs. Jennie Lim please write to her sister Lamoon as soon as possible, as she is now without a home.'

Day after day the *Tribune* carried a large government public notice ordering all civilians to evacuate a stretch of the northern coastline 'purely for precautionary measures'—an advertisement which was presumably reported back to the calm and peace of Chequers, causing Churchill to cable angrily, 'I am concerned about the fullness of the information given in the Singapore papers. . . . Why is it necessary to state that a mile has been evacuated for defensive purposes on the northern side of the island? . . . They seem to give everything away about themselves in the blandest manner. After all, they are defending a fortress and not conducting a Buchmanite revival.'

There were other signs of war. In Singapore the Cold Storage stopped baking its delicious French bread and produced, in common with all other bakers, a new government 'health bread' which resembled a wholemeal brown loaf. As the army fell back across Johore, some of the government food stores were thrown open to the public—though when the news first reached Singapore it was treated as just another rumour. But at night, when Jimmy Glover was in his office, one of his newspaper vans returned from Johore Bahru, the capital of the State, and the driver had two cases of tinned milk which had been given to him.

The next morning Tommy Kitching, the Chief Government Surveyor, received a telephone call from the army. Could his department do a rush job printing new bank-notes? Money was running short, partly owing to army needs, partly because everybody was now forced to pay cash. Yet not far away, in another government department, Mr. Eric Pretty was almost simultaneously being asked to consider the possibility of burning five million dollars in notes, in order to stop the Japanese getting them.

Day by day life became crazier. Tim Hudson drove an old lorry to the main ARP store headquarters in order to get some desperately needed picks and shovels. He found the place deserted. A sign pinned to the door announced: 'Back in four hours.' The man in charge had taken time off to visit the cinema. Two miles away George Hammonds, after locking his car, went into the Cricket Club for a pre-lunch drink, and returned just in time to see two men stealing his car. As they had no key, they had torn the floorboards out of his car and were already starting the ignition with a piece of wire; as he yelled at them, the car leapt away, leaving the floorboards on the ground. George stood there shouting after them, until a member whose name he did not know said quietly, 'Take mine. I'm leaving in an hour.' George drove back to Amber Mansions in a large shiny Chevrolet.

CHAPTER SIX

THE END OF THE MYTH

The Last Days of January

Not until this moment—as the battle for Johore moved inexorably towards disaster in the last days of January—does it appear to have dawned on Churchill that Singapore was indefensible—and, even more terrible, that Britain might have to make what he described as an 'ugly decision' and abandon the island and fortress, diverting reinforcements to Burma. For it was not until January 19 that the myth of Singapore was finally exploded for Churchill himself—the one man above all others who had been taken in by the grand illusion of the fortress that never was.

The news came in the form of a cable from Wavell, in reply to one which Churchill had sent him asking, 'What would happen in the event of your being forced to withdraw on the island?' Churchill posed a series of vital questions. How many troops would be needed? How would landings be prevented? What were the defences on the landward side? Could the 'Fortress Cannon' command the Straits of Johore? Was everything prepared? 'It has always seemed to me,' his cable read, 'that the vital need is to prolong the defence of the Island to the last possible minute, but of course I hope it will not come to this.'

Wavell's reply arrived on January 19. It told him bluntly:

'Until quite recently all plans were based on repulsing seaborne attacks on the Island and holding land attack in Johore or farther North, and little or nothing was done to construct defences on North side of Island to prevent crossing Johore Straits, though arrangements had been made to blow up the causeway.'

Churchill was horrified. In place of the legendary fortress in which he had believed, there was 'the hideous spectacle of the almost naked island'. 'I ought to have known,' he wrote later. 'My advisers ought to have known and I ought to have been told and I ought to have asked. The reason I had not asked . . . was that the possibility of Singapore having no landward defences no more entered into my mind than that of a battleship being launched without a bottom.'

Churchill's immediate reaction was to dictate a blistering minute to General Ismay for the Chiefs of Staff Committee:

'I must confess to being staggered by Wavell's telegram. . . . It never occurred to me for a moment . . . that the gorge of the fortress of Singapore, with its splendid moat half-a-mile wide, was not entirely fortified against an attack from the northward. What is the use of having an island for a fortress if it is not to be made into a citadel?

'To construct a line of detached works, with searchlights and cross-fire combined with immense wiring and obstruction of the swamp area, and to provide the proper ammunition to enable the fortress guns to dominate enemy batteries planted in Johore, was an elementary peace-time provision which it is incredible did not exist in a fortress which has been twenty years building.'

And he added bitterly, 'I warn you this will be one of the greatest scandals that could possibly be exposed.'

To Wavell, Churchill cabled personally:

'I want to make it absolutely clear that I expect every inch of ground to be defended, every scrap of material or defences to be blown to pieces to prevent capture by the enemy, and no question of surrender to be entertained until after protracted fighting among the ruins of Singapore City.'

To the Chiefs of Staff he sent his own ideas for how the 'fortress' should be prepared against attack:

'Let a plan be made at once to do the best possible while the battle in Johore is going forward. The plan should comprise:

(a) An attempt to use the fortress guns on the northern front by firing reduced charges and by running in a certain quantity of high explosive if none exists.

(b) By mining and obstructing the landing-places where any considerable force could gather.

(c) By wiring and laying booby-traps in mangrove swamps and other places.

(d) By constructing field works and strong points, with field artillery and machine-gun cross-fire.

(e) By collecting and taking under our control every conceivable small boat that is found in the Johore Straits or anywhere else within reach.

(f) By planting field batteries at each end of the straits, carefully masked and with searchlights, so as to destroy any enemy boat that may seek to enter the straits.

(g) By forming the nuclei of three or four mobile counter-attack reserve columns upon which the troops when driven out of Johore can be formed.

(h) The entire male population should be employed upon construction defence works. The most rigorous compulsion is to be used, up to the limit where picks and shovels are available.

(i) Not only must the defence of Singapore Island be maintained by every means, but the whole island must be fought for until every single unit and every single strong-point has been separately destroyed.

(j) Finally, the city of Singapore must be converted into a citadel and defended to the death. No surrender can be contemplated.'

There is a note of grim irony in this detailed list of instructions. At least seven of Churchill's points had been contained in the 'list' which Brigadier Simson had compiled for Duff Cooper, and which Duff Cooper had passed on to Churchill. Not even the order had been changed by Churchill. In other words, it had taken Churchill himself to order Percival to implement the precise ideas which the Chief Engineer had been advocating in vain for months.

The Chiefs of Staff sent their version of this dramatic minute to Wavell, though for some unexplained reason they decided not to include the final three paragraphs.

Wavell replied to Churchill in the only way he could —by telling him the doleful truth: 'I am sorry to give you [such a] depressing picture.' Now Churchill was faced with a cruel issue: should the reinforcements already on their way by sea to Singapore be diverted to Burma? 'There was still ample time to turn their prows northwards to Rangoon.' For Churchill realised, as he told the Chiefs of Staff:

> 'Obviously nothing should distract us from the Battle of Singapore, but should Singapore fall quick transference of forces to Burma might be possible. As a strategic object, I regard keeping the Burma Road open as more important than the retention of Singapore.'

That evening he could not make up his mind. In the utmost secrecy—for this was a matter which concerned the Australians deeply—Churchill asked his Chiefs of Staff to consider the problem and meet him later, advising them to bear in mind that

> 'We may, by muddling things and hesitating to take an ugly decision, lose *both* Singapore and the Burma Road.'

By some extraordinary chance the Australians in London obtained a copy of this minute. How this came about has never been explained, but Sir Earle Page, the Australian delegate in London, promptly cabled its contents to Australia. The effect on the Australian cabinet was electric. Mr. Curtin, the Australian premier, cabled an angry protest to Churchill.

> 'After all the assurances we have been given the evacuation of Singapore would be regarded here as an inexcusable betrayal. Singapore is a central fortress in the system of the Empire and local defence. We understood that it was to be made impregnable, and in any event it was to be capable of holding out for a prolonged period until the arrival of the main fleet.
> 'Even in an emergency, diversion of reinforcements should be to the Netherlands East Indies and not to Burma. Anything else would be deeply resented, and might force the Netherlands East Indies to make a separate peace.
> 'On the faith of the proposed flow of reinforcements, we have acted and carried out our part of the bargain. We expect you not to frustrate the whole purpose of evacuation.'

The phrase 'inexcusable betrayal' had an unpleasant ring for the Prime Minister, and though he was later to maintain that Curtin's message had not decided the issue, it is difficult not to infer that this fact *did* influence him to a considerable degree. Churchill became very conscious of 'a hardening of opinion against the abandonment of this renowned key point in the Far East'. And so, though he had 'no doubt what a purely military decision should have been' it was decided to fight on. The British 18th Division (composed of territorial units recruited in East Anglia) now on the long sea route, proceeded to Singapore as planned—even though by January 26, we find Percival signalling Wavell, 'We are fighting all the way, but may be driven back into the Island within a week'. Percival was so worried that he sent a private letter to Wavell, backing up his cable. 'It looks as if we should not be able to hold Johore for more than another three or four days,' he wrote. 'Our total fighter strength is now reduced to nine.'

Singapore was now on the edge of disaster, and, in terms of history, this was the moment when the great city—its normal population doubled to a million—should have been rallied under a dynamic leader with the soul of Raffles to prepare for the rigours and terrors of siege warfare and street fighting. It is easy to conjure up a picture of what might have been—the thousands of troops hurriedly throwing up defence works; the civilians—suddenly aware of the danger upon them—dropping everything to barricade the streets and fortify each corner; the issue of small arms to eager squads of men in ill-assorted uniforms, ready to defend each street and each house to the death; the coolies under fire stoically unloading precious war materials from the docks. Alas, there *was* no dynamic leader. It was all very well for Sir Shenton Thomas to broadcast, 'This is total war, in which the whole population is involved. It will be grim, no doubt, but no more grim than in Britain, Russia and China, and if the people of those countries can stand up to total war, so can we . . . Europeans, Indians, Chinese, Malays—we all stand together side by side, shoulder to shoulder.'

They were 'shoulder to shoulder'—but who was to direct their energies and loyalty? Who was to tell them where, when, how to fight? Who was to feed them? Who would look after their families if they left their jobs? The tragedy of

Singapore was that all men of all creeds were prepared to fight, but the flowery exhortations were never crystallised into direct, unified action. Troops as well as civilians were confused and insecure. For nearly two months they had been fed on pompous pronouncements. A ruthless censorship had hidden the truth from them. Never once in the campaign had loyal and patriotic men had a 'father figure' to whom they could turn and offer to help. And now, at its moment of destiny, Singapore was like a storm-tossed ship without a captain. There was no single mind, no man cast in heroic mould, to direct and control the thousands who awaited the call.

At this very moment of great urgency—and despite Churchill's clarion call to action—it actually took the service chiefs and the civil government ten whole days to thrash out an agreement on rates of pay for the desperately needed coolies. First, the problem was discussed in the Singapore War Council, where the Navy and the RAF demanded conscription of all available labour. Brigadier Simson, now also on the War Council, asked for higher wages, protection during raids and compensation for injury. The civil government inexplicably insisted that special danger pay 'was undesirable since it would lead to inflation'. After three days of argument the government agreed to some increase in wage rates and a measure of compulsion. Yet even so, it took the War Council another five days to agree on details. For now the service commanders said that they had no authority to spend money on increased rates of compensation. The Governor and the three service chiefs thereupon despatched simultaneous cables to London (where, one would have thought, a single cable would have sufficed) asking for a free hand to fix wages. On January 29, an emergency Bill was passed in Singapore announcing the new labour conditions. But it was not until two days later, on January 31, that Whitehall finally capitulated and gave the military authorities a free hand.

By then the Japanese were less than 30 miles away.

In London, Churchill, fearing the worst, asked the House of Commons for a Vote of Confidence on January 27, and during the course of his survey of the war, told the Commons, 'We have had a great deal of bad news lately from the Far East, and I think it highly probable . . . we shall have a great deal more. Wrapped up in this bad news will be many tales
100

of blunders and shortcomings, both in foresight and action.'

George Hammonds heard this speech broadcast to Singapore a few hours later, sitting in the dark, listening to the radio in his flat in Amber Mansions. He turned to Karen and said, 'Churchill's given up the fight. You and the kids are off on the next ship. Don't argue.' Within a couple of days he was told by the government Evacuation Committee she could go 'when you can get her on a boat'.

To all who heard them, Churchill's grave and sombre words —and the clear implications behind them—stood out like a warning beacon. Within a matter of hours, almost minutes, the word had gone out along the grapevine. The four troopships which had recently brought in the 18th Division were due to leave. It was now or never. As though compelled by some instinctive urge for survival, the rush began by civilians to whom the larger issues of the war had now become crystallised into personal, agonising decisions that would affect lives profoundly.

Tim Hudson was off duty that night and was already in bed when an old friend rang him at midnight and told him that his wife was leaving the next day. He urged Tim to get Marjorie away. She was on night duty at the hospital, but Tim decided that she must leave, so he got the car out and drove through the black-out to register her name with the P and O. But to his consternation, when Marjorie returned from the hospital, she refused to go. All through the morning he tried to persuade her but her resistance was so strong that in the end he was forced to phone the P and O and cancel the ticket. 'They thought I was crazy.'

For others the simple equation of 'stay' or 'go' was decided for them. Leslie Hoffman had already booked his wife a place on the *Empress of Japan*. Now suddenly he was told officially that in view of the bitterly anti-Japanese articles he had written, he would, with his Asian blood, be a marked man if the Japanese took Singapore. Official permission had been granted for him to go with his wife. But Leslie's old widowed father was still living in Singapore and Leslie didn't want to leave him alone. Who knew when—if ever—he would return? After the position had been explained, the government immediately gave Leslie's father permission to go too.

Knowing the danger of remaining under Japanese rule, Leslie drove through the black-out to his father's house and told him to pack. But he had reckoned without the old man's stubbornness. His father absolutely refused to budge. 'I've lived in Singapore for 50 years,' he said. 'It's my home, I'm not going to be pushed out by a bunch of Japanese.'

Leslie and his wife implored, begged, cajoled, threatened; it made no difference. Hoffman now found himself faced with a heartbreaking decision. If Singapore fell, he could expect no mercy from the Japanese; he might never again see his wife and unborn child. If he went, he might never again see his father. In the end, he decided to send his wife and stay himself.

During that night there were six Japanese raids, and at dawn George Hammonds received a phone call from the military, telling him that all service wives had been ordered out, that a boat was leaving that night, and it was time for Karen to go—even though 'H.E. will make no evacuation order as he feels it would lower British prestige.' Karen gulped a cup of tea, grabbed a piece of toast and, leaving the children with the amah, set off with George for the P and O office.

The government had centralised all bookings through the P and O which had moved its office from the centre of Singapore to the less dangerous Agency House at Cluny, five miles out of town. When they reached the bottom of the long uphill drive off the main road, George left her, promising to return as soon as he had attended the morning military briefing. Karen's heart sank. In vain police were trying to instil some order. Scores of cars lined the grass verges where the main road met the drive, some of them askew with their wheels sagging down into the ditches. Several had obviously been hit by machine-gun fire. And at the foot of the winding, climbing drive, a long, slow-moving procession of women and children stretched almost out of sight into the office. It was an almost biblical picture—the slowness of it, mothers tugging at their children, on the verge of tears, the hurt, brittle words with which they tried to mask their fear, some with children in their arms, all seeking the shade of the trees that lined the drive. The lucky ones had their amahs with them. The winding, white procession kept to the left-hand side and hardly seemed to move as Karen joined the tail end. Down the opposite side women moved more quickly, aware of a new excitement. They had reached the bungalow, they had got their tickets, they were off. They almost ran to their cars, eager to pick up a suitcase, to be on their way. Karen noticed a friend further up in the queue who wished her good luck—and told her that she had been queueing since midnight.

Twice during the hot, sticky procession towards the office, Japanese air raids forced the women and their whimpering children to take cover in the concrete ditch at the side of the road. But after three hours—during which time George had not returned—Karen Hammonds reached the house. In more normal times this has been the pleasant private residence of the P and O chief. It was a big bungalow, with a handsome porch and a large verandah with rattan shades which could be lowered against the rain. Now it had all the frenzied atmosphere of an evacuee transit camp. True, the orchids in their pots were still hanging from the trees, but the beautiful green lawns had been turned into a muddy brown, whilst indoors the two big downstairs rooms were bare of the 'best furniture' which had been carried upstairs and replaced with rows of cane chairs.

Karen almost stumbled into the welcome shade of the room, and gratefully gulped a long drink offered to her. She found herself facing two tables. One was for booking to Colombo, the other to Britain. She had already decided to go to Britain, but even as she walked towards the 'U.K. table' she remembered George and her resolve weakened. 'I felt I was standing under a sign at a cross roads. I knew it was immensely important that I should not take the wrong road.'

In the hot crowded room, distracted P and O officials struggled to cope with a horde of women, some half fainting in the heat, many on the verge of hysteria, and undecided whether they really wanted to go. It was typical of this undecided state of mind that Karen should turn to an officer and wail, 'I don't really want to go!' At that moment George appeared, gripped her arm, and steered her to the table.

'Come on now,' said Mr. Frank Hammond, the P and O chief kindly, and asked for her passport. Thumbing it through, he made the startling discovery that it had run out.

Hopefully George produced his military and press permit, together with an identity card with which Karen had been issued for civil defence work. It bore a duplicate of her passport photo. Politely but firmly it was rejected and she was told that it wasn't the fault of the P and O; regulations were regulations and she must return to Singapore and get her passport renewed.

In tears Karen set off down the 'way out' side. It took her and George four hours (and two raids) to get the passport renewed, and she was once more able to take her place at the end of a new queue. Finally she reached the 'U.K. table' again and got her 'ticket'—a slip printed on a duplicating machine with her name on it and a few brief embarkation instructions. She was told that mattresses would be provided, but not bed linen. It would be necessary to take her own plate, knife, fork and spoon and some sandwiches for the first few hours. The scrap of paper bore no berth or cabin number.

Karen barely remembered the return journey to Amber Mansions. Her first necessity was to obtain some money for the journey, but by now all the banks were closed. In desperation George phoned the Hong Kong and Shanghai Bank, said he was speaking from the *Malaya Tribune*, and demanded to speak to the manager. 'It created the right impression.' Karen was promised £25 in travellers' cheques which she could collect on her way to the docks. She had little more than an hour left before she had to be on board, no time for goodbyes, just a few minutes in the living-room where so much had happened, and where they had been so happy together. Then George was bundling the suitcases and the children into the back of his shiny new 'Chevvy'.

Karen was to be far luckier than many others—for she had a car, money and a man to help her. But for all too many women and children this was a time of complete confusion. Many did not have the faintest idea what to do. Authority appeared non-existent. No orders were issued to the evacuees and they were left to their own devices. The government could have used the Malaya Broadcasting Company to give them official guidance and advice, but not a word was heard over the radio during this confusing period. Many women who had been evacuated from up-country had neither money nor papers. Yet when they came crowding into the P and O office, they discovered that regulations forbade them obtaining their vital tickets until they had been issued with documents which regularised their positions and gave them the necessary authority to leave.

Leslie Hoffman had been at Cluny helping some friends

when a middle-aged woman, distraught and in tears, arrived at the table with the news that her mother of 81 had lost her passport when ordered out of Kuala Lumpur, and was now in hospital. Both wanted to leave Singapore and her mother was able to travel, but the old lady couldn't get a new passport because all the Japanese photographers had been interned. Hoffman drove back to the *Tribune*, found a staff photographer and was able to send the pair of them gratefully on their way.

Some women were alert enough to by-pass officialdom. One young married woman had been living in a remote rubber plantation and had never been near enough to a government office to have her maiden name changed on her passport. On arrival at the 'U.K. table' with a baby in her arms she was told that her passport was not in order. Refusing to accept defeat, she walked across to the 'Colombo table', stood in front of a different assistant who looked at the 'Miss' on her passport and then at the baby. 'It's mine—illegitimate,' she said curtly—and sailed that night.

Many 'useless mouths' had no idea that the government had agreed to stake their fares home. The government did not want to publicise this news in case it lowered Asian morale. As a result Marjorie Hudson was awakened in the middle of the night by an old friend who had come from up-country with her three children. With three children she should have left weeks before, and it was only when she begged Marjorie for money that she discovered that every shipping agent had been instructed by the government that in cases of hardship. European women with children could 'sign' for the trip.

But many women still resolutely refused to go. Freddy Retz, who had left the hospital after 24 hours of nearly non-stop work, became involved in sucn an argument with Philip Bloom who had come to fetch her that he stopped his car and they had a blazing row. Finally Philip turned to her. 'Well—if you stay, will you marry me?' Without a moment's hesitation Freddy told him that she would—on her birthday, which was February 6. And after that promise they never mentioned the subject of leaving again. Two other people who never mentioned it were Dickie Dickinson and his wife Bunny. 'It never entered either of our heads to go.' Dickinson was obviously doing vital work, and Bunny was in virtual charge of Blood Transfusion. Jimmy Glover's French wife Julienne also refused point blank to leave—

'with typical French vehemence'. So did Marjorie Hudson, despite more arguments. She 'had a job to do' and that was that.

'Well, if you insist on staying, you'd better go out and buy a spade,' said Tim Hudson, pointing to a bold government advertisement in the *Straits Times*. This was a fervent appeal to every householder with even the smallest compound to start growing vegetables. Supplies of fertilisers would be distributed in the near future by the Food Production Office. Eagerly the government announced through the Press, 'Don't put it off till tomorrow—start growing vegetables today!'

All night and half the morning the docks and their approach roads had been heavily attacked by formations of Japanese twin-engined bombers with Zero fighter escorts. Half the big godowns in the docks were raging fires. The smell of rubber mingled with that of burning tar and rope. Hundreds of civilians had been killed, and as the carloads of women approached Collyer Quay and moved off along the waterfront, ambulances kept their motors running while bodies were dug out of the smoking ruins. It was every woman for herself. The police and the Army had long since given up any attempt to marshal the traffic. Cars, driven by husbands or servants, just drove as far as they could—and then people walked. The roads leading to the three-mile dock area were often impassable—not only because of the congested stream of 'useless mouths' on their way, at last and too late, to freedom, but because they clashed head-on with convoys of army lorries, racing to get the military stores away from the docks and into Singapore Island so the ships could sail before the Japanese sank the sitting targets—four huge troopships which had brought in the 18th Division, berthed now at the Main Wharf of the big, rectangular Empire Dock. One had a hole in her iron deck where a bomb had landed that morning, killing 26 men as the troops sweated to unload military equipment. Newly arrived soldiers of the 18th Division sat about on the dockside, lolling on their mountains of luggage and equipment. They had only just been disembarked, and all were in high spirits as they waited to go forward into an action about whose outcome they were pathetically optimistic.

The monsoon rains had ceased, but there were many who would have preferred a wetting to the sultry, steaming, humid weather that made the sea they faced look like a burnished steel tray hurtful to the eyes. The quays, which were seething with women and children and their menfolk who had come to see them off, were so hot that one could feel the heat through shoes. Every inch between the line of godowns and the ships was jammed with gasping women, jostling, or just waiting patiently for their turn to pass through the one small gate where sat a P and O man—one lonely man with a very small table and one pencil—who took down every passenger's name, writing it beautifully but with painful slowness in a ledger.

Among the thousands of people who were converging on the docks, was the Rev. Bennitt, driving his wife and daughter who had passes for the *Empress of Japan*. 'The Rev.' drove them down early past big fires and through air heavy with the smell of burning rubber. Mrs. Bennitt always remembered the look on a British soldier's face as he helped them out of the car and noticed her husband's 'dog collar'. 'Bless us, Rev!' he cried. 'Where did *you* come from?'

Because they had got there early, 'the Rev.' was able to see them on board, but somehow he couldn't bear to stay. Neither could Leslie Hoffman whose wife was also sailing on the *Empress*. As the women disappeared in the throng every man, as though to hide his feelings, made off as quickly as he could.

George Hammonds with Karen and the children reached the docks a little later, for the normal route to their ship had been blocked by a direct hit which had caused a huge fire. On their arrival they saw an indescribable scrum of women, children and luggage—without a single porter or coolie to help. Every man in the labour force had vanished as they stood in the 'sweaty mess of humanity'. With George carrying the suitcases, they moved forward towards the man with the pencil at the rate of a yard every half hour. They were still queuing with other women—including Marjorie Hay and Lucy Buckeridge—when the siren sounded and George felt cold and sick at the thought of the shambles that would result if a bomb fell in their midst. But the planes passed over, the crowd calmed, and the P and O pencil plodded steadily on as the thin trickle of women flowed up the gangway and into the ship. Like the other men, George could not bear to wait. After what seemed like an eternity of pushing and shoving, carrying Karen's luggage, he saw her and the children past the P and O man, and on to the gangplank. Then they

107

vanished into the big vessel just as the sirens sounded again. George dived for the nearest shelter, but when he saw women and children outside, he left and squeezed down by the side of a godown.

As the embarkation proceeded, the hot suffocating day changed into a sunset the colour of blood, to be followed by the swift pink twilight of tropics and a period of blessed darkness. Then a bright moon broke over the edge of the sky, lighting the city, as though to give the women lining the rails of the big ships a last indelible picture of the waterfront of Singapore, once a great thriving port but now almost deserted. Beind the scarred docks they could make out the tall, flimsy Chinese houses cheek by jowl with the more ornate buildings of the merchants and the occasional row of palms. And in the background, the silhouette of the city, sometimes silver, was lit here and there with the crimson glow of fires.

Back in their bungalows the men wrote their own private farewells to those they loved and might never see again. It is better they should go,' wrote 'The Rev.' in his diary. 'We have had each other eight and a half years—eight and a half years with the best wife in the world and nearly five with the loveliest ever daughter.'

In those last few hectic hours before Singapore became a beleaguered city, four ships managed to get away. Two troopships, the *West Point* and the *Wakefield*, left on the Friday, carrying a large number of European women and children and some Asians. Now, a day later, under the tropic moon, the *Empress of Japan* prepared to leave with 1,500 women and children and the *Duchess of Bedford* with 900 on board. And as the big ships sailed out—all to arrive safely at their destinations—the first tired troops of the Imperial forces were preparing to cross the causeway for the last stand in the 'fortress' they did not know was already doomed.

PART TWO

DURING

CHAPTER SEVEN

AWAITING THE ATTACK

Sunday, February 1—Sunday, February 8

As if to compensate for war, the first few days of February were beautiful. It was hot, but the humidity had dropped with the passing of the north-east monsoon, and now only an occasional shower washed the grimy, bomb-scarred city. The burning sun poured on an awakening tropical world that was always at its most exciting after the rains. Thousands of Java sparrows pecked away at the upturned earth of the Cricket Club padang; brightly-coloured birds flashed among the rubber trees. In the Botanic Gardens, monkeys gambolled almost down to the edge of Tyersall Road. And at night a bright moon shone out of a jet black sky laced with stars.

The crossing of the causeway on the night of Friday-Saturday (Jan 30-31) had been such a closely guarded secret that 24 hours elapsed before Singapore woke up on the morning of Sunday, February 1, and read in the local newspapers that the island was invested. Thirty thousand troops had crossed the 1,100-yard causeway, miraculously without a single casualty. The last were the Commanding Officer and the pipers of the Argyll and Sutherland Highlanders, who had fought every inch of the way from the Siamese frontier, and had by now been all but decimated. As the skirl of the pipes faded away at 8.15 a.m. on the Saturday—when the last man was safely on the island—the causeway, which was 40 yards wide, was breached. Railways, water mains, lock gates, boulders weighing a ton or more were blown sky-high, and when the dust had cleared, the water was racing through a gap of 60 feet.

This had been the actual moment—24 hours before Singapore realised it—when the battle of Malaya had ended and the siege of Singapore began. And yet, in the first few beautiful days that followed civilians hardly realised the difference in their lives, for this was the brief interlude between siege and assault. The Japanese had reached the

111

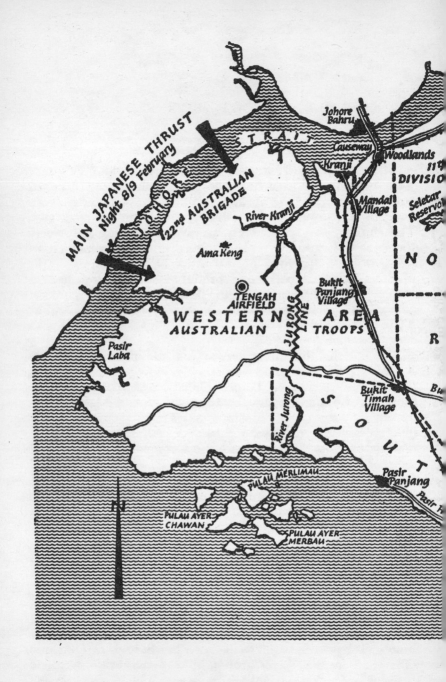

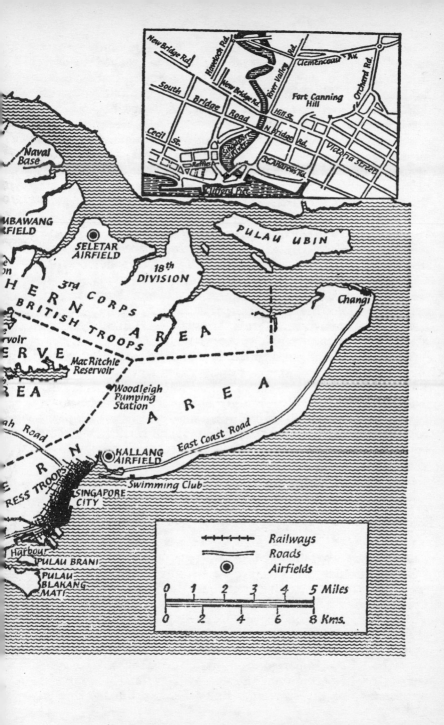

causeway, yet they needed time to re-group and prepare to fall on the island, so that civilians who lived through this lull before the storm seem to have remembered not so much the daily bombing or a Singapore glittering with staff officers, but in retrospect a strange hiatus between two episodes of a tragedy.

It must have been a strange moment of time, for as the British and Japanese prepared for the battle, the opposing armies, with a bizarre irony, could even catch the occasional glimpse of each other. Separated by little more than a thousand yards of water, British troops could at times plainly see Japanese soldiers walking about on the other side of the Straits. It seemed wildly impossible that this 'peace' could ever be interrupted, that the figures they could clearly make out were not law-abiding citizens of Johore. When General Gordon Bennett visited his forward Australian positions he looked across the Straits and saw a Japanese staff car drive along the waterfront. An officer alighted, for all the world as though war were a thousand miles away, and 'had a long gaze at the Island'.

To the people of Singapore, this was the classic beleaguered citadel of military history—stoutly defended, well prepared for siege warfare, and above all surrounded by Churchill's 'splendid moat' across which, given a determined defence, no enemy could hope to force a passage. At first Europeans compared their role in history yet to be written with the embattled defenders of Malta and Moscow, not realising that the circumstances were completely different—that Malta was an impregnable fortress honeycombed with rocky shelters, whereas Singapore was a shelterless, swampy island; that Moscow was the heart of a country whose citizens preferred death to dishonour, whereas Singapore was a hotch-potch of many races with hundreds of thousands of people who hardly knew what the struggle was about.

Their illusions were heightened because everyone knew of the preparations which had been made for just such a moment as this—preparations which seemed adequate for any siege. There was food for six months. Singapore's two largest cinemas, the Capitol and the Pavilion, together with other caches, had been turned into food dumps. Nine thousand cattle had been imported from Bali for slaughtering; there were 125,000 pigs on the island. Milk rationing would be unnecessary as the two large dairy herds normally kept in

114

Johore had crossed the causeway late in January—in fact they could be seen grazing by the roadsides or on the golf course. Hong Kong had capitulated because it had had no water—but this could never happen in Singapore. It was true that the ten million gallons a day normally pumped in from Johore had now been lost, but the island's three reservoirs assured the population of seventeen million gallons a day—more than the island was using under war conditions.

To the civilians in those early days, the feeling was one of unqualified optimism. What the military felt—or did—was, however, a very different matter.

General Percival reckoned that it would take the Japanese 'at least a week' to mount an offensive against the island, and now he and his staff officers set about the complicated task of implementing an overall plan of defence to meet the three Japanese divisions across the Straits of Johore.

Singapore, which Churchill had insisted 'must be fought for until every single unit and every single strong point has been separately destroyed', was, as we have seen, roughly the size and shape of the Isle of Wight, 26 miles across and 14 miles from north to south. Generally undulating, much of it was at that time covered with luxuriant jungle or swamp, together with rubber and coconut plantations and many orchards and small market gardens. In contrast to the massive granite mountains of the mainland, the island boasted nothing higher than two hills in the centre, of which Bukit Timah was the largest, rising to just under 600 feet. The vast majority of the population was concentrated in the city at the island's southern tip, while the few villages were clustered around junctions dividing the excellent roads, or near the 72 miles of coastline, much of it scarred with small creeks or rivers, frequently edged with mangrove swamps. There were virtually no defences apart from those protecting the Naval Base. The two northern shores facing Johore across the Strait—east and west of the shattered causeway—were virtually undefended, as Wavell had discovered to his horror when inspecting the area with Percival early in January.

Percival's indifference—and his preoccupation with not upsetting morale—had been bad enough, for it seemed obvious that an attack must be launched from the mainland, but what is even more difficult to understand is why Percival did nothing *after* Wavell's fateful visit. Wavell had plainly shown his anger, and Wavell was, after all, in supreme command. One would have thought it a simple matter for him to have *ordered* Percival to build up the defences on the northern shores—in other words, to implement Brigadier Simson's suggestions. But, apparently, instead of 'ordering' he 'urged' for as *The War Against Japan* says, 'Despite considerable pressure from Wavell little more was done until the 23rd [January] when an outline plan for the defence of the island was issued, followed by a more detailed one on the 28th. By that time it was too late, for civil labour was no longer available.'[1]

The truth is, of course, that Percival, despite his weak, unprepossessing appearance, was a man of extraordinary stubbornness, and as long as books are written about Singapore, historians will speculate on the character of this military leader who seemed to combine all the opposites in human nature. He had an irritating stubbornness in front of a military map; a completely negative, colourless personality when dealing with a group of men, but a career at staff college which had been brilliant. He had an ability to work out military schemes which looked excellent on paper, but which somehow frequently got bogged down in practice. Even his detractors admit he had a penetrating mind but (as Wavell and Simson had discovered) he did not always take kindly to the advice of others. When Ian Morrison of *The Times* met him he found a man who 'had a mind that saw the difficulties to any scheme before it saw the possibilities'. He would argue endlessly to gain a point (his point) and it is possible that Wavell—clearly anxious to fortify the northern shores—was talked out of his convictions and retired exhausted from the verbal battles.

On paper Percival could match the Japanese strength, for he had approximately 85,000 men to defend the island—but this was on paper only. At least 15,000 were baseline non-combatant, unarmed troops. The infantry battalions (thirteen British, six Australian, seventeen Indian, two Malay, plus two British and one Australian machine-gun battalions)

[1] 'Little provision had been made against the possibility of a struggle on the island itself. Even when this possibility had become acutely obvious as the Japanese forces swept into Johore, nothing was undertaken which reflected the British Prime Minister's demand for heroic measures.'—*The Japanese Thrust* (Official Australian War History).

with supporting artillery and 152 AA guns, were in a pitiable state. Six of the British battalions had only recently landed, the other seven were under strength. The plight of the Australians was even worse. All except one battalion had been 'made up' with many untrained reinforcements. Some had sailed from Australia within two weeks of enlistment. Many hardly knew how to handle a gun. 'The decision to select these untrained Australian reinforcements for Malaya was unfortunate,' said The War Against Japan. The Indian units were also in a woeful state, after bearing the brunt of heavy fighting on the peninsula. Their losses had been appalling, so that all except one battalion included many raw, untrained troops. There was a desperate shortage of good officers.

These were the men on whom Percival could call to face the Japanese across the Strait of Johore, which varied in width from seven hundred to five thousand yards, and where General Yamashita was assembling three crack Japanese divisions—The Imperial Guards, the 5th and the 18th Divisions—the 18th having been landed unopposed in Southern Johore. All were fresh and jungle-trained. They were backed up by strong armoured forces, including tanks. They also had over 200 aircraft against one token squadron of Hurricanes—all that was left of the RAF.

As Percival saw it, he was faced with two broad alternatives. He could either spread out his men along the coast to prevent the Japanese landing on the thirty miles of northern beaches, or alternatively he could hold the coastline only thinly and keep large reserves of troops to fight the battle on Singapore Island itself. Though admitting that 'it was not possible with the forces at our disposal . . . to build up a really strong coastal defence' Percival opted for the first alternative because 'the morale effect of a successful landing would be bad both on the troops and on the civil population'.

No doubt Percival made the right decision, even though he knew he did not have the forces to implement it. But it is intriguing to note how Percival had changed his mind, for now he decided on a strategy for which he did not have sufficient troops because he felt it would be good for morale; yet only a month previously, he had refused Simson permission to erect fixed defences at the very same spot because he felt it would be bad for morale.

Anyway, this was his broad strategy, and the island was split into three areas which covered the entire coastline. The 18th British Division and the 11th Indian Division were placed in the Northern Area which extended along the north coast, from Changi in the east to the causeway. Gordon Bennett's 8th Australian Division was deployed in the Western Area. This stretched from the river Jurong in the south (but west of Singapore city) up to and including the causeway in the north. The less important Southern area was entrusted to the fortress garrison together with locally recruited troops. There was also a small Reserve Area in the centre of the island.

One thing is immediately apparent about the disposition of the forces. Two divisions had been allocated to the area *east* of the causeway, but only one to guard the area *west* of the causeway. This provides yet another extraordinary instance of the way in which Percival insisted on acting against the advice of Wavell. For Wavell (rightly as it turned out) was convinced that the Japanese would attack the north-*west* coast. Percival, on the other hand seems to have had an *idée fixe* that the Japanese would attack the north-*east* coast, despite the fact that Wavell had firmly suggested that the fresher, newly-arrived troops of the 18th British Division should defend the north-west shore, where he was certain the Japanese would be most likely to attack.

Percival was no doubt partly influenced by the fact that 400 Japanese troops had landed on the island of Pulau Ubin —one of the many outlying islands. It lay between the north-east tip of Singapore and Johore. The Japanese met virtually no resistance on this chunk of rock surrounded by muddy shores, and which could never, by the wildest stretch of imagination, have been used as a Japanese springboard for invasion. Even so, Percival told Wavell (no doubt at great lengths) that he believed the Japanese would attack east of the causeway, and in the end, Wavell, probably with a sigh, felt that 'since Percival . . . seemed convinced of the probable direction of the enemy attack' he had to allow the man on the spot the final say in the disposition of his troops.

Possibly it did not make much difference where the troops were placed—the British troops were soft after weeks at sea, whereas the Australian contingent contained many untrained troops—but what did make a difference was yet another extraordinary decision which Percival now took upon his own

118

shoulders. It was one which would rob the Australians of even the slimmest chance of defending their coastline. So obsessed was Percival with his belief that the Japanese would attack the north-east coast that without warning he suddenly ordered Brigadier Simson's Royal Engineers to shift vast quantities of defence material from the north-*west* coast to the north-*east* coast.

All Simson's military training, all his knowledge of military engineering, cried out against the futility of the order. For weeks—though he had received no direct orders from Percival—Simson had been quietly 'stocking' the north-west shores of Singapore Island, which 'everybody, including General Wavell, had predicted as the main danger point owing to the good embarkation facilities available to the enemy on the opposite Johore shore.' At suitable places the Engineers had left stocks of mines, booby traps, Lyon lights, drums of petrol for fires at landing points, barbed wire of all sorts and pickets. Simson had even conceived the idea of stripping the hundreds of derelict cars in the city of their headlamps and batteries to light up the water and the 'killing areas'.

Abruptly Percival ordered the Engineers to transfer this vast quantity of materials. To Simson the order 'was incredible. It was difficult to follow the minds of all the responsible leaders and their staffs on the subject of defence works.' For the north-east coast did, in fact, present insuperable problems to the Japanese if they wished to launch an attack on the island. Simson had previously reconnoitred the Johore shores both sides of the causeway. He had discovered that only to the west of the causeway were there reasonable facilities and road access for embarking men, tanks, stores, for a major attack. No such facilities existed in the marshes and mangrove swamps east of the causeway. Yet there was nothing Simson could do about it. Everything had to be moved—in double-quick time. By a stupendous effort, all the defence stores were moved and dumped east of the causeway by February 5. During that night, however, reports of heavy Japanese troop concentrations facing the north-*west* coast reached Percival, and the following morning Simson was told to move all the material back. By then, of course, it was too late.

It is difficult to know what was going on in Percival's mind at this time. Nothing he did seemed to make sense. This was evident in a conference at which Gordon Bennett (who found the meeting 'depressing') was present. Bennett felt they should appoint a military adviser to the civil government—someone 'who should be the strong man behind the throne, one who could force the civil administration out of its peacetime groove.' Percival seemed impressed with the idea, and, waiting until the other officers had departed, he drew Gordon Bennett aside and asked him if he would take on the job. Bennett said that he would prefer to become Military Governor of Singapore—though he did agree to become military adviser if Shenton Thomas would 'act under his instructions in all things'.

Nothing came of Gordon Bennett's idea, so Percival considered the alternative of taking over complete control himself. He was, after all, in military command, and historically, such a course would have been perfectly proper now the 'fortress' was under siege. His excuse for not doing so was pathetic. Shenton Thomas was the King's representative, and he, Percival, knew nothing of the organisation of the various government departments. He might, he said, even increase confusion rather than diminish it.

Of all this the civilians were, perhaps mercifully, kept in ignorance. There was, however, one fact which could not be hidden from them—the gushing, writhing, black plumes of smoke from two huge fires far to the north. They were the oil dumps at the Naval Base, and they had been burning for days. The ominous clouds had drifted across the green island and now started to darken the sky above the city itself. At first people had jumped to the natural conclusion that Japanese aircraft had scored two lucky hits. But slowly, rumour began to spread that this was not the work of the Japanese, but of the British. It seemed absurd of course, yet the stories persisted, and when Hammonds questioned his military friends who could normally be relied upon to help him, they closed up like clams—until suddenly, the truth was revealed to him in an off-the-record Press conference.

The briefing room was crowded. Local newspapermen, foreign correspondents—with British, American and Australian newspapers predominating—jammed the stuffy room in the Cathay Building where staff officers sometimes held their background talks. Hammonds had been warned that the meeting promised to be historic. The briefing officer gave a few preliminary remarks ('a softening-up process' whispered the correspondent next to Hammonds) before he finally came to the point.

There had been a lot of speculation, he said (in so many words about the fires at the Naval Base. He felt he should put the correspondents 'in the picture'. Suddenly, as Hammonds always remembered, the room full of tough newspapermen became suddenly silent and aware of impending drama, the sense of momentous news. None, however, could have guessed the whole truth—that not only had the British fired the oil dumps, but that the entire Naval Base had been evacuated by the Royal Navy. A note of despair at the useless waste creeps into George Hammonds's notes. 'Never throughout all the fighting—all the defeats—did I ever feel such a sense of utter dismay,' he wrote. 'It seemed impossible that this naval fortress which had cost £60 million and taken seventeen years to build could have been thrown away like this—without even a fight for it.'

This was the place where six million cubic feet of earth had been excavated when hills had been swept aside and a river deflected; where eight million cubic feet of earth had been used to reclaim swampland before construction had even been started. Out of nothing a vast and mighty base had arisen, with pewter-coloured oil tanks holding a million gallons of fuel, with machine shops, underground munition dumps, dry docks, graving docks, giant cranes, a floating dock so big that 60,000 men could stand on its bottom, 22 square miles of deep sea anchorage. There was even a self-contained town for thousands of men with cinemas, churches and seventeen football fields. This was Britain's great symbol of naval dominance in the Pacific Ocean, and it had been built for one reason, and one reason only; for just such a moment of destiny as Britain now faced. And in all this story of equivocation, of ineptitude, of the myth so assiduously fostered, nothing can match in grim irony the fact that when the moment of destiny finally did arrive, the base was valueless and impotent.

Worse was yet to come. After a series of probing questions the briefing officer was finally forced to admit that the base had in fact been evacuated *before* the troops had crossed the causeway. 'But I thought they'd been withdrawn to the island to defend the Base?' one voice asked. There was no answer. Nor could there be, for the Navy had pulled out—leaving the Japanese thousands of pounds' worth of equipment.

Over the next few days George Hammonds was able to piece together the incredible chain of events which had brought about this catastrophe—a catastrophe that was to have a shattering effect on the morale of troops, from whom the guilty secret could not be hidden for long.

Most of the few naval vessels had already gone, but there still remained several hundred men and a labour force of some thousands, and it appears that on January 21 the Admiralty had warned Rear-Admiral Spooner, the Naval Commander-in-Chief, to get his skilled personnel—many of them civilians—away from the base. When the Army had been ordered to withdraw to the island, Spooner had decided to transfer the entire European naval and civilian dockyard staff to Singapore. This move was made on January 28; by January 31, however, he had done more; even before the island had been invested, he had unaccountably sent most of them to Ceylon, leaving only a few to give technical advice to the Army unit which would be responsible for the work of demolition. Perhaps because the Army felt bitter at 'being left to carry the baby', senior officers quietly let slip another astounding item of news. For some extraordinary reason, Spooner had not mentioned either to Malaya Command or even to General Percival personally, that an elaborate scorched earth scheme, which should have been carried out by the naval dockyard staff, had been handed over to Percival's troops.[2] Not only that, but without telling anybody, the silent service had silently disbanded its invaluable civilian labour force—a force used to working in danger areas and which the Army would have welcomed. Not a word of this had reached Percival—but when finally it did reach him and his senior officers, their natural conclusion was that Whitehall and the Navy had already given up the fight. In his diary Gordon Bennett summed it up in his characteristic Australian forthright manner, 'This demolition . . . even before we withdrew from the mainland reflects the lack of confidence in our cause. . . . It is an admission of defeat.' Later, *The War Against Japan* was to emphasise

[2] 'Operational command was assumed by Percival but despite the urgency of the situation no overall control of both civil and military affairs was established.'—*The Japanese Thrust*.

that 'The hurried evacuation of the Base left an unfortunate impression in the minds of many soldiers who did not know that the Admiral, although perhaps precipitately, was acting under instructions'.

We have a picture of the bewildering scene that greeted the first troops when they stumbled on the deserted acres of this once-thriving nerve centre, for George Hammonds visited the Base with some correspondents, including Ian Morrison, who described it as 'my most tragic memory of the whole Malayan campaign'.

Lolling Indian sentries at the gates waved them inside without bothering to enquire what they wanted. They walked past deserted barracks which had housed a labour force of 12,000 Asians; near the empty administration offices an acre of ground was littered with equipment—everything from shirts and truncheons to gas masks and wooden lockers. The great crane that could lift out an entire gun turret was still in working order; enormous ships' boilers stood in the boiler shop awaiting the Japanese navy, together with lathes, spares for seaplanes, shelves of radio equipment, scores of boxes of valves; one warehouse was filled with huge coils of rope, wire or cord. In the causeway George could still see the upper works of the giant floating dock that had been towed all the way from England.

To Hammonds it looked as though every man had bolted at a moment's notice in panic, and though this was not true (and much of the equipment was valueless to the Japanese) conditions on the Base did give that impression. A football still lay by the goalposts of one pitch. In the Mess Hall was a table of half-finished meals. The cooking galleys were crowded with opened boxes of cutlery and plates, and pans—some still dirty—to feed thousands, as though a hurried meal had been interrupted. In the barracks half-cleaned belts and buckles lay on un-made beds. 'It was like the *Marie Celeste*.' Flies moved busily among the edible rubbish, swarming away in angry black clouds as the rats came out. Scavenger dogs—lean and hungry and mean—fought over morsels of food or scratched and bit at closed doors behind which they could smell food.

A party of troops arrived in four trucks on a 'legitimate scrounge'. Hundreds of tropical shirts and shorts and boots were tossed unceremoniously into one lorry—to be used by men who had hardly changed their clothing during the long retreat; other soldiers raided a warehouse stacked with cases

123

of bully beef, tinned fruit and cigarettes, and as one man filled his pocket with fags he turned to George Hammonds and said, 'Blimey! It's like pinching the rings off a warm body.'

In fact, as George was to discover, the Army needed 120 lorries, each making three trips a night for a week, to remove the portable equipment left behind by the Navy.

Though the siege of Singapore had indubitably started—and it would have been difficult for anybody to deny the fact—those newspaper correspondents still remaining on the island now received an incredible order: on no account must they use the word siege in their cables. To the amazement of Hammonds, the word was also banned from the columns of the local Press. The word siege, said the briefing officer solemnly, was bad for local morale. The word investment should be used instead. However, after some heated argument the spokesman did finally give the irate newspapermen permision to say that Singapore was 'besieged'. Bewildered, George Hammonds asked what was the difference, while as Ian Morrison pointed out in his elegant prose, 'it was inconsistent to permit the use of a certain English verb but to deny us the use of the noun which is cognate with that verb, for possible ill effects which that English noun might have on a population whose native tongue was not English'. (In fact, when Morrison cabled to *The Times* the censor struck out the word 'siege' but inadvertently put in a word that does not exist, so that Morrison's cable reaching London started 'The besiegement of Singapore began. . . .')

Relations between the Press and the censors had been deteriorating for weeks—as, understandably, they frequently do in times of stress and crisis—but suddenly they took a turn for the better with the appointment on the War Council of Rob Scott, a young Scotsman whose propaganda skill had long been a byword in Asia, but whose opportunities to look after the Press had until now been limited.

Scott had been appointed Director of the Far Eastern Bureau of the Ministry of Information just before the Malayan war. He was 35, with 'a broad open face, a dark moustache, very Scottish both in voice and manner'. A man of tireless energy, he was always accessible. But though his brief had been to organise propaganda, and though he was known to every newspaper correspondent, he had not been able to help them as much as he would have liked over such problems as censorship. Now, however, Scott was suddenly asked to become a member of the War Council, sitting together with the Governor and the commanding officers of the three forces.

Such was his personality that within a few days he was threatening to resign from the War Council unless he was given full control over Press and censorship. He was immediately granted the powers.

It was a small thing that had caused Scott to become so angry, but it was the sort of ridiculous incident that emphasised the incredible gulf existing between officialdom and the ordinary people. A United Press correspondent, Harold Guard, had written a homely little story about his everyday life in Singapore—how he had done his own washing in his bombed house, how he had bought a leg of pork and cooked it. It was the sort of 'human interest' story that thousands of women would read. The censors, however, thought otherwise. Who could possibly be interested in reading about pork in grave times like these? There was something sinister, mysterious, about this seemingly innocuous article. It was passed on to the Military Intelligence. They too did not like the look of what must surely be an elaborate code. The upshot was that Guard was brusquely ordered up to Fort Canning for interrogation and told that he could send no more messages of any sort out of the 'invested' city— until a furious Rob Scott heard about it, had the decision rescinded and then personally demanded more powers. Friction between the Press and government diminished from that moment.

To the civilians a new hazard was now added to the ruthless daily bombing. Early in February the Japanese opened harassing artillery fire from the mainland. Long-range guns sited on high ground in Johore were able to bring in their range, not only the island's four airfields, but the entire city as well. And this was unlike anything else the civilians had ever imagined or expected. In a way they had become fatalistically used to the whistle of falling bombs; they had learned to take the dull thud of the anti-aircraft guns for granted, even the regular sight of unopposed Japanese aircraft lazily peeling away after dropping their bomb loads. The raids, too, were launched with an almost clockwork punctuality, and the civilians could tell from the whistle where the bombs were likely to fall. Few bothered to take shelter except when the raiders were directly overhead.

Now, however, an utterly different and altogether more menacing element entered their lives. There was something almost inhuman about this sound which they had never heard before—a low whine in the distance that slowly crept up the scale until it became a wild, screaming noise culminating in a piercing crescendo. And no one knew where the noise would end.

Marjorie Hudson had just driven her husband to Dunlop's godown, and was queuing for her butter ration in the Cold Storage when the first shell landed in Orchard Road. 'At first nobody had any idea what the sound was,' she remembered later, 'the noise seemed to hang in the air for an age. I felt as though I'd been hypnotised—I can't describe the terrible scream—then a soldier shouted, "It's a shell!" and the queue scattered and I dived under a counter. I can't remember what happened to the others.' Freddy Retz heard it too. 'At first I thought it was an automobile revving its motor.'

Now, too, the raids were being stepped up. Using four repaired airfields in Johore, the Japanese were sending not only dive bombers but fighters to cruise low over the city, machine-gunning the streets or dropping showers of small anti-personnel bombs which burst in the air into hundreds of tiny, sharp fragments of shrapnel. The pockmarks of war showed more and more. Hardly a street did not have its gaping hole or a jagged dusty ruin to mark the path of a bomb or shell, though some places seemed to bear charmed lives. The Cricket Club had only been bombed once. Robinson's was never hit again after the first night—and was to remain open for business right to the end. The Singapore Club was untouched except for shrapnel scars. But in some parts of Chinatown entire streets had been obliterated. The Singapore railway station had been badly damaged. In the nearby dock area half the godowns had gone up in flames and civilian labour was now so acutely short that, as Gordon Bennett noted, 'the unloading of the ships was slow, the men working only one shift per day. That leaves the ship idle for two-thirds of the day in a constantly bombed area.'

By the end of the first week of the siege at least two hundred people a day were being killed—not including those whose bodies were never found. Raids could no longer always be signalled by sirens. The blue sky and the sun were obliterated by smoke from the burning oil tanks that hung over the city. Each day there was mounting evidence of an uglier mood—particularly among the troops. Bewildered knots of men wandered, 'grimy, lost, leaderless, without orders'. They were sprawled haphazardly all over Singapore, seemingly without anyone to direct them. Without warning, Tommy Kitching found the compound of his house filled with convalescent soldiers 'who all looked hale and hearty'. The road from Tim Hudson's house to Orchard Road was blocked for hour after hour because a column of troops could not find an officer to tell them which turning to take. Many of the troops were desperate with fatigue—but often they could not find their units and had to sleep on the floor of the YMCA after a supper of tea and buns. Others who did manage to find their commanding officers still had nowhere to sleep —because there were not enough tents, and billeting officers had been unable to requisition enough rooms. Gunners could not find their guns, army cooks could not find their raw materials. Inevitably, drunken, dishevelled troops appeared, reeling around the main squares, waving bottles of cheap liquor. (Crème-de-Menthe was a great favourite.) Their mood became more bitter—and more belligerent—with each new raid or rumour.

Sometimes the sullen troops became violent. 'Willie' Watt, head of the famous Singapore import firm of McAlister's, a straight-backed Scot well over six feet tall, was being driven to his office after an all-night stint with the Observer Corps when two drunken soldiers forced their way into his car during a traffic jam and started making insulting remarks about chauffeur-driven, non-fighting civilians. Willie—who had fought in World War One—was fifty, but not the man to accept the insults passively. He managed to get one soldier by the scruff of the neck and hurl him out of his car; as the second followed, however, he landed a vicious swipe with his rifle butt across Willie's arm and almost broke it. Willie spent weeks with his arm in a sling.

Looting was rapidly becoming widespread. Buckeridge was clanging along to a fire when a bunch of drunks, amused by his beard, jeered, 'Let it burn, dad! It's too late.' They started to pelt him with big, oblong 'missiles', two of which landed by his side in the front seat. They turned out to be cartons of cigarettes. Leslie Hoffman was on his way home when he noticed, with the precise eye of a newspaperman, a

127

Chinese boy laboriously trying to ride a brand-new bicycle far too big for him. A group of Chinese children in nearby Beach Road were playing in an enormous abandoned American car. Farther on, a family outside a smashed dwelling was eating rice when a tiny naked girl ran breathlessly towards them carrying a chicken. The mother guiltily bundled it under her clothes and hurried inside the ruins.

In Government House Shenton Thomas struggled to 'live according to his station'. Each morning after a breakfast —which invariably ended with toast and marmalade—the cook brought the day's menu for his approval, though lunch was now largely reduced to cold cuts. Shenton Thomas, however, insisted on guests wearing collars and ties, though he dispensed with dinner jackets in the evenings. He now faced an urgent, new personal problem. His wife had been taken seriously ill. The doctor diagnosed it as amoebic dysentery —which meant that it was quite impossible for her to go to the shelter in the grounds. Yet the bombing raids had killed several of his staff, torn a vast hole in one corner of the enormous white 'palace', and now the Japanese guns suddenly found the range of Government House. Firing from Johore, at 24,000 yards' range, and aided by an artillery spotting balloon floating high over the Strait, they bombarded the Governor's residence with devastating accuracy. Lady Thomas could not leave her bed, but the Governor's ADC did the best he could. Using every spare mattress he could find, together with bales of wool sent up to Government House by the Red Cross, the ADC made a shelter of sorts under and around the big banqueting table in the formal ground floor dining-room. The small entry hole was just high enough to allow the Governor's wife to be wheeled in on a very low stretcher.

In the chaos of this 'phoney war' the civilians and a host of refugees felt more and more bewildered. Almost everything they were told seemed to be contradictory. In his 'Battle of Singapore' Order of the Day, Percival had made great play of phrases like 'the enemy within our gate', 'loose talk' and 'rumour-mongering'—all calculated to alarm civilians (when in fact there was virtually no 'fifth column'). A few days later Wavell issued his Order of the Day, in which he said that 'our part is to gain time for the great reinforcements' which he promised would arrive. Yet in the next breath he demanded that 'we must leave nothing

128

behind undestroyed that would be of the least service to the enemy . . . I look to you all to fight this battle without further thought of retreat.' To the million bombed, shelled civilians with their backs to the sea, it was not clear how anybody could retreat from a beleaguered island, nor how the scorched earth policy which Wavell demanded would be of help to the reinforcements which he had promised were on their way.

There was no inspiration to the civilians, no direct appeal to them, no leaders to whom they could turn, no clarion calls to take up arms. No wonder that the Rev. Bennitt—a highly intelligent man—was primarily concerned with the problem of making his will (leaving one copy with the Bishop and posting another to his wife) or dismayed when 'I played bridge too long, and made a fool of myself in the last rubber through sheer exhaustion.'

While some played bridge or quietly got drunk, others, as Ian Morrison discovered, formed queues outside the cinemas. With a rare understanding, Morrison did not think it was altogether complacency. 'I could understand that people should prefer to watch a film rather than sit around mopingly waiting for news of the fighting.' Flt. Lieut. Arthur Donahue of Minnesota, the first American to fly with the RAF in Britain, was now flying one of the last Hurricanes in Singapore. He was given a couple of hours' leave after days of non-stop flying and went with some friends to *Ziegfeld Girl* at the Alhambra Theatre. 'The shock was quite rude for us when it was over; completely lost in the lovely atmosphere of American girls and song and gaiety and peace, we stepped out into the teeming oriental traffic and the sweltering tropical sun to be reminded that we were halfway round the world from America, with our enemies only a few miles away.'

Small pleasures (or small problems) loomed larger than life. The Rev. Bennitt noted with satisfaction that 'the Municipality fixed us a gas heater' for his hot bath. Tim Hudson was delighted when he unexpectedly acquired 24 tins of sardines for $5; Freddy Retz was equally pleased to pick up a dozen special dry ginger ale and two bottles of salt ('very hard to find'). Hoffman took time off for a haircut at Robinson's 'where all was normal, the place full of people having their morning coffee'. George Hammonds received his monthly bill for $4.50 from the Swimming Club and felt that 'I suppose we've got to go on supporting them but they might cut down the sub when nobody uses the place'.

It was a curious, unreal existence. There were now more soldiers than ever before on the island and despite the anticipation of impending battle—to say nothing of impending defeat—the first thing the troops did when they got an hour's leave was to buy souvenirs to take home. The small shops and stalls in the narrow, stifling Change Alley—traditional bargain hunter's paradise linking Raffles Place with Collyer Quay—were jammed with more customers than in peacetime.

In Raffles Place, Robinson's reported more over-the-counter sales than ever before—which helped to offset the collapse of their up-country trade. Kelly and Walsh reported increased sales of 'serious books'. Round the corner in Battery Road, Mrs. Lily Jackson worked on at Maynards the chemists, superintending Elizabeth Arden beauty treatments. Fraser and Neave still bottled their soda water; Tiger beer was still brewed; the brickworks carried on making bricks—while Percival was planning his scorched earth policy. Wearne's garage in Orchard Road was inundated with minor repair jobs because cattle from the dairy herds had reached the outlying districts and motorists regularly hit them in the black-out.

At night you had to book a table if you wanted to go to Raffles. The Cricket Club was filled with noisy drinkers, and many members went there directly from offices or ARP headquarters for a quick shower because the Club was centrally placed. At the sole remaining 'World', a soldier had to queue for half an hour before he could get a 7d. dance with a taxi girl—unless he invested in a roll of tickets, and waved them, whereupon the girl (who got a percentage) would attach herself to him for the rest of the evening—until 'God Save the King' that is, when her polite but firm amah or mother would whisk her away from a disappointed soldier and take her home in a rickshaw.

For some the war brought sudden riches. Since December—when all the Japanese fishermen had been interned—Singapore had suffered from an acute shortage of the delicious fish that abounded in the coastal waters, for the Malay fishermen now only caught sufficient for themselves. The Chinese did not make good fishermen—until a few enterprising ones discovered that after Japanese raids on the docks (in which many bombs fell in the sea) hundreds of dead or stunned fish floated by the waterfront waiting to be picked up.

Sometimes acts of kindness had unforeseen sequels. Marjorie Hudson was asleep one afternoon, after night duty at the General Hospital, when Mei Ling, her amah, announced that two soldiers insisted on seeing her. Marjorie got up, sleepy-eyed—to be confronted by two muscular Australians whose faces were vaguely familiar. 'Don't you remember us?' asked one in pained tones. Suddenly she did. They had been brought into the hospital slightly wounded, and after treatment she had felt sorry for them, and had taken them home for a square meal. Now they wanted to show their gratitude. One solemnly presented her with a Mills bomb. 'If the Japs try to rape you,' he explained gravely, 'just pull out the pin. Then you'll know nothing.'

For many, life had changed drastically. Now that Karen had gone, George Hammonds left Amber Mansions and moved into Dulverton with the Glovers. Leslie Hoffman, also a grass widower, moved in with his 80-year-old father into the house where he had been brought up in St. Michael's Road, a rambling old bungalow on stilts that raised it six feet off the ground in a compound cluttered with frangipani and tulip trees. The house lay out in the suburbs on the way to Serangoon, and nothing in it had really changed—including the old Chinese amah—since Leslie had been born there 26 years previously. The first thing Leslie did was to go out and buy a powerful short-wave radio set. 'When the balloon goes up,' he told Hammonds, 'I'm going to be in touch with the rest of the world.'

Hoffman's wife had left, but other women still refused to go. Tim Hudson spent hours vainly trying to persuade Marjorie to leave. So did Jimmy Glover, but Julienne also refused adamantly—until the *Tribune* received a direct hit.

It happened at noon. Glover had gone to see Rob Scott at his headquarters in the Cathay Building, but Scott was in conference, so Glover had stayed talking to Rob's confidential secretary, Irene Kenny, 'a jewel among war-time secretaries. She never batted an eyelid when fifty bombers were overhead, and she had to be driven to take shelter.' Glover always reckoned that Irene Kenny was his 'barometer'; he knew that Rob Scott would never allow her to stay if Singapore were doomed; but while she was still at her desk there was still hope.

Scott came in. He was dressed in his local Volunteer Defence Corps uniform, which he even wore at the War Council meetings until the admiral, the general and the air marshal, embarrassed by the uniform of a corporal, 'gave me a mild ticking off'. Scott was tired, for he had been on duty that night. He was relaxing with one of his acrid cheroots, when the sirens went. From the fourth floor of the Cathay the two men could see the raid—a 'terrible and awe-inspiring sight' as 27 Japanese aircraft bombed the docks and Anson Road area. To Glover it looked as though the entire *Tribune* area was being pattern-bombed, and somehow he drove there through the dust and smoke. His premonition had been right. The *Tribune* offices were a shambles of broken, twisted machinery—a nightmare ending to the dream he had realised. One look told Glover that tomorrow's *Tribune* could never be printed in the wrecked building. The staff was rushed out to Glover's emergency printing plant at his home, and the *Tribune*—printed in the compound— came out the next day as usual, with relays of cars taking the papers in batches to the Cathay, where Glover had organised a central distribution depot. That was the day when Glover put down his wife's name on the P and O roster.

This was also the day when Britain lost the only vessel out of all convoys of reinforcements that arrived. She was the *Empress of Asia*—an old tub loaded with automatic weapons, heavier guns and other war material, mostly for the 18th Division. One of a convoy of four ships bringing in supplies, she fell astern as the vessels passed through the Sunda Strait in the early morning. When she was only seven miles from Singapore, nine Japanese dive-bombers spotted her and set her on fire. Though the loss of life was small when she sank, all the precious equipment was lost.

There was one cheerful note in this period of gloomy waiting. On Friday, February 6—Freddy's birthday—she and Philip Bloom were married. Both were on day duty at the General Hospital, and they had arranged to take an hour off during the morning, though a heavy raid at 10 o'clock almost wrecked their plans. Freddy—the only American girl in the hospital—was in 'Comforts Corner' near the X-ray Department, and Philip was in the operating room when a bomb scored a direct hit on the X-ray Department. Philip, knowing Freddy was near there, started to run. Then he slowed down—'I realised the danger of panic'—and walked slowly towards the shattered room—to find Freddy on the floor, under the bulky form of an RAF orderly.

Freddy had brought a clean uniform to the hospital, but now it was ruined, and 'looked as though it had been worn down a coal mine'. However, she borrowed a clean white uniform from a colleague ('Mind you return it by lunchtime') and about eleven o'clock she and Philip set off for the registrar's office in Fullerton Building, stopping on the way at da Silva's, the jewellers, in High Street. They had seen the perfect star sapphire there, which Philip wanted to present to her as a combined engagement and birthday ring. Time after time they had tried to sneak an hour off to buy it, but had never been able to leave the hospital before the shops closed. Philip had, however, telephoned to say they would call on this particular morning.

They stopped the car at da Silva's—to find not only his shop, but every jeweller's in High Street boarded up after the raid. Philip banged and rattled the big iron bar across the wooden shutters, but obviously the place was empty. They were on the point of getting into the car when Philip spotted a street trader with a tray of jewels on the ground in front of him. He had no 'stars'—but he did have a beautiful cabochon sapphire, so Freddy got her ring.

They had barely reached Fullerton Building before the sirens sounded again. This big building had a 'business as usual' system of its own so that the General Post Office on the ground floor and government offices above could function during raids. Tommy Kitching—who had his surveyor's offices there—had knocked out all the glass in the partly air-conditioned building, and boarded up windows. Certain sections were 'safe spots' where people could work during alerts until roof-spotters sounded klaxons to indicate aircraft were directly overhead.

One room in the registrar's office was in a 'safe spot'—the other wasn't. The registrar was elderly, a little worried, and anxious to get this routine (and to him unromantic) chore over as quickly as possible. Despite the sirens, he agreed to start the ceremony in the 'safe spot'. Philip and Freddy stood there, suitably solemn. The registrar started intoning (he was the sort who did intone) when the roof-spotters' klaxon went

—and that meant a mad rush to shelters under the stairway, where they spent ten minutes until they heard the 'raiders passed' signal.

'Now, where *were* we?' asked the registrar benignly, and Freddy, secretly amused at this evidence of British phlegm, suggested, 'Can't we start all over again?' They did. Then the klaxons went again—and back they scuttled under the stairs. All this took a considerable time 'and Philip kept on looking at his watch, apparently forgetting that this was a highly important day in our lives, for he never stopped muttering, "I mustn't be late back".'

Finally they were married. The 'ceremony' was followed by a brief embrace, the perfunctory congratulations of the registrar, and then Mr. and Mrs. Philip Bloom were driving pell-mell back to the hospital. 'See you this evening,' cried Philip before leaving for his office. 'We'll have a celebration *somehow*.'

Freddy ran towards the nurses' changing rooms, and returned the clean white uniform to her colleague, changing back into the old one. 'You'd better hurry,' said the nurse, 'there's a whole crowd at "Comforts Corner".'

When Freddy got there, Mrs. Graham-White, the frail, 'lady-like' wife of Archdeacon Graham-White, was vainly trying to look after a queue of grimy, half-naked sailors—survivors from the *Empress of Asia*. She had distributed mugs of steaming tea, but as Freddy reached the long line of men—some wearing nothing but towels round their waists—Mrs. Graham-White turned to her thankfully, and announced blandly to the men, 'This is Freddy. You'll be glad to hear, gentlemen, that she got married just a few minutes ago.' And then as though to apologise for this unseemly conduct, she added vaguely, 'She's American.'

One sailor started to cheer. The others took it up—and that was Freddy's wedding reception. She was toasted by a queue of grimy, unkempt men, clutching towels round their waists with one hand, holding up mugs of tea with the other.

Philip had promised her 'a night out to celebrate' but by now the shelling made evening excursions too difficult so he drove her back to the flat instead. He had tried in vain to buy some champagne, but Jim Henry, the neighbour who lived above, came down with an extra bottle of Scotch, and that, it seemed, was to be their 'celebration'—until they got a welcome surprise. They were sitting on the verandah when a big lorry swept into the drive, and in the dark, a cheerful voice shouted, 'It's Jim Patterson.'

Patterson was an old friend of Freddy's from up-country to whom she had written giving her address. He had no idea that this was her wedding night, but he was a cheerful, gregarious character, and when Freddy cried, 'Hi! I've just got married!' he shouted back, 'Fine! I've brought you just the right present.'

He had. To their astonishment, the lorry was filled with an unlimited supply of champagne. Philip, Freddy and Jim Henry ran outside with torches, and with an assumed non-chalance Patterson said, 'Help yourself!' and heaved not one, but two cases of vintage champagne out of the capacious interior. 'Plenty more where that came from!' he cried cheerfully.

There was a simple explanation. Patterson had hitch-hiked all the way from up-country, one jump ahead of the Japanese. Every time he had found an abandoned car, he had driven it southwards until there was no more petrol in the tank. Then he had walked on until he came across another. The last abandoned vehicle had been this lorry loaded with champagne. He had driven it across the causeway towards the end of January, hidden it, and now had, quite by chance, chosen this day to visit them.

The Blooms spent 'a hilarious evening' but they never saw Patterson again, possibly because within two days, the shelling became so bad around the Chatsworth Road area, they decided it was safer to live in the General Hospital. (Jim Henry, their neighbour, moved out too.) Freddy took her pictures off the wall, threw the frames away and packed the pictures in the one suitcase she took with her. She gave Marsha, her amah, all her Malay money and begged her to go to her kampong. Then they left in Philip's car—after one last, lingering look at the 'Green Spot' which she never saw again.

Three days later the house was obliterated by shell fire.

It was about this time that Tim Hudson made an uncensored broadcast which was to bring him local fame. Like many Europeans (even intelligent ones), he still entertained some undefined hope that a miracle would occur to save the island. And it was in this frame of mind that he asked the heads of the Malayan Broadcasting Company to allow him to give an uncensored talk. He had spent weeks now helping to dig out corpses of people, many of whom could have been saved had there been sufficient shelters, or even blast walls. He begged the right to speak his mind—and indeed, announced firmly but politely that otherwise he would rather stop broadcasting. The situation was delicate. Tim Hudson had without question become their star speaker, with a big following. Yet the MBC was a government department. Somewhat to Hudson's surprise, however, the MBC agreed. No doubt the many alert minds working for the MBC were as bored as the listeners with the uninspiring programmes which government policy had forced them to broadcast. And Hudson—so they felt—could be trusted. He was a man who knew what he was talking about.

Hudson gave his broadcast after the news that night and when Marjorie heard it in the nurses' common room, 'I went pale at the anger and bitterness in his voice'. She was convinced he would be arrested.

'It's no use telling people that Malta has had thousands of air raids, and has stuck it out,' said Hudson over the air, 'or that Chungking has had worse than we have had. They have ideal shelters. Singapore has nothing except drains and odd slit trenches. The official shelter policy has been bungled.' He went further. 'Scores of tin miners have arrived in Singapore from up-country. They have specialised knowledge —but nothing specialised to do. I urge the government to round them up and put them to work tunnelling into the hills around the town. Many hills are of soft earth and tunnelling would be easy. There are thousands of coconut trees that could easily be cut down to shore the tunnels. And if the government says it can't find the labour, I'll guarantee to go out and get it myself.'

The effect was electric. Listeners jammed the phones— though Eric Davis, head of the MBC, managed to get through to Hudson and tell him to return immediately to the Cathay, and Hudson remembers, 'I drove down expecting a rocket—not that I gave a damn.' But the moment he walked into the office, Eric Davis—in khaki shorts and canary-coloured stockings—got up, gripped his hand and said, 'I want to shake your hand. If there's any trouble, I'll be behind you.'[3]

[3] In his book *Singapore Goes off the Air*, Giles Playfair, who was working on the MBC at the time, wrote, 'Hudson himself is fairly typical of the hard-working majority of Europeans, though he's prob-

136

Because, of course, there would be trouble—for, after all, the Malayan Broadcasting Corporation was a government institution, and was supposed to reflect government opinion.

There was, however, another underlying, deeper reason why Hudson's broadcast caused dismay in government circles. Though he had been broadcasting to the people of Singapore, he was unwittingly the first man to let the outside world—particularly Britain—know the pitiable state of the civilians under shelling and bombing—news which the censors had successfully suppressed since early December.

For weeks, foreign correspondents based in Singapore had been trying to write articles about the lack of defences and shelters against air attack. Every attempt had been ruthlessly censored. As George Hammonds put it, 'Shelters was a dirty word and you were never allowed to mention it'. There had, however, always been one exception to censorship. Since the MBC was a government department anything that went out on the air was 'censor-free'. If a correspondent quoted 'as announced on MBC' his despatch automatically passed the censor, who naturally assumed this to be a reflection of government policy.

George Hammonds heard Hudson's talk and was round at the Cathay within five minutes begging for a copy of the script. He knew that once the government tumbled to this unexpected loop-hole, officials would do everything to stop the story reaching London. He managed to file to Britain within half an hour. And so, for the first time, London learned something of the grim way in which a million civilians were living and suffering—and how little had been done for them.

Even the *Straits Times* was astounded, and in a leading article the next morning said,

'Divisional Warden Hudson seems to be the chief unofficial spokesman for Singapore's Air Raid Precautions Department. We say "unofficial" because the very forthright nature of some of Mr. Hudson's remarks is so entirely out of tune with what we are accustomed

ably more critical, more aggressive, more fearless than most of them —more determined to push the administration into some kind of action or to assume the responsibilities of leadership himself. To my mind he's one of the men whose names shouldn't be forgotten when this war is over, and whatever the eventual fate of Singapore he deserves praise and recognition.'

to hear from official spokesmen. The most surprising thing about his campaign for more vigorous action is that he is allowed to conduct it from the studios of the Malaya Broadcasting Corporation.'

The first government reaction was one of unconcealed anger. Hudson was called to ARP headquarters and told formally that 'several senior members of the government are displeased with what you've said. You've done more harm than good. Your talk was a serious blow to public morale.' During the afternoon, however, he was summoned to another meeting—this time of a very different character, for the invitation came from none other than Brigadier Simson. Hudson—like all who came in contact with him—found Simson 'extremely charming and courteous, and most anxious to help', for Simson said, in so many words, 'Try and put your ideas into practice. You can have anything you want—money isn't important—though you'll have to find the labour.'

Hudson was able to tell Simson that scores of European tin miners who had been evacuated from up-country had already phoned the MBC studios offering to help. They would supervise the tunnelling and Tim was sure that his own coolie force would help. Within a few hours Hudson had commandeered a fleet of old lorries, and had started chopping down coconut palms, and was digging scores of tunnels to be shored up with timber. They undoubtedly saved hundreds of lives.

Hudson's broadcast resulted in a complete reversal of the official government shelter policy; but as he wrote, 'The tragedy is that it's all too late now. If they would have listened to me at the beginning, who knows what would have happened, and how many more would be alive today.'

Soon after dawn on February 8, Tim Hudson and Buck Buckeridge were taking a shower in the Cricket Club after a night spent fighting a big fire near South Bridge Road. As they walked into the locker-room, George Hammonds waved a good-morning. Then almost casually he mentioned that a Free French boat was leaving that night. She was one of the last convoy, in which the *Empress of Asia* had been sunk —and did they know Jimmy Glover's wife? She was going on it.

Hudson and Buckeridge looked at each other. The same

138

thought crossed both their minds. It was now or never. Hardly bothering to thank Hammonds for the vital news he had imparted Buckeridge drove to Robinson's and Hudson to the General Hospital.

Marjorie Hudson was on duty, but Tim sent a message that he must speak to her immediately. He waited patiently for twenty minutes before she came out into the hospital grounds and Tim beckoned her to sit in the car. There 'we had the only serious quarrel in our lives.' To Marjorie it was running away. She felt that in her way she was doing a job as important as he was. To Tim the argument was simple: 'If I'm caught, it's going to be ten times better for me if I know you're safe.' They argued for half an hour, with Marjorie in tears, but finally—perhaps more from exhaustion than a change of heart—Marjorie gave in. She went back in the hospital 'feeling terribly guilty and in tears' as she said her good-byes. Tim's klaxoning cut them short and when she came out, still in uniform, he drove her straight to Cluny. They queued for two hours, but when they finally reached the Agency House, the P and O officer recognised Hudson in his uniform and gave Marjorie her chit immediately—warning her that the *Felix Roussel* was sailing that night, and she hadn't a minute to spare.

Only one thing Marjorie insisted on. 'I won't go—and I mean it, Tim—without saying good-bye to Mei Ling.' They drove from Cluny to their bungalow in silence. Tim gave her five minutes to pack a suitcase and say her farewells, and when Marjorie finally walked across the lawn to the garage, Mei Ling stood on the verandah. Mei Ling's last words to her were, 'Better you go. I look after the tuan.'

'That was the worst moment of all—when I really felt guilty,' wrote Marjorie later.

Buckeridge had the same difficulty in persuading Lucy, but luckily they had not needed to waste the best part of a day queuing at Cluny. One of the P and O men worked with Buckeridge in the AFS, and Buck was able to go straight in. He got the chit, didn't bother to look at it, and drove to Robinson's, picked up Lucy and drove as far as he could towards the *Felix Roussel* which was berthed at the far end of Keppel Harbour.

At the same time Jimmy Glover and George Hammonds were driving Julienne to the docks. It took them over three hours to cover the three miles from Collyer Quay to the wharf. Nobody had organised parking. Cars cluttered up the dockside; often they had been driven by women who were departing and who had then just abandoned them. There was nobody to take them away. There were no porters, no volunteers to help the scores of unattached women and their children. 'The result of all this,' Glover noted later, 'was that over 300 passengers failed to reach the wharf in time, and the ship had to leave without them.'

Tim Hudson was already on the quayside with Marjorie, looking around for Buckeridge and Lucy, as they had agreed to stick together so the wives could try and share a cabin. Though they had been warned to bring only hand luggage, there was utter confusion when some arrived with carpets, packing cases of furniture, while two highly-placed wives insisted (and succeeded) in having their cars hoisted on board during a raid.

Buckeridge was the first to reach a large four-berth cabin. Two women had already laid claims to two berths, but the other two were empty. A French steward bustled along, took the P and O chit, put Lucy's suitcase on one bunk, then looked at the two other ladies—and at Buck. Once again he glanced at the slip of paper that served as a ticket, and said almost apologetically, 'But m'sieu, you can't sleep with these strange ladies.'

'Me! I'm not going!' grinned Buck.

The steward pointed to the ticket. Buckeridge's friend at the P and O had quietly made it out to 'Mr. and Mrs.' 'It was the most agonising moment I've ever faced,' said Buck, for it was not as though he had deliberately decided to run away. Here, suddenly, with a raid in progress, he was on a big ship —perhaps the last to leave—and with a ticket. 'But of course,' wrote Buck that night in his diary, 'it couldn't be done. I couldn't rat.'

Tim Hudson was also tempted. At the foot of the gangway a sergeant stopped him, saying that passengers only were allowed on board. Tim, who was in uniform, said he merely wanted to carry his wife's suitcase to her cabin. The sergeant waved him on, but just as Tim started to climb the steep gangplank he felt a tug at his shoulder and the sergeant muttered, 'If you've got any sense you'll stay on board. And you won't be the only one. There's no hope here, mate.'

In the cabin the steward politely informed the four of them that the ship wouldn't be sailing for some time, so if they
140

would care to have a drink the bar was open. It seems incredible, but so it was—providing a pathetic echo of the boisterous good-bye scenes that always take place when a ship is sailing. The main lounge was jammed with men and women having their last farewell drinks with forced cheerfulness, almost as though the women were going home on leave. Hudson and Buckeridge faced the age-old problem of fighting their way to the bar where, in Buck's words, 'we watched an extremely slow bar steward carefully take an order, select a bottle, methodically pour a drink, hand it over, do a little arithmetic on a slip of paper, dollars to sterling, count the money, hand out the change, pick up a glass, polish it, hold it to the light, and take another order'. Somehow, Buckeridge managed to get four bottles of beer and some glasses and carried them headhigh to a table, where they had a last drink before their brief farewells.

Long before the *Felix Roussel* sailed that night for Bombay, the men had left. Jimmy Glover and George Hammonds had returned to Dulverton where there was work to be done getting out the next day's paper. Hudson, oppressed by the thought of returning to his bungalow in Stevens Road, had half decided to sleep at his ARP headquarters, when Buckeridge suggested he should spend the night at his flat over the Central Fire Station, and Tim gratefully accepted the offer.

After a scratch meal of sardines and bully beef and beer, the two men sat on the balcony of the station drinking a last stengah. It was a starry night, with the silhouette of St. Andrews Cathedral in front of them. Shortly after ten o'clock the black sky was broken by a red and then a blue rocket bursting far to the north. The stars seemed to hang in the air for a moment, then the sky was black again.

'What a time for fireworks!' cried Buckeridge, who never lost his sense of humour.

'Maybe distress signals,' said Hudson more soberly.

In fact, the red and blue rockets had been fired by the Japanese—to announce that the first crack troops of the 18th Chrysanthemum Division had crossed the Strait and had landed successfully on the island.

CHAPTER EIGHT

THE ASSAULT

Sunday night, February 8—Thursday night, February 12

In all the catalogue of ineffectual leadership, unfortunate decisions and wrangling in high places which contributed to the fall of Singapore, nothing is quite so puzzling as the virtual absence of any deterrent action during the last precious hours of daylight before the Japanese attacked. It is not as though the attackers took the defenders completely by surprise. Everything pointed to an imminent assault on the north-west coast of the island, and even though Percival had to bear in mind the danger of feint attacks, it is hard to believe that a modern general could so easily ignore what was happening around him.

At dawn on this fateful Sunday a daring Australian patrol, which had silently crossed the Straits of Johore during the night and penetrated nearly two miles into enemy country, returned with highly disquieting news. They had seen clear evidence of massive troop concentrations opposite the Australian sector, west of the causeway. As they skirted the jungle-lined roads opposite their shores, they had seen for themselves how they were choked with military traffic. The inland creeks were jammed with collapsible boats. Here was vital information which should have made the commanders set to work at once, planning new troop formations. Unfortunately the dawn report did not reach General Percival until 3.30 that afternoon. Why, has never been explained.

Long before Percival had received the delayed message, however, the patrol's news was corroborated by direct action. At dawn the Japanese launched savage and sustained bombing attacks on the forward Australian positions. Flying from their airstrips in Johore, fighters and light bombers came in low over the coconut palms in wave after wave, for hour after hour. Some planes scattered anti-personnel bombs. Others swept into shallow dives, their machine-guns blazing. The Australians, entrenched in hurried, often makeshift defences in

142

jungle country or plantations of coconut or rubber, could do nothing but stick it out. Which to their credit they did.

These sustained attacks might not in themselves have been enough to convince Percival that landings would follow shortly but they were only a mild foretaste of what was to come. By mid-morning the Japanese planes were being rested, and then the Japanese opened up with the most fearful barrage of the entire campaign. For hours during the blazing day enemy guns remorselessly pounded the Australian positions. By sundown they had wreaked such damage that every telephone line between the Australian units and headquarters had been cut. And yet British artillery hardly opened up in reply. Here—unless the Japanese were executing a colossal bluff—was clear evidence of a probable point of attack. And this in turn meant that somewhere in the rubber jungle across the Strait large groups of men were waiting for zero hour, together with concentrations of landing craft, artillery, army vehicles—in short, all the complicated paraphernalia required to launch an attack on a heavily defended island. True, the British had virtually no aircraft to spare, yet a sustained counter-barrage would surely have done something towards disrupting the highly organised Japanese plans. Instead the Japanese were permitted to carry them out with little or no interference.

Even after sunset, when the barrage against the Australians increased, if anything, in intensity, the British guns remained silent. Why? Incredible though it may seem, 'Neither Malaya Command nor Western Area [i.e. Percival or Bennett] was seriously perturbed by this,' says *The War Against Japan*, 'each apparently thinking that it was the first of a number of days of softening up, or that the enemy would switch the bombardment back next day to the Causeway and northeastern shores of the Island. As a result no orders were given during the evening for artillery fire to be brought down on the probable enemy forming-up places.'

Had this extraordinary decision been the judgment of generals who did not believe the Japanese were ready to attack, it might have been understandable. But this was far from being the case. In point of fact, General Percival had predicted that the Japanese would require a week to prepare. He had been right—but now when the week was up, he refused to believe in his own judgment. Ironically, Percival was wrong on two counts. He was certain the Japanese would attack the north-

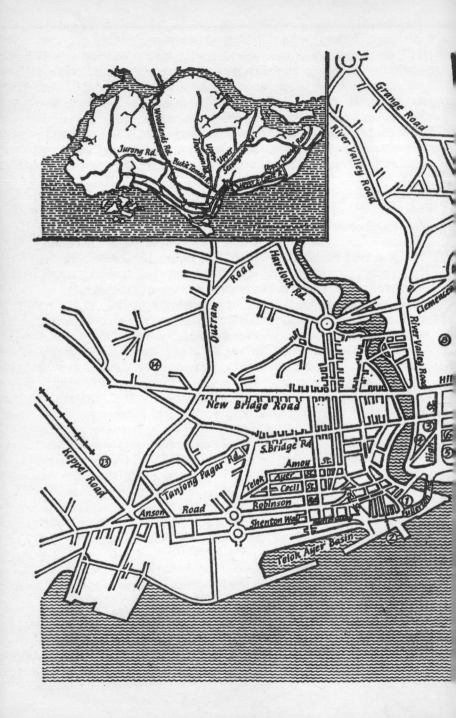

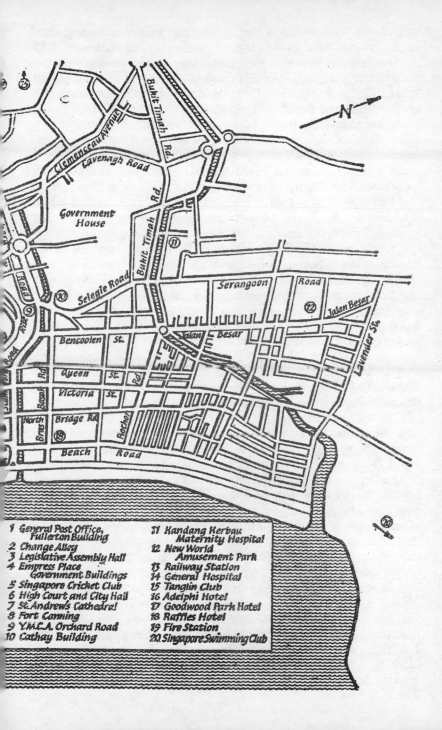

N

1 General Post Office,
   Fullerton Building
2 Change Alley
3 Legislative Assembly Hall
4 Empress Place
   Government Buildings
5 Singapore Cricket Club
6 High Court and City Hall
7 St. Andrew's Cathedral
8 Fort Canning
9 Y.M.C.A. Orchard Road
10 Cathay Building

11 Kandang Kerbau
   Maternity Hospital
12 New World
   Amusement Park
13 Railway Station
14 General Hospital
15 Tanglin Club
16 Adelphi Hotel
17 Goodwood Park Hotel
18 Raffles Hotel
19 Fire Station
20 Singapore Swimming Club

east shore and stuck to this rankling fear which was un-founded; he gave the Japanese eight days to prepare, and ignored this when his judgment was right.

In a story of so many 'ifs' and 'buts', no one can be sure what difference it would have made to the ultimate outcome of the siege had Percival opened up a counter-barrage; prob-ably none, though it might have lengthened the defence by a few days. A curtain of shells on the Japanese positions might have made it impossible for the enemy to cut *all* Allied com-munications lines in the north-west of the island, and this was to prove the gateway to disaster in the coming night.

At half past ten the enemy attacked. The Japanese had made intensive preparations. They had evacuated every civilian from a coastal zone ten miles deep. They had set up their military headquarters in the imposing brick and green-tiled Imperial Palace of the Sultan of Johore, which dominated the Strait, and which had a high square tower from where General Yamashita the next morning could plainly see his troops winding their way inland. Three divisions had been assembled together with 3,000 vehicles, 200 collapsible launches powered by outboard motors and a hundred larger landing craft. For a week they had (as we now know) been carrying out practice landings day and night in the countless creeks and small rivers jutting into the secret hiding-places of the rubber plantations. The 4,000 troops selected for the first assault wave were all veterans of fighting in China. Now after dusk—and secure in the knowl-edge that they would not be exposed to air attack—the spear-head troops carried their boats on their shoulders several miles from the inland creeks to the shore.

The first troops attacked on a broad front between two bays on the north-west coast of the island—Tanjong Buloh and Tanjong Murai (Tanjong is the Malay word for promontory) —under cover of devastating artillery and mortar fire. The first Australian sentries on the Singapore shoreline spotted the boats bobbing across the black water. The alarm was given, and hundreds of Australians opened a withering fire. The first wave of enemy troops was destroyed. So were many in the second wave. Yet such success could not continue, for the Australians were fighting against one overwhelming disadvantage. According to plan, the killing area in the Strait should suddenly have become as light as day—illumin-ated by scores of brilliant searchlights, which were there, waiting to be switched on so the defenders could blow the

146

enemy clean out of the water. Instead there was blackness everywhere, and the Australians could only fire haphazardly against invisible targets. How could they be sure where the weaving small boats were? All they could see was the occasional blacker shadow against the water, all they could hear as a guide was the high whine of outboard motors. Men cursed and shouted for light as they stumbled against each other in the dark. And still the small rubber boats came on relentlessly, cloaked in blackness. And then, too, what had happened to the artillery at this critical moment? A counter-barrage had been planned for the moment of the attack. Instead, British guns remained mute.

There was a simple, tragic explanation, though the Australians defending the beaches could not know it at that time. Nobody was able to get a signal to either the searchlight teams or the guns. Long before the Japanese had begun to scramble ashore, every line of communication had been cut —and no instructions ever reached either the searchlight crews or the artillery. And without those signals they could not go into action. In other circumstances, the searchlight teams might have been adventurous enough to use their own initiative to throw their beams across the water without waiting for orders, but it happened that they had been given the most explicit instructions that on no account were searchlights to be switched on until the signal was given. Apparently it was thought if they were lit too soon they would be destroyed by the Japanese.

Thus it was left to the infantry to send up SOS signals before a few guns opened fire—but by then the Japanese were ashore along the entire front, and before the Australians realised what was happening, they were fighting with the bayonet in the damp, sombre plantations, and the Japanese, as always, seemed to be everywhere—in front, behind, on either side, infiltrating swiftly behind disorganised pockets of Allied troops cut off from their colleagues. Swarming through the close, intricate country, each Japanese party was led by an officer with a compass strapped to his wrist. Carefully avoiding any frontal attacks, they sought out the gaps in the Australian lines and pushed through behind them. Once the Australians—who had no compasses—lost sight of the Strait and were attacked from the rear, they did not even know which direction they faced in the maze of the

147

jungle, lit only by the stabs of light from gunfire and the occasional Japanese barge burning offshore.

By one a.m. the Australians were withdrawing from their forward positions. It was a catastrophe of the first magnitude, of which Kenneth Attiwill,[1] who fought throughout the campaign, gave a graphic picture: 'Groups of men became separated from their comrades in the bewildering darkness. Others lost their way. Many died. Some straggled back as far as Bukit Timah. Others even reached Singapore City, and long before they could be picked up, re-organised and sent back, the disorganisation was complete. The effect of the withdrawals was to dislocate the whole brigade area, and by ten o'clock on the morning of the 9th—less than twelve hours after the assault had been sighted—the 22nd Australian Brigade, on whose fighting power had rested the defence of the north-western area of the Island, was no longer a conclusive fighting force.'

By then nearly 4,000 Japanese had secured a firm foothold on the island. Their forward elements were already advancing towards Tengah airfield, west of the city. And by then the High Command had issued its first communiqué, in which it announced with irritating blandness that 'Offensive action is being taken to mop up the enemy'. To anyone familiar with Percival's polite little white lies, it was possible to read between the lines, though no doubt some civilians were left with the impression that the few foolhardy Japanese on the island would soon be wiped out. Percival, however, suffered from no such delusions himself, for in his battle report to Wavell he said bluntly that the 'Enemy landed in force on west coast last night and has penetrated about five miles . . . situation is undoubtedly serious in view of the very extended coastline which we have to watch. Have made plan for concentrating forces to cover Singapore if this becomes necessary.'

He had, indeed. The plan was top secret, but unfortunately it leaked out—with disastrous results.

During the night few people in Singapore City had the remotest idea of what was happening barely 20 miles away, though everybody could hear—and had heard all day—the muffled hammering of the guns to the north. At times it sounded like a far-off storm—an illusion that was heightened

[1] In *The Singapore Story*.

when, during the evening, a brief but violent thunderstorm drenched the city. As the thunder clapped directly overhead, it was as though the distant storm had finally come closer—until, in each period of silence that followed, the sullen sound of the distant guns echoed through the streets, with the rain hissing down on the skeletons of bombed, charred buildings.

A few civilians knew what was happening. Shenton Thomas was having a last nightcap when Percival telephoned him with the news. Freddy Bloom had finished extra duties and was walking through a corridor to her room in the General Hospital when an army sister bustled up and whispered conspiratorially, 'It's started!' Leslie Hoffman had a hunch—but no more than a hunch—so telephoned a friend in Bukit Timah, the village on the main road linking Singapore and the causeway. 'I don't know anything,' said the friend, 'except that all hell's broken loose over to the west, and I can't sleep for the noise.' Buckeridge was not told anything, but though technically off duty, received a friendly warning to stand by 'in case of urgent calls'. 'I've been standing by for a couple of months,' he retorted drily, 'so another night won't hurt me.' Around midnight, an army contact phoned Jimmy Glover at Dulverton and told him that ' a small party of Japanese' had landed on the west coast—but warned him that on no account must the news be released before the official communiqué had been issued. There was nothing he could do, so Glover told the boy not to awaken him or Hammonds unless the nearby AA guns went into action, and they both slept through the night, with Glover 'subconsciously aware of the fitfully increased tempo of the artillery activity on the north of the island'. They were both up before dawn, however, for the *Tribune* had to be printed and on the streets before lunch.

About nine o'clock the official news of the landing was announced on the radio. Ian Morrison was in the press room at the Cathay starting to type out a story of the bombardment for *The Times* when the news came through. He had no time to think, but tore the piece of paper out of his typewriter, crunched it into a ball, and started a new despatch. Leslie Hoffman had driven to the Cathay in his open MG sports car to pick up any news on his way to Dulverton. As he ran down the stone steps after hearing the bulletin, knots of bewildered men and women were already clus-

tering round the entrance instinctively knowing the importance of the building and waiting hopefully for fragments
of information. When he drove off, he saw other groups of
anxious men and women outside the Supreme Court. Men
of all races—Europeans, Malays, Chinese, Indians—jostled
round the entrances to all the public buildings, as though
gathering some strength from the proximity to officialdom,
as though it somehow eased the intolerable suspense that
he could already sense around him. Driving past St. Andrews
Cathedral, he saw a most unusual sight for a Monday morning—streams of men and women crossing the green sward and
going into the church to pray.

At Dulverton, Hammonds was looking over Glover's
shoulder as the communiqué, which had been phoned to them,
was typed out, and muttered, 'Aren't you glad you got
Julienne away?' Glover must have been relieved—for it seemed
that the Japanese, who were thrusting inland from the north-
west coast, could not be more than thirteen miles away from
Dulverton. Not that they had any time to reflect on anything except one fact: if the Japanese advance were not
held, the *Tribune* might be driven from its emergency printing
office in a matter of hours.

'It's all over bar the shouting,' Leslie Hoffman said to Hammonds when he arrived, 'you'd better pack a suitcase while
you've still got time.'

It says much for the loyalty of the Asian workmen setting
type, proof-reading, preparing the flat-bed press, that the
Tribune came out at all that morning, for 'the war and the
noises of war were coming closer'. Several hidden artillery
positions had been established in the jungle not far from
Glover's bungalow—and they were obviously inflicting damage
on the Japanese troops for throughout the morning the area
was raided at half-hourly intervals by Japanese planes searching for the guns. From the verandah of Dulverton, Glover
and Hammonds could easily see the enemy aircraft screeching down, like Nazi Stukas, into shallow dive-bombing attacks.
Miraculously, Dulverton escaped damage. At a time when
water mains and telephones were being disrupted all over
the island, Glover was still able to phone to the Cathay and
keep in touch, while the special electric cable he had had
installed for his machines bore a charmed life. Bombs tore
up the surrounding compounds. The dusty spurts of machine-
gun bullets danced in straight, savage lines on either side of
150

the cable. But apart from the occasional nervous flicker the power kept on—and the men in the attap shed remained at their machines.

When the first wet copies were gathered off the press, Glover loaded them in his car and took them down to his distributing centre at the Cathay. Hammonds took the second load, Hoffman the third. They faced increased hazards in getting through to the centre of the city along roads virtually monopolised by military traffic. After he had dumped his last load of newspapers, Glover climbed the stone steps of the Cathay to have a word with Rob Scott. The moment he entered the office he noticed that Irene Kenny had vanished. 'The barometer had fallen.' And when he asked for news of her, Scott replied that he had ordered her to leave—at half an hour's notice. She had been furious. There had ben an outbreak of tears and protest, but Scott had packed her into a car which had stopped for five minutes at the YWCA to allow her to pack a grip, and then taken her straight to the airport.

'What does that mean in terms of your opinion of holding out?' asked Glover.

'Oh! They've dropped a shade—say 49 to 51,' replied Scott with a smile.

By now it must have been clear to those in authority that the island was doomed, and Brigadier Simson was urgently demanding from Sir Thomas Shenton the right to put a comprehensive scorched earth policy into practice. Churchill had uncompromisingly made it clear that he expected 'every scrap of material . . . to be blown to pieces to prevent capture by the enemy' but so far little had been done, even though as far back as early January Simson had suggested to the Governor that 'a phased programme of destruction' should be prepared and approved. Simson wanted at all costs to avoid a repetition of the disaster at Penang when much valuable equipment had been left for the Japanese. Despite his urgent representations to the government, however, Simson had been unable to extract any decision until towards the end of January.

Though on the surface it would seem to have been a relatively simple matter for a beleaguered city to implement its Prime Minister's orders to blow up anything that might be useful to the enemy, the situation was fraught with certain

151

complications. The Governor was still responsible for civil affairs—and he had to consider the fact that if or when the city capitulated, many of the Asian businessmen would no doubt try to carry on as best they could. The military naturally wanted to deny as much as possible to the enemy, but since Percival had refused to assume the authority of military governor, Shenton Thomas did in fact have the last word on what should, or should not, be done to the hundred or so major civil installations.

Simson wanted *carte blanche* to deal with them all as soon as possible, and on the evening after the Japanese landing, the two men sat on the Governor's favourite verandah overlooking the city, sipping their stengahs. The Brigadier tried to emphasise the need for speed. His arguments were simple but cogent. Time after time during the retreat down the peninsula engineers had been unable to get government sanction to destroy items like tin dredgers or stocks of rubber until too late. It had been physically impossible to get the orders through—with the result that the Japanese had been presented with a great deal of valuable material. He wanted at all costs to avoid delay. The Governor, however, felt Simson was taking too pessimistic a view of events to come, and had made up his mind what should be done. Public services such as gas, electricity, water and sewage were to remain untouched. The Governor would also undertake to arrange for the demolition of rubber and tin stocks and the radio station. Though Simson might have chafed with a secret impatience, and felt he could get the job done more quickly, he could not cavil at these decisions, for though Churchill had demanded complete denial, such a course was incompatible with a fight to the death. It was one thing for an army to scorch the earth as it retreated; it was quite a different matter for an army to scorch the earth of a fortress it had been ordered to defend to the last man.

But then the Governor dropped a bombshell. After going through the list of civil plants, he told Simson politely but firmly that he refused to sanction the destruction of about forty Chinese-owned engineering works. As Simson listened open-mouthed, the Governor calmly crossed them off the list. There were big workshops, many equipped with the latest and most modern machinery. Others were stacked with brand new vehicles.

Simson, who could hardly believe his ears, cried, 'But
152

they'll be invaluable to the Japanese. *Why*, sir? What's the reason?'

The Governor held up his whisky glass and gazed reflectively into it before uttering, quite calmly, a phrase that seemed destined to haunt Simson throughout the campaign. Echoing the words of General Percival at another, earlier, historic meeting, Shenton Thomas said simply, but with complete finality, 'It would be bad for morale.'

The Governor 'gave me one hard, long look' and then said coldly, 'I would remind you, Simson, that we haven't lost the island yet.'

And that was all he would say on the matter. Most of the more important Chinese engineering works were left in running order for the enemy—and Simson could only study the names still left on his list: some forty-seven British-owned plants. These he could deny to the enemy, together with vast quantities of liquor and stocks of petrol and oil which would be destroyed by the military authorities or the oil companies themselves.

The Governor's decision 'resulted in the enemy receiving a welcome present of new vehicles and well-equipped workshops':[2] and we can only surmise the reasons behind it. Of course the Governor was rightly proud of the way in which he 'looked after the natives' who would have to carry on after any surrender. He believed Malaya was their country and that he was there to protect them (against themselves if necessary). But one must also remember that the Governor's responsibilities, though unchanged in theory, had in practice been whittled away. Duff Cooper had seen to that—and so had a war which had not only swept across a country, but had swept away the cobwebs of colonial government. Slowly but relentlessly the Governor had found himself becoming more and more of a figurehead, whose many friends could plainly see how miserable he was at not being permitted to do more than sign unimportant papers and make 'public appearances'. Even his critics admit that Shenton Thomas was incapable of a mean action, and without any doubt he believed that the Chinese would have to 'carry on' and must be left with the means to do it—though this theory hardly tallied with the ruthless way in which all fishing boats had been smashed up or sunk. Ironically, there is no doubt that Shenton Thomas would have been appalled had anyone sug-

2 *The War Against Japan.*

gested that his decision was hindering the global war effort.

The meeting broke up shortly before dinner. Curiously enough, neither man had mentioned the problem of destroying the vital machinery and facilities in the sprawling dockyards. These were run by the Singapore Harbour Board, which was a law unto itself with its own electricity plant, even its own wardens and fire brigades. In view of what was to happen in a few hours, however, it was a significant and unfortunate omission on the Governor's part.

Simson had already gathered sufficient men to start the demolition work. Men from the Public Works Department (the PWD), together with courageous Chinese and Indian volunteers, started the complicated task of destroying the machinery of the forty-seven firms. They faced tremendous physical hazards, for the shelling of the city was beginning to assume drumfire proportions, while one air raid followed another so swiftly they seemed to be incessant. The firms were also scattered far and wide, and were often difficult to reach, while some presented serious technical problems for engineers and PWD men. Thorneycroft's ship repair and boat-building yards at Tanjong Rhu, five miles east of the city, covered nearly 12 acres and employed 700 people under Mr. Stewart Owler, its managing director. The sprawling boatyards and repair shops, the slipways by the shore, the machine rooms and power plants, represented the best part of a life's work to the senior Europeans who worked there. It was heart-breaking—but so generous was the co-operation that the denial team largely finished the work of destruction in twenty-four hours.

Not all firms were so co-operative. Some plants were only destroyed 'despite the active opposition of the owners or their agent'. Several owners did everything possible to delay the denial scheme. Some lodged personal appeals with the Governor. Big plants with head offices in Britain, Australia or India petitioned their home governments for exemption. In one or two cases there were hand-to-hand scuffles as Europeans tried forcibly to prevent Simson's men from doing their job. 'British firms were most reluctant,' wrote Simson later, 'and one or two put every obstacle in the way of the PWD when demolition was finally ordered.'

Perhaps the worst case of all concerned a big garage. There was no question that it had to be rendered unserviceable—even the Governor had admitted this by leaving it

154

on Simson's list. So, thinking that this was just one more 'job to be done', Simson's men went round and started work. Unknown to them, however, the garage had powerful friends at court. So powerful, in fact, that Simson's men were actually in the process of destroying workshops and vehicles belonging to the garage when to their astonishment they were abruptly ordered to stop. The owners were able to wave a slip of paper before their eyes. Written instructions to exempt them had been received directly from the government —with the result that, as Simson noted wryly, 'the enemy reaped the advantage.'

By contrast, few civilians attempted to defy the order to smash up the liquor stocks. The horror stories of the Japanese drunken rampage in Hong Kong were too fresh in people's minds to be forgotten or ignored. Sir Shenton Thomas had not only announced that a total ban on all liquor would come into force at noon on Friday the 13th, but had ordered big firms to start smashing up their stocks immediately. The Customs led the way by breaking tens of thousands of bottles of hard liquor, though as Buckeridge pointed out to Hudson, 'That didn't hurt. Since when have the Customs had any feelings?'

All over the city, people were destroying their own precious stocks, in some cases the results of years of 'collecting'. Jimmy Glover had for years been storing the finest French wines for the time when he and Julienne would retire to Cameron Highlands, up-country. Now, he and George Hammonds spent the evening 'smashing bottles of precious liquid from some of the finest vineyards in France'.

Buckeridge was helping out at Robinson's after one of Lucy's colleagues had phoned, saying, 'We've got half a million dollars' worth of strong stuff—and we've got to smash it all up by Friday. We need volunteers.'

For the best part of a day and a half—while the customers in the store had no inkling of what was happening—Chinese boys lugged case after case of whisky, gin and brandy out of Robinson's cellars into a courtyard behind the store where other boys were waiting to rip off the tops. There, a team of six men smashed the bottles in the only way possible—by hurling them one by one at a brick wall opposite. 'I never realised,' wrote Buckeridge in his diary, 'just how long it takes to pull twelve bottles out of a case, then throw them against a wall.'

Something else had to be destroyed—bank notes. And this was even hotter work than smashing bottles under a blazing sun, for the notes had to be burned under the watchful eye of a senior official. The task fell to Eric Pretty, the Acting Federal Secretary. Despite the run on money, the Treasury reserves still totalled $5 million, and early in the morning Pretty went to the vaults below the government offices in Empress Place, not far from Fullerton Building. In the next cellar was the furnace used by the government to destroy confidential papers. It took a day to burn the money, for though there was a fair proportion of $100 bills, 'it seemed to me,' said Pretty, 'as though there were an awful lot of fives and tens.' Pretty could not just allow the messengers to toss the bundles into the furnace. Each batch had to be checked and the numbers of the notes recorded as the boys brought them in from the vaults. 'I never imagined I'd have so much money to burn,' sighed Pretty.

All this work of destruction—to say nothing of the problem of living—was being enacted against a grim background of increased shelling and bombing. Chinatown was badly hit time and again, and it was after one typical raid in one of the poorest districts that Rob Scott and Ian Morrison found 'a marvellous atmosphere of helpfulness and fellow-feeling. One could not help admiring these people who, with so little direction from above, were doing what they could.'

Malays, an Arab with a fez, some Chinese, a couple of European wardens, were digging the victims out of a ruin that had received a direct hit. Scott and Morrison seized shovels and started digging too. In all they found thirteen bodies, and all the time a ring of stoic Chinese—many of them children—stood watching. At last Scott reached the body of a woman so mutilated one could hardly recognise it. And then something happened. As Scott lifted the body out of the hole, a group of children started howling miserably, with one little girl, obviously the eldest, struggling and crying and trying to make herself understood. Realising that she was the daughter, Scott held her back. 'She continued to struggle and was trying to say something through her tears.'

Eventually, with the aid of a Chinese, Scott discovered what it was. 'Her mother had some money tied in a sash round her waist. The little girl wanted the money. She was afraid that someone might take it away.' Rob Scott bent down, unfastened the red sash tied round the woman's waist, and

156

found a purse containing four dollars and a few small coins. 'It was probably the family's entire worldly wealth.' Scott gave it to the little girl, who snatched it without a word, though 'her crying became a snuffle'. Scott found nothing cynical or grasping about the little girl's action. It was the natural reaction of generations of Chinese, scratching a bare living out of the soil.

Not only was Chinatown bombed ruthlessly. The Japanese now singled out Orchard Road as a target for their guns. This wide straight street was the main military link between the city and military headquarters at Fort Canning, and the Japanese regarded it as a legitimate military target—despite the presence of the Cold Storage, the Municipal market and other big shops. All day long the military traffic tore along it, running the gauntlet of the shells that whined and crashed. Half the buildings seemed to have been hit by now. Abandoned or burned-out cars littered every corner. Water gushed along the deep gullies from unmended pipes. Here and there bodies lay waiting to be collected, many of them civilians, for people had to live, they had to eat. George Hammonds, like everyone else, had to buy food. He usually went to the Municipal market at 5.30 a.m., parking his car at the corner of Cuppage Road. On this Tuesday there was not much to buy at the market, for only a handful of apathetic Chinese stood around in the vast hall lit by guttering candles. After buying some vegetables, George went across the road to the Cold Storage, which was almost as empty as the market, with barely a dozen civilians wandering in the enormous building. At least in the Cold Storage George bought ample stocks of butter and bacon.

After driving over to Robinson's to get a haircut, George walked out into Raffles Place. With the heat of a new stifling day pressing down and the bright sun already hurting his eyes, Hammonds wiped his glasses, pulled a cigarette from his round tin, and lingered on the steps of the big store for a few minutes. He remembers the scene vividly. The famous square—the real heart of white Singapore—had hardly been touched. Even the noises of war were muffled by the high buildings, and the square was filled with people of all colours—some in white ducks, some in shorts, others in sarongs—either busy or unconcerned, going in and out of shops, talking at the corners. An Indian street trader squatting on the pathway dozed over his tray of cheap

157

trinkets; a Malay driver was fast asleep at the wheel of a tuan's parked car; a food hawker bobbed along, two containers dangling from the bamboo across his shoulders; an old, bearded white man in shorts, sports shirt and sandals came out of Kelly and Walsh, the booksellers, clutching a big new volume with a shiny cover—and was already dipping eagerly into it as he brushed past George on his way into Robinson's, perhaps for a coffee and a read. Two Chinese workmen were walking along arguing when one suddenly turned to the other with an obvious insult. In a flash they were brawling. Out of nowhere a policeman appeared to separate them. 'It all seemed so normal,' wrote George, 'it made even Orchard Road seem a long, long way off.'

But then all Singapore in those hectic, tragic days was a confused pattern, a world in which each and every man had to face up to his own problems. The Rev. Bennitt faced one which only he and his conscience could resolve. The Bishop of Singapore had told him that, though he hoped the Japanese would allow some clergy to remain at liberty, he was sure some would have to be interned. If this happened, he felt that Bennitt should be classed as 'non-essential' and be interned with the other civilians.

'The Rev.', who had never missed an hour of his double duties at the Cathedral and Yoch Eng first aid post, accepted the decision stoically—until a friend suddenly appeared with a suitcase and announced that a small coastal vessel was going to make a dash for Java. He begged 'The Rev.' to come along. An interned priest, he argued, was less valuable than a priest at liberty. After wrestling with his conscience, Bennitt went to the cathedral and wrote a note to the Bishop saying he was leaving. Packing a suitcase hurriedly, he got out his car and drove his friend to the docks, reaching the rendezvous during a raid. As they scrambled out of the car they had to step over bodies lying in the street. A wounded child was crying piteously and instinctively 'The Rev.' bent down to comfort it, while his friend urged him to hurry, shouting that there was not a moment to lose.

As he calmed the child and it stopped whimpering, 'The Rev.' looked up. The ship—perhaps the last chance to escape —was there in front of his eyes. His friend was yelling for him to come. And suddenly 'The Rev.' stood up, shook his head and waved his hand. Of course he couldn't go. If he could comfort people now, how many would he be able to
158

comfort and help in the long years of captivity? Without a word he watched his friend disappear into the ship. Then he drove back from the blazing docks to the cathedral and destroyed the note.

Not far from the cathedral the Governor was still trying to 'carry on as usual'. On the one hand he was still holding a daily 'collar and tie' conference at Government House—but the shelling was so bad that he had moved his bed to the corner of a downstairs drawing-room, while his wife spent the night under the dining-room table. He made almost daily visits to heavily bombed areas in an effort to bolster morale —and to answer the Japanese, who were now using the captured radio at Penang to announce that he and Lady Thomas had run away.

The grounds of Government House—to say nothing of the city—were not only plastered with bombs, but with an incredible assortment of enemy leaflets. One bore a crudely drawn picture of a girl languishing in the arms of a soldier, with the puzzling caption 'Nightmare of your neglected wife: "Oh Tommy! I am going crazy." ' Another announced that Singapore was rioting, that British and Australian troops were secretly evacuating the island. It urged the Asian troops to 'Pack up your troubles in your old kit bag and co-operate with the Nippon Army.' A third bore a drawing of an obese British planter lolling under a fiery sun. Yet another showed a gluttonous British officer tucking into steak and chips while his starving Indian troops looked on with drooling lips. 'Leaflet collecting' became a passion with hundreds of Chinese children who had never collected cigarette cards in their lives.

On the other hand, adults were busy collecting something quite different—a few surreptitious bottles of precious liquor to hide before the Governor's edict that all stocks must be destroyed. The big stocks had already gone down the drains, but, understandably, many civilians felt they had the right to save the odd bottle 'for an emergency'. 'Willie' Watt— still nursing his bad arm after the swipe by a drunken soldier —hid several bottles of Scotch in the thick coarse lalang behind his bungalow; Tim Hudson put a couple of bottles in his godown, and two more at home.

On the last 'wet' night in Singapore before sales of drinks were banned, more than a few civilians had their share of drink—particularly at the Cricket Club, for Buckeridge was

159

not alone in feeling, 'Just imagine the Cricket Club without being able to get a stengah. I had to go and mourn at the funeral.' The club had a stock of 150 cases of whisky, to say nothing of other liquor, and members flocked to drink as much as possible. All but two of the club stewards had left, and for once the moderate measure that normally comprised the Singapore stengah was forgotten. Perspiring Chinese boys filled everyone's glass with anything up to four fingers of whisky before adding a splash of Fraser and Neave's soda. The only thing lacking was water for those who preferred a *whisky ayer*. As Buckeridge noted, 'Though nobody could have had the remotest idea how payment was to be exacted, members still had to go through the rigmarole of signing chits for each drink'.

Despite the finality of the occasion, despite the desperation of these last days, few if any of the so-called 'whisky-swilling planters' got drunk—perhaps because they knew that scores of wounded were being temporarily housed in a wing of the club after a hospital with 100 patients had been trapped during a hasty Allied withdrawal. After dark its ambulances had rumbled back to Singapore under the very noses of the Japanese—only to find there was nowhere for the wounded to go. Patients, nurses, orderlies were housed in the Club until the Victoria Theatre across the way was turned into a hospital of two hundred beds.

As the rate of wounded—both military and civilian—increased daily, every available building was turned into makeshift hospitals. Even St. Andrews Cathedral became a first aid post. Chairs, pews, hymn books, hassocks were hurriedly cleared from the nave to make room for stretchers and beds. The vestry was turned into an operating theatre. Nurses and doctors moved in with bottles of antiseptic, rolls of bandages, splints and drugs. By nightfall, the Rev. Bennitt was recording in his diary, 'It was a strange sight to look down from the east end of the famous building and see rows of wounded men lying on the floor, orderlies and doctors doing their rounds among them with pinpricks of lighted cigarettes showing in the dark corners'.

About half the casualties were British, half Australian; there was even one Japanese soldier among them. Hundreds of wounded men received their first treatment in the cathedral. Doctors and nurses worked round the clock, and when the taps dried up, volunteers carried pails from the nearest broken water mains. And soon, round the corner in the beautiful green churchyard, the first rough crosses were being placed over the graves of those who had died.

The devotion and courage of the Asian nurses at all the hospitals were magnificent. They never faltered. During heavy shelling, Freddy Bloom saw a young Chinese nurse at the General kneel down beside a wounded soldier, shield his body with hers, and as the screaming shells fell around, cover the man's ears with her hands to blot out the sound. Some instances of 'devotion to duty' would have been almost comic if tragedy had not been so close. Boys who had served meals to the tuans in Ward Four—the first-class European male ward—found it impossible to absorb the fact that three or four men now shared one room. Yet, despite the shelling, they still insisted on serving the scratch meals of bully beef on trays complete with tray cloths, and cruets carefully set out, with the silverwork shining.

Every hospital had its quota of direct hits though nothing matched the terror raid on the Tyersall Indian Hospital, a hutted camp with attap roofs north-west of the city. Shortly after lunch a wave of Japanese medium bombers attacked it, even though the buildings were clearly marked with red crosses. The hastily-built camp was a fire-trap, dry as tinder, and long before the brigades arrived, it was one sheet of searing flame. 'It was the worst sight I ever saw,' said Buckeridge. 'Every building was an inferno—and you couldn't get from one to another.' Stretcher patients were roasted to death in their beds. Those who could walk attempted to escape but often could not force their way through flames up to thirty feet high. Buckeridge remembers how 'half a dozen men screaming with pain suddenly rushed out into the open. They were in flames from head to feet'. The smell of burning flesh made scores of helpers vomit as they worked. The screams of the trapped overshadowed every other noise—even the staccato rattle of machine-gun fire, for now Japanese fighters swooped low over the furnace, machine-gunning the rescuers and those wounded who had been got out and laid on the grass away from the huts. Many who had managed miraculously to escape were killed in cold blood as they lay there waiting to be moved. Over two hundred patients died.

It was about this time that a remarkable woman doctor enters the story. Dr. Cicely Williams, unmarried, was 47 at the time, and at the outbreak of war had been quietly working in a hospital up-country. Tall, good-looking, with an infectious sense of humour that masked an iron determination, she had made her way to Singapore and asked 'for a job of work'. Somewhat to her astonishment, she was asked if she could take charge of a group of children, some of them air raid victims, others orphans. She had only sporadic help. She had little in the way of equipment—and now suddenly 'out of the blue I found myself mother of 120 children'. She managed to house the ill-assorted babies in the Tan Tock Seng Hospital on the outskirts of the city, where doctors visited her during the day 'when possible'—which was not often. With the aid of the few nurses and amahs she had managed to round up, together with one or two volunteers, Cicely Williams housed, fed, washed her suddenly-acquired family of tots. A born organiser, she 'scrounged' milk and other baby foods, and at times she even had to help with the cooking. But not only was she 'mother' to 120 children—she had 'a full-time job' as doctor to them, for her charges not only included babies orphaned in raids, crying for their mothers, but many others who were either ill with tropical diseases or in a state of shock.

Alone at night, Cicely Williams coped as best she could, helped only by Asian volunteers. Sometimes even she had to leave the children—as on the night when she heard the clanging of an ambulance bell at the hospital entrance, and ran out just as the ambulance disappeared down the drive. Shells were bursting everywhere—but there, on the front steps, was a tiny, whimpering bundle. At first she thought the driver had bolted because of the shelling, but when she took the baby inside, one look told her it had diphtheria—and she had 120 children in the same building. She could not keep the child at Tan Tock Seng for an instant. There was only one thing to be done—get the baby to the Middleton Infectious Diseases Hospital in Pegu Road. But that was half a mile away, and the only car had broken down, while the phone had long since ceased to function. Apart from a few Asian helpers, she was on her own. Carrying the baby, Cicely Williams set off in the shelling and walked the half mile to the Middleton, handed the baby over, and walked back—arriving just as the amah in charge of a ward of year-old babies threw up her hands and cried, 'Ta boleh Tahan!' ('I can't stand it!') and bolted. Cicely Williams spent the rest of the night in the ward with wounded children who had the screaming horrors.

A day or two after the beginning of the assault, a startling rumour swept through the civilian women of the nursing services—both professional and volunteers—working at the General Hospital. It was nothing less than a report that all British and Australian military sisters and nurses were about to be evacuated—leaving the civilian nurses behind. The 'General' had been rained with bombs and shells. Since Freddy Bloom's wedding day—when she had survived a direct hit near the X-ray department—several more bombs had landed on the hospital, and she herself had had some narrow escapes. Understandably many women were in danger of becoming jittery. Yet the hundreds of civilian women of all races carried on courageously—some in the large hospitals, others at first aid posts. They had to work in 12-hour shifts. At times there was such a shortage of water that doctors and nurses operating on raid casualties had to wash their hands and sterilise their instruments in soda water. Women used to a dozen servants now gratefully slept in the nearest corridor—if it were not already crowded with wounded. Some volunteer nurses were weighed down by agonising personal problems, particularly those who had had no news for weeks of husbands fighting in the Local Defence Volunteers. Yet in all the bloody history that was being written during the siege, they worked quietly, efficiently and unremittingly, drawing strength and courage from the trained professionals who now—so it was said—were going to pull out.

Dr. R. B. MacGregor, the energetic Director of Civilian Medical Services, felt he had to scotch the rumour—if, indeed, it were only a rumour—without delay, or the morale of his civilians would plummet, particularly as he had promised his civil government sisters and nurses and MAS volunteers the same opportunities for evacuation as military nursing sisters. Dr. MacGregor immediately sought out Shenton Thomas for some assurance that the whispers were unfounded, and it happens that, at a time when virtually all written records were lost in the confusion, we do have a carefully compiled list of times and meetings between the chief figures in this drama, which was to have such an unsavoury climax.

On Tuesday, February 8, MacGregor told Shenton Thomas

that by and large there was no question of the civilian nurses wanting to leave. 'The majority are willing to carry on under the same conditions as the military sisters,' he said, though admitting that 'some MAS are showing signs of strain,' and should be given a chance to go if they wished. The first and most important point that needed clearing up, however, was the future movements of the Army sisters.

The Governor promised to make enquiries. That same evening he met General Percival, and asked him bluntly, 'Is there any proposal to evacuate Army sisters?' Percival looked astonished at the direct question. Sir Shenton Thomas remembered that he 'seemed surprised that I should ask'. In any event, Percival replied emphatically, 'No. None at all.'

This was the reply the Governor had expected, and at 7.30 the next morning he telephoned Dr. MacGregor that the Army sisters were definitely staying. He had had the news directly from Percival. Sir Shenton suggested that the regular civil nursing staff and the MAS should be asked to volunteer to remain, but added, 'Those who don't volunteer should be given the chance to leave without the stigma of desertion.'

Dr. MacGregor now called all the civilian nurses together and addressed them. It must have been a dramatic meeting. Freddy Bloom remembers that the evening was suffocating as they all trooped into one of the lecture rooms. There was no raid on, but the evidence of war was all about them. Half the windows had been smashed, and outside they could see fires burning. Hot and sweating, the group of women waited for the doctor to speak.

Dr. MacGregor told them there was no foundation for the rumours that the Army sisters would leave—they had been scotched by Percival himself. Yet he did not minimise the dangers that lay ahead. Though every woman was doing invaluable work, he could not force them to stay, but he did ask them to volunteer. Reassured by the news, every European civilian government sister and every volunteer in the MAS decided to remain.

Dr. MacGregor then turned to the Asian nurses—professional and volunteers—and asked how they felt about staying, for their case was rather different—many of them could have returned to their kampongs.

From the back of the group a voice piped up, 'What are *you* going to do, sir?'

164

Slightly flabbergasted, MacGregor retorted, 'Why—stay, of course!'

Almost simultaneously every voice joined in a chorus, 'Then we stay too!'

Not one of them knew that within a matter of days every single military sister and nurse in Singapore—except one who refused to go—would have been quietly evacuated, that without a word they would have left their wounded behind, to be tended by a totally inadequate staff of civilian sisters helped only by a band of semi-trained volunteers.

The exception was a remarkable young Scotswoman, Elizabeth Petrie, who had joined up in Singapore, had served with Indian units on the Siamese border, and fought her way down the peninsula. She flatly refused to leave the wounded. The other Army sisters' had not, of course, 'deserted'. The Army had posted them to other areas, but they had done so without a word to the civil government, and despite Percival's categorical assurance that such a step was far from his mind. Shenton Thomas remembered someone coming up to him and exclaiming bitterly, 'The ideals of Florence Nightingale have been scrapped in favour of safety first'.[3]

This extraordinary action would have been easier to understand had it been decided to get these battle-trained sisters away to serve elsewhere. But, in fact, the decision was an error, the result of a chance remark—as Shenton Thomas discovered when, fuming at what he considered a betrayal of his civilians, he demanded an explanation from an embarrassed Percival. The order had been given by an officer —without reference to higher authority—after Percival had made a casual remark that 'The Australians seem to have an unduly large number of sisters.' Presumably the officer had taken this to mean that they ought to go. In any event, the officer had made the decision himself—and the entire staff, British as well as Australians, had been ordered to go. One can sympathise with Shenton Thomas's bitterness, and at the retort he made to Percival: 'Apparently the army places the welfare of its sisters before the care of the wounded'.

The Army sisters were not the only ones to be evacuated

[3] Over 200 civilian nurses and MAS women were interned, though only four service women were interned; three were the wives of high-ranking soldiers who elected to remain. The fourth was Elizabeth Petrie.

in circumstances amounting almost to secrecy. Another extraordinary evacuation now took place, and again without the one man who should have been told being informed—this time Brigadier Simson.

For now it was the senior European officials of the all-important Singapore Harbour Board who quietly left the island. The Harbour Board, as we have seen, was a self-contained unit, run on autocratic lines by officials who brooked no interference. Its record during the campaign had not been particularly noteworthy, though its staff had not been found wanting in bravery. But it had 'decided not to erect shelters along its extent of some miles of great wharves; and the decision has been criticised'.[4] The lack of shelters had resulted in the frequent refusal by coolies to unload vital war materials from the convoys. And notwithstanding the fact that the harbour area was a legitimate target for bombing, the Board had foolishly allowed vast stocks of food (including 12,000 tons of flour) to be stored in some of its sixty-five cavernous godowns. Much of it had gone up in flames before Brigadier Simson's men managed to start transferring stocks to safer areas 'after considerable pressure on the Governor and the Chairman.'

Shenton Thomas had barely ended his conversation with MacGregor on the Wednesday morning when Japanese bombers started a savage attack on the dock areas. There had been a good turn-out of coolies doubtless attracted by the new improved pay rates and guarantees of compensation for which Simson had fought. The Brigadier had by this time been bombed out of his own house, and—at the suggestion of Shenton Thomas—was living at Government House, and it was there that he was called urgently to the telephone.

On the line was the officer in charge of parties working in the dock area, and in an agitated voice he said, 'Sir, I have to report that all the senior Europeans working for the Harbour Board have gone—left the island.'

Simson at first thought there must be some mistake. The Governor had laid down in unequivocal terms that no Europeans could leave the island without permission.

'We've managed to get a labour force here,' the officer added, 'but there's nobody left to tell them what to do.'

'I'll get on to Rodgers, the chairman,' Simson suggested on the phone.

4 From *The Civil Defence of Malaya.*

'Rodgers!' The officer gave a short laugh. 'He's gone like the rest, sir.' Then he added something that Simson found even more difficult to believe. 'The story down here, sir, is that the Governor gave them permission to go.'

In fact the Harbour Board officials—like the Army sisters —had not 'done a bunk'. Shenton Thomas had previously received a cable from Whitehall saying that if Singapore could not be held, senior Harbour Board staff should be evacuated. They were trained men who would be needed in India. Simson, however, was quite unaware of this, even though he had the responsibility of finding labour for the docks.

The Governor's study was at the far end of the house, and it was there that Simson asked Shenton Thomas why he had evacuated the Harbour Board. Thomas explained the telegram he had received. 'Well, you might at least have let me know,' said an aggrieved Simson. 'The coolies at the docks are probably being killed at this very moment.'

The Governor had the grace to apologise. In the stress of events, the matter 'had slipped his mind'.

All that Simson could do was to arrange for the Engineers and the Public Works Department to destroy the valuable machinery and equipment which the Harbour Board Europeans—like the Navy at the Base—had 'forgotten' to deny to the enemy.

Now that the Harbour Board had ceased to function as a separate unit, much of this heavily-bombed area came under the protection of Tim Hudson and his ARP team at Tiong Bahru, and that very afternoon 54 twin-engined bombers launched one of the heaviest raids of the campaign.

It was an oppressive afternoon. The blue skies of the morning had turned into slate grey clouds which looked as though they would burst with heat or rain. Nothing stirred in the bare, breathless schoolrooms which had been turned into his headquarters—looking somehow empty and unused now that all the schools had been closed. Normally, the Chinese wardens 'on call' would have been full of their own particular brand of boisterous fun. Sometimes they played football in the schoolyard. But not today. Today it was too stifling. Every 'roster bed' used by the night wardens was filled with snoring, sleeping men, and Tim Hudson himself had dozed off in the headmaster's study, slumped in a rattan chair.

At precisely eleven minutes past two, the direct phone

from ARP headquarters startled him into wakefulness. Raiders were on their way. Hudson sounded the klaxon, but even as he ran out into the schoolyard the planes were overhead, flying 'with the sort of uninterrupted precision I used to see at an air show'. They appeared almost motionless.

'Get ready to move. They're over the docks,' yelled Hudson, knowing from experience what to expect. The wardens ran for their assorted vehicles, lined up with bonnets pointing to the school gates. Behind them was an ancient lorry which Hudson had transformed into a mobile canteen with a tea urn. This was under the charge of a young Chinese with an unruly fringe of black hair and the unlikely nickname of Wee-Wee, and who had become the mascot of Tiong Bahru. As they all prepared to move, with Hudson leading the way in his Hillman, Tim could actually see the planes drop their bomb loads at the same moment. 'It was like looking at a film,' he remembered. 'The sticks of bombs seemed to float down so slowly I couldn't believe it was real.' As usual, the Japanese bomb aimers had waited for the leading pilot to give his signal. All had then dropped their bombs at the same time, and it seems that the peculiar sunless pewter colour of the afternoon sky provided just the right lighting to show up the bombs, for hundreds of people saw them as clearly as Hudson had done.

All this had happened in a second. The bombs had not even reached the ground before the wardens were racing for the docks. Shattering explosions rocked the cars on their way, then the aircraft turned lazily in a semi-circle above the inferno they had created. One stick of bombs hit a fuel dump, triggering off explosions and sheets of flame shooting hundreds of feet into the air. Another hit a godown filled with rubber. A third set some stocks of sugar on fire. As Hudson and his men reached Keppel Harbour, a twisting column of acrid smoke darkened the grey sky like an umbrella. In the outer roads—a few hundred yards off shore—a Chinese junk was blazing furiously, and Hudson could make out figures jumping over the side, into water daubed with patches of blazing oil. Before Hudson could do anything, three of his Chinese wardens, jabbering and pointing, were running to a sampan by the edge of the docks. A fourth gesticulating figure chased them. Hudson just caught a glimpse of Wee-Wee's black fringe as he darted past. The Chinese tea boy was actually grinning. He caught the others up, jumped in
168

the big sampan, and then set off frantically for the burning junk and the black dots bobbing in the water around it.

Hudson could not stay. Flames from the fuel dump were roaring across Keppel Road, west of the railway station, and were already licking the flimsy shophouses around Kampong Bahru Road behind. Here, hundreds of Chinese families had refused to leave the ramshackle rooms they called home —four-storey buildings so flimsy, so jerry-built, they looked as though a puff of wind would blow them down. Out of every window brightly-coloured washing hung on poles. Children crawled in the gutters, oblivious of the black smoke curling around them. Stoic old ladies squatted by their front doors, as though ignorant of the disaster a few hundred yards away. One family had re-started a late, interrupted lunch. Squatting on their hams in a circle, their chopsticks dipped rhythmically into a bowl of rice flavoured, perhaps, with a few morsels of fish. To them, and to those around them, the bombs had missed. The raid was over—and they were alive. Nothing else mattered.

Hudson's first thought had been to get everyone out of the street in case the fire spread, but then he vaguely heard a fire bell clanging behind him, and the next moment Buckeridge was shouting in his ear, 'Don't worry about the houses— they'll be all right. It's the sawmill behind.' Buckeridge's men were running, unwinding their hoses. 'Clear out of the sawmill,' yelled Buckeridge. 'One spark from the oil dump and the whole damn lot'll go up like a bomb.'

Here lay the real danger. This was one of twenty or so sawmill areas in Singapore, for sawing timber was a major Chinese industry, and the mills presented one of the gravest fire hazards in the city. This particular mill—like most others —had grown by the side of a tidal creek up which logs were floated, so Buckeridge was running his fire hoses down to the shallow, dirty water. The other side of the mill, which covered about an acre, backed up against Chinese houses. In one corner were stocks of petrol and oil to drive the saws. In another were drums of paint. In another was a small mountain of shavings and scantlings. The flick of a cigarette lighter could have turned them into a roaring furnace.

As Hudson forced his way inside the untidy yard, past stacks of newly-sawn planks, he saw to his dismay that this mill was a timber box factory, and that fifty or so men were quietly working to the whine of saws, the noise of men sweeping up shavings, hammering planks into boxes, shouting for tins of paint—all this despite the fact that, apart from the narrow, shallow creek of water, the mill was hemmed in by inflammable approaches. Hudson yelled to one of his Chinese wardens to get the workers out, but it seemed impossible to make them understand. With an almost supercilious arrogance they seemed to be saying, 'You may be scared, but we're not'. Like the people in the adjacent street, they felt the raid had passed them by, so what was all the fuss about?

Not a man spoke a word of English, and as they stood shouting and arguing, it was obvious to Hudson that the Chinese warden was helpless. But then something happened that sent them scattering, running for their lives. It was a sound that Hudson had been secretly dreading—the low whine of a shell, rapidly reaching a crescendo.

The shell scored a direct hit on the paint shop. As Tim threw himself behind a shed at the other end of the yard, the ramshackle building burst into fragments smothered in flames. One after another, the drums of paint exploded with a noise like that of anti-aircraft 'pom-pom' fire. Something soft and wet hit Hudson. It was the decapitated, bloody body of a man—half a body, really—which had been tossed across the open space.

Hudson's only thought was to get rid of the drums of petrol at the other side of the yard. Half dazed by blast and heat, he groped his way across the yard.

'Our only chance is to get them into the creek,' he shouted. 'We've got to try and float the stuff away.'

Buckeridge appeared. He had brought one trailer pump round a back way, and already had a hose drawing water from the creek. His men were playing it on the huge pile of shavings. Another trailer rattled up as Hudson and his men started to roll the fuel drums towards the water. More shells followed, but now they screamed over into the docks. One by one the wardens rolled the drums into the creek. Three Chinese wardens waded in and started pushing them into deeper water.

As Buckeridge tried to prevent the fire spreading—he let the paint shop burn itself out—other trailer pumps were dealing with big fires on the docks. Meanwhile Hudson's men were piling up the dead in one corner and trying to make the score or so wounded men as comfortable as possible. Hudson had sent a messenger back to Tiong Bahru to phone for three ambulances. Finally one arrived. Two had set off—

all that could be spared—but one had broken down on the way. The ambulance men loaded up the most seriously wounded and drove off with clanging bells. Tim could do nothing about the dead, except leave them piled up in a corner. The wounded presented a much more pressing problem.

'I'd better take as many as I can to the General,' Hudson said to his number two, and managed to squeeze three Chinese carpenters with bloody head wounds into the Hillman. Just as they were about to set off, Japanese raiders appeared again, but, as Buckeridge noted in his diary that night, 'They flew right over. Obviously they didn't see me.'

Tearing up Cantonment Road with his groaning passengers, Hudson branched left at the corner of Outram Road and reached the General Hospital in a few minutes, where, as orderlies carried the wounded inside, he lit his first cigarette since the raid had started. He remembered afterwards how wonderful those first few puffs were—until suddenly he saw something so horrifying that the cigarette dropped from his mouth.

As Tim watched, a melancholy procession was wending its way towards him. At first, Tim hardly noticed them, but then he saw they were orderlies carrying corpses. They moved towards a place where the once beautiful gardens and lawns had been torn apart to make way for two vast pits, one forty feet long, the other stretching for at least a hundred yards.

Impelled by a morbid fascination, Tim moved towards the closest pit. It was half-filled with bodies, neatly laid out in tightly packed rows. 'It reminded me of nothing so much as a gigantic tin of sardines.' As he stood there, rooted, and with a handkerchief over his nose to shut out the overwhelming stench, half a dozen more Chinese orderlies came down the steps of the hospital carrying more bodies. Carefully they laid the European bodies at one end of the pit, the Asians at the other, and covered them quickly with a sprinkling of lime.

Hudson was aware that a nurse was standing beside him and he mumbled an apology. In an American accent she replied, "Don't apologise—I understand.' Then she added, 'They bury them at opposite ends for religious reasons.'

Something in the voice made Hudson look at her more closely. He saw a good-looking woman, almost dropping with fatigue, a grimy, dirt-streaked face above a uniform covered with blood, and at first he did not recognise her. But then neither did she recognise him—until suddenly, because of the way she spoke, Tim cried, 'It's Freddy Retz, isn't it?'

'Freddy *Bloom*, please!'

'Of course. I'd heard a rumour that you'd got married. When was it?'

'Last Friday.' Freddy looked at Tim's grey, lined face, the shoulders bent with weariness, his uniform also smeared with blood, and she said, 'I heard you on the radio. Fine.'

'Too late,' said Tim tiredly.

'Marjorie got away all right?'

'As far as I know. How's it with you?'

Tim remembers that, despite the surroundings, Freddy gave 'a sort of chuckle' and told him that she couldn't complain—especially as she'd had a bath that morning. Water was becoming so short by now that it was practically impossible to bathe, 'but I did get one this morning. A Chinese nurse told me that she'd prepared a tub of hot water for cleaning bloodstained uniforms. She let me have a dip first. Boy! Was it good!—I could have stayed in all day. The only thing was,' she added, 'it was my job to wash the uniforms.'

Tim Hudson always remembered that brief scene in the hospital grounds. For some reason he could never understand, it was etched in his memory like a dream that recurs, so that much later he would sometimes re-live the whole scene—the scarred earth of the once-beautiful grounds, the men piling more bodies into the huge pit, the stench, the pretty young American nurse barely able to keep on her feet. And perhaps it was the last words she spoke that tugged always at his memory.

'It's a long time since we last met,' said Freddy.

Hudson's brain was so fuddled with weariness that he hadn't the faintest idea what she meant.

'Don't you remember?' she jogged his memory. 'Sunday morning drinks at the Sea View.'

Of course. The last day before it had all started—the crowded tables at the Sea View, the women in shorts singing 'There'll always be an England'. It was another age, another life, and to hide his emotion, Tim said good-bye almost gruffly and strode away.

When one analyses these first few days of desperate fighting, the gloomy picture that emerges is one of almost total confusion. Everything that could go wrong went wrong—and there was no bad luck about it. Fuddled errors of judgment, panic retreats against orders, the unaccountable leaking of a top secret plan, even Wavell's final visit to the island —all contributed to a distressing military debacle rarely if ever equalled in British military history.

It was now a simple battle for survival, yet there appeared to be no overall plan, and consequently the defensive manœuvres during these two days degenerated into a series of decisions in which each local commander hardly seemed to care (or know) what anyone else was doing. Though the fighting was being carried out over a comparatively small area—and at first the defenders greatly outnumbered the attackers—all coherent plans (if ever they truly existed) seemed to have vanished into the powder-laden hot air or the deep recesses of the rubber jungles and swamp, so that now, looking back, all that happened during the first critical days takes on a strange, nightmarish quality. Time and again apparently unaccountable decisions were taken. The Japanese would be unable to advance—until for no apparent reason Allied opposition melted away. At one bizarre moment the Japanese were down to their last hundred rounds per man—while the British defenders were burying their ammunition in pits.

From the start of their invasion, Japanese troops had been advancing towards Tengah airfield which had to be held, so both Percival and Gordon Bennett agreed that the only chance was to launch a counter-attack in force. It was planned —yet for several reasons, some obscure, it never took place. The attack was to have been led by Brigadier Taylor, commanding an Australian brigade, but when Gordon Bennett managed to get through to him on the field telephone and enquired how the attack was progressing, Taylor, according to the astonished Bennett, 'replied that just as the advance was to commence, the enemy attacked in strength and that his line had fallen back behind the [Tengah] aerodrome. This meant that the aerodrome was in enemy hands.' In fact the retreat was so swift that the Japanese found fresh bread and soup on the dining tables. Bennett could hardly believe the news, and nobody has ever explained why Taylor should have abandoned the airfield, though it is significant that when Bennett spoke later to Taylor, Bennett noted that 'he seemed confused'. Percival was also to blame, for he had a small command reserve, to say nothing of two divisions guarding the unattacked north-east shores. Yet Percival was loath to throw them into the Western Area because he was still convinced the Japanese might attack in the north-east, so that, as *The War Against Japan* puts it, 'The fleeting opportunity to launch a counter-attack . . . and confine the enemy to the north-west corner of the Island was lost.'

Despite the loss of Tengah airfield, however, the Japanese were still in the north-west of the island, and there was still one hope of pinning them there and preventing them pushing in towards the city. It was necessary to defend a partly reconnoitred and prepared stretch of country between Tengah and Singapore. Two or three miles long it was euphemistically called the Jurong Line, and consisted of undulating jungle and swamp country linking the headwaters of two broad rivers, the Jurong and the Kranji, the former flowing due south, the latter due north. (The Jurong spilled into the sea on the southern shores of the island, the Kranji flowed into the Strait of Johore a mile west of the causeway.) The two rivers and the country between them did in fact slice the island in two from north to south, and if this natural line could be held, the Japanese would be contained in the western part of the island.

There were enough troops to defend the Jurong Line against a frontal attack—but there was one grave danger. What would happen if the Japanese landed between the mouth of the Kranji and the causeway? They would obviously be able to turn the Jurong Line. This was precisely what the Japanese planned to do, and once again they obligingly gave the British clear notice of their intention, for while the battle was raging around Tengah in the West, Japanese artillery started a massive barrage on the mile-long strip of coastline between the mouth of the Kranji and the point where the causeway reached the island.

Here was an exact copy-book replica of what had occurred before the first Japanese landings. The Australian positions were dive-bombed and pounded mercilessly. At one stage of the barrage, sixty-seven Japanese shells were landing every ten minutes. Yet again Percival refused to commit troops to this newly-threatened area, even though, as *The War Against Japan* points out, 'The only way . . . was to leave the north-eastern coastline defended by a skeleton garrison with a high proportion of machine-guns, and to withdraw the 18th Division. . . . The risk was not great; the threat of a landing on the north-eastern sector had receded.'

No such 'risk' was taken, and when evening came, and the first units of the Japanese Imperial Guards were being ferried across the Straits near the causeway, we find Percival drawing up a plan for the defence of Singapore City. It seems that by now he feared the worst, and had decided that, if the inevitable did happen, troops should fall back to a perimeter that would include Kallang airfield near the city, and two of the three island reservoirs. During the evening he called in two of his three senior commanders (Gordon Bennett could not leave his headquarters) and explained his plans to them verbally, enjoining them to the strictest secrecy. After they had left about midnight, Percival issued the plan in writing as a 'secret and personal instruction' for the three commanders and a few senior members of his staff. Secrecy was absolutely essential. Morale was bad enough anyway, and there was no point in depressing and alarming officers in the battle areas.

The wisdom of Percival's insistence on secrecy became apparent almost before his clerk had finished typing the plan, for suddenly—and most unexpectedly—morale at headquarters was given a rousing, exciting fillip. The crack Japanese guards attempting to land between the causeway and the mouth of the Kranji were being thrown back into the water.

At first Percival could hardly believe it—partly because Brigadier Maxwell, commanding the Australians in the causeway area, had already requested permission to withdraw to a line farther inland. Gordon Bennett had curtly refused, and told him his men must fight it out. And now this was just what they were doing—magnificently. As the minutes ticked by, Percival waited impatiently for news via Gordon Bennett. After half an hour it came—good news. Even though the Japanese landing barges carried mortars which they fired at speed, throwing up a screen of spray from a creeping barrage, the Australians were forcing most of them back, while those Japanese who did manage to gain a foothold on the muddy bank found themselves facing a stubborn, determined defence quite out of character with what they had been led to expect. Nothing they could do would dislodge the Australians, who were dug in five hundred yards from the shore line. The few Japanese who tried to rush the swamp and undergrowth were raked with machine-gun fire. At times the ranges were down to ten yards.

As the night wore on, the line still held, and in the early hours of the morning news was rushed to Percival that the Japanese had apparently given up the attempt to land. It was true. As we now know, the commander of the landing troops had sent a signal to General Yamashita in the Sultan of Johore's palace, asking for permission to call the attack off and endeavour to land elsewhere the following evening.

Yamashita was undecided. He decided to wait until dawn —which was only a few hours away—and instructed his intelligence officers to wake him with a fresh report from the causeway area at that time. And when it came everything had suddenly, unaccountably, inexplicably changed. The stubborn, heroic resistance of the night had vanished. The line the Japanese had been unable to dent was no longer there and, to Yamashita's astonishment, he was told that 'all resistance had melted away'. How this tragic reversal had come about at a moment of heroic defence has never been fully explained. All we know is that Brigadier Maxwell ordered his troops to retire, and insisted later that he had been given permission to withdraw. Gordon Bennett insisted with equal vehemence that he had never been given such permission. Whatever happened, by dawn on the 10th the causeway area had been abandoned and the road to Singapore lay open.

If this disaster were not enough, another now followed hard on its heels—and this, too, was never explained. For somebody in Gordon Bennett's Western Area—the culprit has never been identified—issued Percival's 'secret and personal' plan for the last-ditch defence of the city to subordinate commanders. Moreover, it was issued as a military order to be obeyed in certain circumstances. From that moment on the 10th, the commanders in the field acted on the instructions —and their own initiative. When Brigadier Taylor (who had already 'seemed confused' to Gordon Bennett) received the order 'its limited nature escaped him'. He read it through— and interpreted it as meaning that he and his men should retreat immediately to new positions. He did so. Bennett later 'tersely reproved him for his actions'[5] but by then it was too late. The last pretence at any coherent plan of defence had

5 *The Japanese Thrust.*

vanished, and nor is this to be wondered at, for as *The War Against Japan* commented,

> 'To these weary and distracted officers, sorely in need of reinforcements and encouragement to fight on despite their difficulties, the receipt of such an order was tantamount to an admission that the higher command regarded the situation as hopeless. The psychological effect of this order had a considerable bearing on their actions during the 10th. A study of events on that day shows clearly that throughout it Western Area failed to co-ordinate the actions of its subordinate formations. ... Thus, despite the fact that the enemy during the day had done nothing more than probe defences with his advance troops, the Jurong Line was abandoned . . .'

On this critical day Wavell flew in to visit the island. Everywhere the fronts were shrinking. He was horrified to hear that the Jurong Line had been abandoned and immediately, over the head of Percival, ordered a counter-attack which was a disaster, resulting in even more confusion 'and in the destruction in detail of the forces involved'.

Wavell's unfortunate decision to launch a counter-attack was possibly inspired by an extraordinary telegram from Churchill which had reached him just before he had flown out of Java. Churchill 'no longer nursed illusions about the protracted defence of Singapore. The only question was how long.' No doubt the Prime Minister was worried by the effect an ignoble defeat would have on American public opinion, and was determined that the 'fortress' should fight for as long as humanly possible, for in his cable to Wavell, he said:

> 'I think you ought to realise the way we view the situation in Singapore. It was reported to Cabinet by the CIGS [Chief of Imperial General Staff] that Percival has over 100,000 men, of whom 33,000 are British and 17,000 Australian. It is doubtful whether the Japanese have as many in the whole Malay Peninsula. . . . In these circumstances the defenders must greatly outnumber Japanese forces who have crossed the straits, and in a well-contested battle they should destroy them. There must at this stage be no thought of saving the troops or sparing the population. The battle must be

fought to the bitter end at all costs. The 18th Division has a chance to make its name in history. Commanders and senior officers should die with their troops. The honour of the British Empire and of the British Army is at stake. I rely on you to show no mercy to weakness in any form. With the Russians fighting as they are and the Americans so stubborn at Luzon, the whole reputation of our country and our race is involved. It is expected that every unit will be brought into close contact with the enemy and fight it out.'

However eloquent and inspiring, this was hardly the sort of cable to send to a hard-pressed commander, for it took no account of the fact that control of the air and the sea had long since been lost, nor that the Japanese had about two hundred tanks and Britain had none; nor that the bulk of the vast body of Empire troops was inexperienced, badly trained, yet pitted against veteran fighters blooded in the war against China. Even worse was the absurd comparison with the fighting between the Americans and the Japanese in Luzon. There were no crack Japanese troops in the Philippines (they were sent there from Singapore after the fall) and Corregidor was in fact a genuine fortress.

Wavell, however, did nothing to tone down this injudicious cable; instead he issued an Order of the Day dated February 10, in which he made use of every argument put forward by Churchill—and indeed almost the same words. It bore an extraordinary similarity to the original:

'It is certain that our troops on Singapore Island heavily outnumber any Japanese who have crossed the Straits. We must destroy them.

'Our whole fighting reputation is at stake and the honour of the British Empire. The Americans have held out in the Bataan Peninsula against far heavier odds; the Russians are turning back the picked strength of the Germans; the Chinese, with almost a complete lack of modern equipment, have held back the Japanese for four and a half years. It will be disgraceful if we yield our boasted Fortress of Singapore to inferior enemy forces.

'There must be no thought of sparing the troops or

civilian population, and no mercy must be shown to weakness in any shape or form. Commanders and senior officers must lead their troops and if necessary die with them. There must be no question or thought of surrender. Every unit must fight it out to the end and in close contact with the enemy.

'Please see that the above is brought to the notice of all Senior Officers and by them to the troops.

'I look to you and to your men to fight to the end to prove that the fighting spirit that won our Empire still exists to enable us to defend it.'

This might have been all very well for local consumption —or it could have been had Percival's secret retreat plan not been leaked—but it had one unfortunate repercussion. For these mischievous if inspiring words appeared in several British newspapers. Naturally they gave the people of Britain an utterly wrong picture of superior Allied forces who did not apparently have the courage to defend the 'boasted fortress of Singapore' against inferior enemy forces. Nor did the words bear any relation to Wavell's real feelings, for when he started drafting a reply to Churchill, he did not attempt to hide the fact that 'Morale of some troops is not good, and none is as high as I should like to see. . . . Everything is being done to produce a more offensive spirit and optimistic outlook, but I cannot pretend that these efforts have been entirely successful up to date.'

This was to be Wavell's last visit to the island, and during the day he drove with General Percival to see Gordon Bennett near Bukit Timah village. The Australian headquarters were heavily bombed at the time and as Percival put it, there was the 'unedifying spectacle of three General officers going to ground under tables or any other cover that was available'. They were in fact lucky not to be killed, for one Japanese bomb scored a direct hit on Bennett's own office. It failed to explode.

That evening Wavell called to see Sir Shenton Thomas, and was appalled to discover how ill Lady Thomas was. He tried to insist that she should fly out of Singapore with him, but Lady Thomas would not hear of it.

He had one last decision to make before returning to Java by flying boat at midnight. Wavell ordered all serviceable aircraft and RAF personnel to the Dutch East Indies. Kallang, the last airfield on the island in Allied hands, was 'so pitted with bomb craters that it was no longer usable'.

For days the RAF pilots had fought brilliantly against overwhelming odds, even though the few remaining aircraft had been pinned down to Kallang, the boggy, swampy airfield near the city. Even this had been kept open only by teams working round the clock on the 750-yard-long landing strip. The British losses had been severe. Out of 'the meagre reinforcements' of fifty-one Hurricanes which had arrived in crates in mid-January, only twenty-six remained serviceable by the end of the month, and even these had rapidly dwindled. By now only eight Hurricanes and six ancient Buffalos were left to carry on the fight. This token force attempted to prevent the Japanese from dive-bombing troops and broke up enemy attacks on shipping. On their last full day's flying over Singapore Island—and without any real ground control—they shot down six Japanese bombers and damaged fourteen more.

Among the last to fly out his Hurricane was Flight Lieutenant Arthur Donahue, the American with the RAF. Together with the other officers, he had been billeted in the Sea View Hotel, where civilian guests had a standing offer of a bottle of champagne for every Japanese aircraft shot down. When the order arrived for Donahue and his colleagues to leave, the old civilians clinging on in the Sea View—the 'useless mouths' which Churchill had in vain asked to be evacuated weeks previously—could not believe it. 'No matter how bad the news,' Donahue noted, 'as long as they could see the RAF flying, they felt there was hope.' Donahue left an indelible picture of his last sight of Singapore as he flew away:

'My final memory of Singapore, as it appeared to me looking back for the last time, is of a bright green little country, resting on the edge of the bluest sea I'd ever seen, lovely . . . except where the dark tragic mantle of smoke ran across its middle and beyond, covering and darkening the city on the seashore.

'The city itself, with huge leaping red fires in its north and south parts, appeared to rest on the floor of a vast cavern formed by the sinister curtains of black

180

smoke which rose from beyond and towered over it, prophetically, like a great over-hanging cloak of doom.'[6]

While Flight Lieutenant Donahue and his colleagues in the RAF were flying out to Java, a stunned Jimmy Glover and a bewildered George Hammonds were preparing to leave by sea. They, too, had in effect been ordered out by the military, though as late as lunch-time on February 11, when Glover had gone to the Cathay to make sure the distribution of the *Tribune* was proceeding smoothly, he had not had the faintest idea that this would be his last day on the Island, nor that this would be the last issue of the newspaper that was his life.

He had spent a wretched morning for, since defeat now seemed certain, he had decided to take his two dogs to Forbes, the veterinary surgeon in Bukit Timah Road, and have them put down. He could not bear the thought of them being ill-treated by the Japanese. At the vet's he had joined a queue of Europeans, each with their unsuspecting dogs. Tim Hudson had been there with his two cocker spaniels. Many men had been in tears. 'Despising myself thoroughly,' Glover remembered, 'I handed them over to the attendant and watched them led away. I have hated myself for this act ever since.'

It was in this frame of mind that he reached the Cathay and made his way to the Press office. The first person he saw was Captain Steele, senior Press Officer, who asked him abruptly, 'Have you got a suitcase packed?' Glover told him it was in his car.

'Good,' said Steele. 'You're leaving tonight if you're lucky.'

Glover's immediate reaction was to blurt out, 'But what about tomorrow's paper?'

'There'll be no tomorrow's paper,' retorted Steele. 'You and Hammonds are leaving with all the other press correspondents.'

At this moment Hammonds was making his final trip from Dulverton with the last few copies of the *Tribune*, and wondering if he would ever reach the centre of the city, for as he drove gingerly towards Orchard Road, 'it was like no-man's-land.' Trees were slumped awkwardly across the road, attap huts burned in a nearby kampong, shells burst around his

[6] Donahue won the D.F.C. in the Malayan campaign and wrote an excellent account of his experiences in *Last Flight From Singapore*. He was killed later in the war.

Chevrolet as he reached a road block manned by a handful of British soldiers, including one tall blond boy stripped to the waist and holding an automatic rifle. George gave him a free copy of the *Tribune* and passed his tin of cigarettes round. As the young soldier waved him through he cried cheerfully, 'Better not come back—the Japs are coming this way. They must have seen that sign!' He jerked his gun in the direction of an enormous street hoarding. It bore the words, 'Join the army and see the world.'

Somehow Hammonds reached the Cathay, to find Glover and Captain Steele. As they waited for the other correspondents to be rounded up, Leslie Hoffman rushed in to say good-bye. Hammonds tried to persuade him to come along, but Leslie, with that engaging grin of his, just said, 'Don't worry about me—I'll become part of the scenery.'

That night Glover and Hammonds carried their suitcases aboard an ancient coastal steamer which had been elevated to the status of 'naval sloop'. There they waited until darkness had fallen, when Hammonds walked aft and took his last look at the city ringed with fires. Then, as the improvised man-o'-war slid stealthily away and turned her prow to the south, Hammonds found a corner on the cluttered, oily deck and tried to blot out everything in sleep.

Another party was also leaving that night—none other than Rob Scott and his staff, for he knew that all of them would be on the Japanese 'wanted' lists, and in any event, there was no point in keeping open a Ministry of Information office. Scott had always planned to remain with a reduced staff right to the end. Indeed 'I had not anticipated that this last group would get away if Singapore fell'. But now he rounded up his team of ten men, together with the skeleton staff of the Malaya Broadcasting Corporation, of which Scott was a governor. Eric Davis of the MBC had at first refused to go. He was still broadcasting with improvised emergency equipment, even though one station was under continual shell fire. In the end, Scott had to order him to leave, and late on the 11th they all set off to board H.M.S. *Giang Bee*, an ancient 1,200-ton Chinese-owned coaster which was requisitioned by the Navy, and which carried a four-inch gun and depth charges. Here they ran into a problem: the captain would take only 25 on board, and refused point blank to include the two women on the MBC staff. The *Giang Bee* was offensively armed, he said, and thus to the Japanese would be a warship.

Scott and his staff of ten men were taken on board, together with the MBC engineers. The rest of the MBC staff—including Eric Davis and the two girls—were taken to another vessel. (Davis was never heard of again.)

For some extraordinary reason the Navy now ordered all the Malays who formed the backbone of the crew to be sent ashore, leaving the ship without stokers, deckhands, stewards, signallers or radio operators, and this unaccountable order was soon followed by another, when the British Naval Shipping Control ordered the *Giang Bee* back into Singapore's inner harbour and instructed the Captain to take on two hundred old men, women and children. In vain he pointed out that he had only four lifeboats, each designed to carry thirty-two passengers. His only crew consisted of a handful of RNVR officers and those passengers who had volunteered. He did not have enough food and water. All his pleas were curtly overruled by the Naval Shipping Control. It was to prove a disastrous error of judgment on their part.

Later that night the *Giang Bee* slid out of harbour. The MBC engineers became radio operators. Scott's servant Chu Yu-Min—who had been with him for thirteen years in all parts of China—became cook 'and produced a meal out of whatever he could lay hands on'. And Scott himself? 'Well, I weighed over fourteen stone, so I volunteered as a stoker, doing the midnight to four a.m. watch.'

The following morning, Singapore awoke to find a new kind of newspaper on the streets. During the evening—as Hammonds had been leaving—Shenton Thomas had decided to take over the *Straits Times* as a government printing office. A member of his Publicity Department was appointed Acting Editor, and between them they rounded up an assorted batch of Singhalese linotype operators, Chinese printers, Asian sub-editors and one reporter. The staff camped in the office. Despite the bombing and shelling, they managed to produce 7,000 copies of a single sheet edition of the *Straits Times* on the morning of the 12th. All the Tamil newspaper sellers had vanished but the Governor arranged for despatch-riders to deliver bundles to all the ARP posts.

The paper was quarto size, and the first issue contained only six news items, with the 'lead' story consisting of the latest communiqué—eight unadorned paragraphs with no comment, no colour, no interpretation. It was, as usual, studded with the meaningless phrases Singaporeans had come to know so well—'enemy pressure slackened during the night. . . . It is hoped to stabilise our position. . . . Elsewhere there is no change in the situation.' Of the other five stories, one noted a modest cash contribution to the Malaya War Fund and two had nothing whatsoever to do with the war in Malaya. As Kenneth Attiwill dryly commented, 'To look at these news-sheets now is to wonder whether the courage and enterprise of the staff were worth it.'

On this same day Leslie Hoffman—now out of a job—determined to make one last effort to persuade his old father to try and escape. He had heard that several boats planned to leave for the Dutch East Indies on Friday the 13th. Leslie felt that if his father would only go, he too might be able to reach Australia and rejoin his wife.

The congestion in the centre of the city was now so widespread that he found the utmost difficulty in getting through it. Many Asians had 'given the city up', producing a new and frightening problem. Roads and squares in the heart of Singapore, already crowded with military vehicles, now began to be jammed with long streams of Chinese and Indian civilians who were heading for the east of the island—anywhere, so long as it was away from the advancing Japanese. To Hoffman, crouched in the small seat of his sports car, it had all the pathetic vividness of the first newsreel of the French fleeing before the Germans. Wrinkled old men and women carried everything they possessed on their backs, staggering under immense loads—beds, bedding, bits of furniture. Women followed carrying food—usually sacks of rice—and every child was loaded with precious possessions. One lucky family had found an abandoned rickshaw. An old wizened woman—she might have been a grandmother—had been put between the shafts to pull the load. Behind her a man carried a bed on his back, a woman two sacks of rice tied together. Half a dozen children straggled along, with pots and pans or dishes dangling on their backs. Where they were making for didn't seem to matter—or that was Hoffman's impression. The Japanese were on the island—that was enough. A kind of dumb instinct compelled them to get out of the city; probably they felt they stood a better chance of survival in the village kampongs. As Hoffman approached the big open space by the Cricket Club padang he had to slow down for a family which had managed to find an empty coffin. They had loaded it up and were now carrying it—irreverent pall bearers—by its heavy brass handles. Once the pride and joy of Singapore, the civil centre now bore the stark evidence of recent raids—smashed windows, uprooted trees, lighting poles torn down, and on every side the skeletons of burned-out cars and lorries. Behind the Victoria Theatre was a huge column of smoke. As Hoffman moved off inch by inch towards the edge of the city, he was halted by three electricity pylons which had been almost uprooted. They were still standing, but at drunken angles.

It took Hoffman nearly an hour, driving along the roads choked with military traffic and refugees, to reach his father's bungalow in the Serangoon area, which was well to the east of the city, and comparatively quiet.

At eighty, Hoffman's father was a grand old man and full of fight. But his obstinacy seemed to have increased with each succeeding year. Since the day when Leslie and his wife had tried in vain to persuade his father to leave, he had never brought up the subject, for though his reason had insisted that Singapore was doomed, perhaps in his heart he had entertained (in common with so many others) the vague hope that a miracle would occur to disprove his forebodings. Now, however, it was different. Now there could be no hope. As he walked into the big airy living-room where he had spent his childhood, and saw his father hunched by the verandah in a long chair, he determined that this time there would be no nonsense. He would *make* him go—whether his father liked the idea or not.

In fact, Leslie Hoffman failed completely. He found his old father more obdurate, more difficult than ever. This was his city. This was his home, and he was going to sit it out. It made no difference that Leslie quoted Churchill's demand that 'useless mouths' should be evacuated. His father hardly seemed to hear when Leslie painted lurid word pictures of Japanese atrocities, especially against men with Chinese blood in them. He hardly bothered to reply when his son asked him if he relished the prospect of starving under the new masters of Malaya who would be completely indifferent to the welfare of old and 'useless' men. They must have argued for over an hour—though as Hoffman wryly remembered, 'the arguments were rather one-sided, for I did all the talking; and my father just kept on shaking his head'.

Eventually the old man ordered some pale Chinese tea for himself, and Leslie searched the refrigerator for a bottle of cold Tiger beer. It was, he remembered, a beautiful afternoon. Apart from the growl of distant gunfire, the war seemed at that moment curiously remote as they looked over the compound, with its luxuriant creepers and exotic blossoms. Only the smell of cordite in the air, instead of Singapore's own special smell, brought Hoffman back to reality.

Then, after his father had put down his small cup of eggshell china, he turned to his son and said something which Leslie would never forget in the days and nights to come. For his father, it was a long speech. 'What does a few years of misery matter in the world's history of suffering? All this will pass over. It's just another storm, my boy. I'm not going to run off to hospital just because I might get my feet wet.' By now—as Friday the 13th approached—the battle for the island had been irretrievably lost, and it was only a question of time. Japanese tanks thundering down the Bukit Timah Road had captured the strategic hill and then the village, together with vast military stores of food and petrol. Hand to hand fighting had flared up in places whose very names were evocative of 'the good old days'—on the racecourse, across the greens and fairways of the Singapore Gold Club, at the Dairy Farm. General Percival, who had been operating from an advanced headquarters in Sime Road near the Golf Club, had been awakened at dawn by Japanese machine-gun fire barely a mile distant. He made his way to the famous Bukit Timah Road and drove along it as far as he dared, to find in the early morning that 'This great road, usually so full of traffic, was almost deserted. Japanese aircraft were floating about, unopposed except for our anti-aircraft fire, looking for targets. One felt terribly naked driving up that wide road in a lone motor car.' Then this strange, complicated man added a rare cry from the heart, a cry that echoed the feelings of a million civilians now trapped inside a perimeter that had shrunk to two and a half miles. 'Why, I asked myself, does Britain, our improvident Britain, with all her great resources, allow her sons to fight without any air support?'[7]

Yet Percival knew that he could not surrender, despite the fact that General Yamashita had sent him a courteous 'airmail' invitation to do so, dropping a note addressed 'To

[7] Percival, *The War in Malaya.*

186

the High Command of the British Army' from a Japanese aircraft. It read:

'Your Excellency,
   I, the High Command of the Nippon Army based on the spirit of Japanese chivalry, have the honour of presenting this note to Your Excellency advising you to surrender the whole force in Malaya.
   'My sincere respect is due to your army which, true to the traditional spirit of Great Britain, is bravely defending Singapore which now stands isolated and unaided. Many fierce and gallant fights have been fought by your gallant men and officers, to the honour of British warriorship. But the developments of the general war situation has already sealed the fate of Singapore, and the continuation of futile resistance would only serve to inflict direct harm and injuries to thousands of non-combatants living in the city, throwing them into further miseries and horrors of war, but also would not add anything to the honour of your army.
   'I expect that Your Excellency accepting my advice will give up this meaningless and desperate resistance and promptly order the entire front to cease hostilities and will despatch at the same time your parliamentaire according to the procedure shown at the end of this note. If on the contrary, Your Excellency should neglect my advice and the present resistance be continued, I shall be obliged, though reluctantly from humanitarian considerations, to order my army to make annihilating attacks on Singapore.
   'In closing this note of advice, I pay again my sincere respects to Your Excellency.
                              (signed) Tomoyuki Yamashita.

1. The Parliamentaire should proceed to the Bukit Timah Road.
2. The Parliamentaire should bear a large white flag and the Union Jack.'

Whatever Percival might have felt, he was faced with Churchill's firm dictum that 'there must be no thought of sparing the troops or the civil population.' He cabled Yamashita's message to Wavell, adding with unconscious irony,

187

'Have no means of dropping message, so do not propose to make reply, which would of course in any case be negative.'

On the 12th, Government House received its worst shelling so far, though Shenton Thomas still refused to evacuate the building despite one direct hit, which he described in his diary, 'House shelled. Several boys [i.e. house servants] underneath at back of house killed by direct hit, including my boy, three Ghurkas and an amah. Twelve in all. My boy and a bedroom boy were lying exposed to view. No sign of hurt, but covered with yellow dust and unrecognisable. Ah Ling, my head boy, went under house to look for more but reported none. Later we heard that others were missing, so I went down with Simson and found four or five including an amah and two Ghurkas in one passage. All like statues, sitting or kneeling, and no marks.'

By sundown Allied forces had withdrawn to a line roughly similar to that outlined in Percival's secret plan, but no one for a moment was optimistic enough to believe it could be held for long.

Mr. V. G. Bowden, Australian government representative in Singapore, had to cable Canberra that 'a group of Australians and others' had boarded a vessel without authority and sailed for Java. The city was crowded with sullen, armed deserters 'in greater numbers' (according to *The War Against Japan*) 'than could be controlled by the Military Police'. Now at last, morale was beginning to crack.

CHAPTER NINE

BLACK FRIDAY

Friday, February 13

It was a beautiful morning, of a kind which only the tropics can produce, and then only occasionally. The light was not yet harsh when Tim Hudson awoke in the headmaster's study —his 'bedroom'—at Tiong Bahru, where he was by now spending most nights. He pulled on his khaki slacks quickly, and walked into the common room where the indefatigable Wee-Wee, grinning below his mop of unruly black hair, was pouring out ugly-coloured, stewed tea to several wardens 'on call'. A plate of corned beef slices and some bread stood in the middle of the table. Breakfast.

The tea was undrinkable—a fact which Tim pointed out in forceful, unmistakable language to Wee-Wee. 'I make fresh tea for you, tuan.' He bustled away, and Tim picked up the second issue of Government's single sheet newspaper, several copies of which had been delivered to ARP posts for distribution. The main headline read 'Japanese Suffer Huge Casualties in Singapore' but the story below, which contained only five paragraphs culled from British and Australian newspapers, told him nothing. Nor did the other items. One dealt with a meeting between Nehru and Chiang-Kai-shek, another with an American plan to raise an air force of two million men. It all seemed so remote, as though the newspaper had been edited thousands of miles away by people completely uninterested in this island a few degrees north of the equator. There was nothing in the way of inspiration, if one excepted a new slogan mysteriously appearing for the first time below the masthead and consisting of a phrase from a broadcast by the Governor, 'Singapore Must Stand; it SHALL Stand.' And underneath that, Hudson—who had lost all sense of time—suddenly noted, with a chilling sense of foreboding, the date: it was Friday the thirteenth.

Hudson was never to get his cup of freshly-brewed tea for he had barely tossed the useless newspaper back on the table when the drone of bombers overhead brought every warden to his feet and the room emptied in a mad scramble. Ironically, Hudson probably owed his life to the fact that, having slept late, he was still in his slippers. As the other wardens made off in the direction of the 'operations room', Hudson ran back to his bedroom for his shoes—and at that moment a stick of bombs straddled the school.

Tim Hudson never knew what hit him. One moment he was sitting on the edge of his hard camp bed, the next he was waking up, as though from a nightmare, spluttering and choking in the smoke-filled room. He was on the floor. Dimly he registered the fact that the camp bed had been blown half through the open window. He had a vague impression of men hammering on the door, shouting in Chinese as they tried to break it down, to force their way in. Gingerly he got to his feet. No bones seemed to have been broken, though an egg-sized lump decorated the back of his head. The pounding continued, for the door had become jammed

189

when a desk had been blown across the room. Hudson managed to tug it away and the door collapsed.

'We thought you'd been killed,' gasped one of the Chinese as they stumbled in.

'Never mind me—what's happened?' cried Tim. Still dazed, he stumbled outside—and stopped aghast. In a few swift seconds, half the school had been pulped into a pile of rubble over which the dust still hung like a morning mist. Girders and roof supports stuck out at crazy angles. Three of the six cars in the yard had been twisted into scrap. Bodies lay everywhere in the grotesque, uncomfortable attitudes of death. 'It was nothing compared with some of the other incidents,' wrote Hudson later, 'but the fact that it was *ours* made me see it quite differently. Until the bombing of Tiong Bahru, I had sized up every incident with a cold, professional eye. Now, for the first time, I knew what the others felt like when they lost their friends.' Seven men had been killed—including Wee-Wee. With a sick feeling in his stomach, Tim found him slumped, head down, over the counter of his mobile canteen—almost as though he had fallen asleep while making the tea.

The phone was dead—yet it was imperative to get on to ARP control. Tim's car was undamaged, so telling one of the Chinese to take charge of the wounded, he decided to race up to the General Hospital, barely half a mile away. The first thing was to get the ambulances down to Tiong Bahru. The second was to decide where the post should now operate.

After hurried consultations, it was decided to move Tim's post into the College of Medicine in the hospital grounds. A tired doctor took him into the assembly hall and pointing, said, 'Your lot can take that corner—at least it's got a phone.' It was better than nothing, and with the help of a couple of lorries, the move from Tiong Bahru was completed swiftly. There was very little left to be carted away after the ambulances had taken the wounded and the bodies had been piled up in a corner to await the burial squad. All except one body, for almost on an impulse Tim went over to the wreck of the mobile canteen of which they had all been so proud, and lifted up the slack body of Wee-Wee. There were others among the wardens who had been closer to Tim, others he had respected and liked more, but in a curious way Wee-Wee, with his grin and tousled hair, had become a sort of mascot to the post. Tim managed to get him into the untidy interior of the Hillman and drove up to the General. There he carried the light body towards the burial pit. At least one man from Tiong Bahru would have a mourner at his funeral.

Tim Hudson never forgot that moment—though he was unaware of something else that was happening within sight, but behind his back. Freddy Bloom saw it all—a complete, biblical picture which she, too, would never forget, for she had been detailed to wait on the steps for Dr. Cicely Williams's 120 children who had been evacuated, and were now coming to the hospital. At one side of the 'picture' as she stood in the porch was the bearded man against the burning skyline, holding the limp, small body across his two arms in front of him, before he gently lowered it into the pit. And coming up the drive towards her was a pitiful straggling, winding procession of scores of children. A few could toddle. Others were being carried. Some were laughing. Some had bandaged heads, or arms in slings. Stretcher cases followed at the tail end.

The composite picture—of the beginning and the end of life—was there and gone in an instant as Freddy hurried forward to help.

For Dr. Cicely Williams and her family of children the day had started in earnest at dawn when the shelling around Tan Tock Seng hospital had become so intense that 'I simply cannot imagine why we were not hit—bits of metal seemed to be flying about everywhere'. She had picked up the babies in armfuls and put them under beds with three or four mattresses, and tried to snatch a few minutes' sleep under her bed. She seemed to have barely closed her eyes, however, when she was awakened with the news that the hospital had to be evacuated—in twelve minutes. Ambulances were already on their way to pick up her charges. The Bishop of Singapore arrived with some MAS volunteers to help, and between them they loaded the ambulances with the children—sick, wounded, orphaned, mentally defective and some in plaster frames.

In ten ambulances they set off to cross the six miles of cratered roads that separated Tan Tock Seng from the General Hospital. Cicely Williams drove ahead to find out where she would have to put the children—and discovered that she had been allotted the Dental Department—or rather

191

the floor of the Department. 'There was floor and that was that.' A woman of infinite resource, she managed to persuade three amahs to help her clean it out while Freddy Bloom waited at the hospital entrance to tell the convoy of babies which direction to take across the spreading grounds.

By the time the babies arrived the floor of the Dental Department was at least clean, and Cicely Williams had managed to persuade the hospital to provide a few mattresses. There was, however, a much more pressing problem. She had no food, and many of the children were already whimpering with hunger. Cicely Williams had to go 'on the scrounge'.

Food was valueless unless she could cook it, and she had no utensils. So she started with a visit to the surgical stores, where she managed to borrow a couple of large saucepans. Then she made a 'determined onslaught' on the man in charge of the hospital storeroom, who was horrified to learn that 120 more mouths needed feeding—small mouths, moreover, which needed special food. Grudgingly he gave her a bag of rice, some tins of milk and loaves of bread, a few packets of prunes—and some beef bones. He also let her have two coalpots and a bag of charcoal for the small fire of embers used when cooking with these locally made pots.

Now at least she had food, fuel and utensils. At first she had hoped to set up her kitchen on the verandah of the Dental Department, but one glance showed her this would be impossible because of flying shrapnel. In the end she started cooking rice in the coal-pots in one of the dental rooms. And, when it came to heating the milk, she had a stroke of luck. Though there was no gas stove, the gas supply was still on in the dental mechanic's section, with its array of false teeth that had never been fitted. And there were a couple of bunsen burners. Just the thing for heating milk.

Somehow Cicely Williams lived through this awful day, often without help. Three of the wounded babies died. Many were still shell-shocked. They were a motley assortment—Chinese, with faces that looked prematurely crinkled, Indian babies with pools of eyes, Malays—and even a couple of European orphans, never to be identified. It made no difference to Cicely Williams, even though she lacked all modern sanitary arrangements. There were no such things as nappies.

Lt.-Gen. A.E. Percival, General Officer
Commanding, Malaya

Lt.-Gen. H. Gordon Bennett, General
Officer Commanding all Australian
troops

Marjorie Hudson

Tim Hudson

Gen. Sir Archibald Wavell inspects Singapore's defences, including one of the notorious 15-inch guns which faced the wrong way. With him are the C.F.D. (Commander Fixed Defences) and Maj.-Gen. Keith Simmons, General Officer Commanding Singapore Fortress

Key men from England, Australia, China, Thailand, Malaya and the Far East Command meet in conference at Singapore. (l. to r. Air Chief Marshal Sir Robert Brooke-Popham, C-in-C Far East, The Rt. Hon. Sir Alfred Duff Cooper, Churchill's special envoy, Sir Earle Page, Australia, Sir Archibald Clarke-Keer, British Ambassador, Chungking, Sir Shenton Thomas, Governor of Malaya)

A view of the Singapore River, showing the Elgin Bridge – scene of one of the most dramatic fires, when this "mechano-like construction" was hit by a Japanese bomb

"Lease and Lend" material from the U.S.A. arrives at Singapore Docks

"Transit Camp" among the rubber trees for newly-arrived R.A.F. personnel

Malayan rescue workers among the wreckage in Raffles Place after the first Japanese raid

The last days at Singapore – the evacuation of women and children during the Japanese onslaught

Native houses reduced to smouldering ruins after the Japanese bombers have passed over

General Percival on his way to surrender the British stronghold to Japanese General Yamashita

British prisoners in the hands of the Japanese after the surrender

But when the children were fed and quieter, she raided the storerooms again and found a supply of mackintosh sheets. That helped. Then for most of the day, Cicely Williams, the 'mother' who had never had any children of her own, was busy cleaning, washing, feeding and doctoring the strange, polyglot family she had inherited.

Cicely Williams was not alone in facing almost superhuman difficulties. Across the grounds, in the hospital proper, each of the four major operating theatres had two operating tables in use 24 hours a day, manned by surgeons like Professor J. K. Munro, who worked in relays, four hours in the theatre, eight resting. Water was so short that Munro remembers 'a basin of water carried from a supply outside the theatre had to serve for washing the hands for several operations.' This was the day—the unlucky 13th—when a shell exploded on the roof of one of the operating rooms where Dr. Neil Ramsay was performing a delicate brain operation on a wounded Chinese. Half the roof seemed to cave in. The doctor and nurses were covered with plaster. Pieces of cement hit the doctor on the head, another knocked out a nurse. Calmly Dr. Ramsay went on with the operation —and just as calmly the theatre sister, her face looking as though it had been dusted with flour, stood impassively by his side, handing out the instruments until the two-hour operation was over.

To Tim Hudson it was 'a hectic, brave, tragic day'. Almost the first instruction he received in his new headquarters was 'ARP wardens must bury the dead as best they can, anywhere, anyhow.' Sometimes his phone functioned, sometimes it unaccountably went dead. More and more he and other divisional commanders had to rely on their Chinese despatch riders, of whom Hudson wrote, 'Still they came with reports of incidents. Brave lads, these Chinese despatch riders who rode through bombing and shelling as best they could, carrying on as best they could.' It was a day of cryptic messages from outlying posts to HQ—'Japanese approaching—please give instructions' and the answer 'Withdraw or disperse to your homes, whichever you think best'.

The whole city reeked with a compound of decaying bodies, burning flesh, smoke and cordite, as General Gordon Bennett recorded in his diary, when 'I made my way through the now deserted streets of Singapore, streets that previously were a seething mass of industrious humanity, I could smell the blast of aerial bombs in the air. There was devastation everywhere. The shops were shattered and deserted.'

Yet there were moments of faith. When Leslie Hoffman went into St. Andrews Cathedral, and walked along the nave —still filled with wounded—he came across a dozen soldiers in one corner behind the choir. They were on their knees praying, then rose and one man with a mouth organ started to play 'Onward Christian Soldiers'. The men joined in, and their voices must have carried out into the nave, for Hoffman could hear the reedy sound of wounded men trying to sing.

More than war, more than bombs and shells, more than the shadow of defeat, Friday the 13th left a lasting legacy of bitterness which persists to this day, because of another extraordinary 'secret' evacuation. The manner in which Naval technicians, then the army sisters and senior Harbour Board officials had been stealthily evacuated had been bad enough. Now, however, 87 members of the Singapore Public Works Department (PWD), including their chief, Group Captain Nunn, suddenly left the island. And Nunn had been expressly told by the Governor that he had to stick to his post.

Nunn was a curious man, whose character, it would seem, left something to be desired. In view of what later happened it is interesting to record that Shenton Thomas plainly remembered (and made notes of) two occasions in February when Nunn made special visits to Government House to ask what he should do if it became obvious that the island would have to capitulate. On the first occasion the Governor reminded Nunn of a Standing Order forbidding any head of a civil government department to leave the island. 'If the worse comes to the worst,' he told Nunn firmly, 'your proper place is at your departmental headquarters.' When Nunn again raised the question, 'it made me wonder,' noted the Governor, 'whether he was ready to pack up.' The discussion was quite brief, for as the Governor added, 'The subject was a most distasteful one and I should have preferred to look upon it as one that could not possibly be raised.' Nunn, however, had a wife who flatly refused to leave unless he did. And it seems obvious that he had for some time realised that his only chance of saving her would be for him to get away too.

Now Brigadier Simson enters this tangled story. Early on

194

the morning of Black Friday he received a phone call asking him to report at Fort Canning at nine a.m. for an important conference. By the time Simson arrived, the room was crowded with officers. Rear-Admiral Spooner, the Naval C-in-C, was in the chair. Air Vice-Marshal Pulford was present. Simson squeezed his way to a small chair and sat down.

The meeting had been called to plan an urgent evacuation that very afternoon of about three thousand key men— military and civilian—who would be useful to the war effort elsewhere. They were to go on dozens of small boats that lay in the harbour, and after the various branches of the forces had been given their allotments, the Admiral told Brigadier Simson that he was being allowed three hundred places. The Admiral pointed out deliberately that 'They are for younger technical men, who will continue the struggle from overseas'.

There was no time to be lost. Evacuees had to report with hand luggage at Telok Ayer basin at four o'clock that afternoon. Before Simson left, Spooner warned him that, since this might be the last official evacuation, the strictest secrecy was necessary, and he stressed again that this was for 'key men' and 'young men'—though he did add that if Simson could not collect three hundred in time, he could make up his allotment with women and children. But it was made quite plain that this was not to become a civilian evacuation of old and sick or even women on compassionate grounds. It was a military plan to save key men—which was doubtless why the conference had taken place at military headquarters, under the presidency of an admiral.

The meeting broke up about 11.30, and Simson had phone messages sent to Nunn, Bisseker and the President of the Municipal Council, asking them to meet him at the Municipal Offices at 12.30.

He still had nearly an hour before the meeting, and though there was no doubt in his mind that this was 'a military show', Simson felt he should go and tell the Governor what had occurred, so he drove up to Government House. Civilian evacuation normally came under the Governor's wing, but this was a military exercise, and Simson noted that 'I remember no dissent,' except that 'the Governor suggested the Civilian Evacuation Committee should be represented'. Simson readily agreed—especially as, apart from anything

195

else, he was already very doubtful if, with half the phones down, he could find three hundred key men in the few hours that remained. By the time Simson had reached the Municipal Offices, Mr. S. M. Middlebrook, a member of the Evacuation Committee, had arrived. Middlebrook later made a detailed report of everything that happened.

In view of the time factor—and the great difficulty of rounding up the people concerned—Simson decided to give fifty passes to Bisseker, his number two, to be distributed to important businessmen. He gave 125 to the Evacuation Committee for Europeans and Asians on their list; he kept fifty for himself, with the idea of distributing them to officials on services like the railways which had now come to a stop. He gave the remaining 75 passes to Nunn for the PWD, which totalled 105 men. He warned Nunn, however, that an adequate party of PWD officers must be left to finish urgent demolitions under Mr. McConechy, the State Engineer, a man of immense zeal and loyalty who was working night and day with Simson on scorching the earth.

Nunn soon had his list of names ready—and it was headed by his own name, together with that of his wife. Simson immediately objected. Heads of departments had been specifically ordered to stick to their posts 'until,' in the words of the Governor, 'the flag was hauled down.' Nunn then made the ingenious excuse that as he held the rank of Group Captain in the RAF Reserve, 'I could be useful in aerodrome construction in Java'. Simson didn't like the idea, but he was, after all, occupied with far too many problems to spend all afternoon arguing about a list of names. That was the job of each head of department, so he left Nunn to act according to his conscience.

As soon as he reached his office Nunn started signing passes, when in strode McConechy. Without a word—and despite Simson's warning that McConechy must carry on—Nunn wrote something on a piece of paper and handed it to the Scotsman.

'What's this?' asked McConechy, who also kept a detailed record of everything that happened that day.

'A ticket for you on a boat leaving this afternoon,' replied Nunn.

McConechy asked on whose authority it was issued and received the extraordinary (and quite untrue) assurance, 'The

Governor's'. And when McConechy asked to see it, Nunn replied evasively, 'It's a verbal instruction.'

McConechy asked how many passes Nunn was signing. Nunn replied that he had 75. 'But there are 105 engineer officers in the department,' cried McConechy. 'What's going to happen to the rest?'

Nunn hesitated, then replied. 'It'll be just too bad for them,' at which McConechy replied, 'I don't want your ticket. I've got a son-in-law and a brother-in-law in Singapore. I'll stand by them. Good afternoon!'

By 3.30, there was pandemonium at the docks, and when Middlebrook of the Evacuation Committee arrived to make sure his nominees—many of them Chinese—got away, he found 'a milling mob round the gates with armed military police on guard'. A young lieutenant sat on a table facing the gates, nursing a tommy-gun across his knees. Several leading Chinese and Europeans were trying to get through the gates, but there appeared to be some trouble over the passes. Middlebrook explained to the military police who he was and forced his way through to the young lieutenant who showed him his orders. There was no mention of Simson's passes, and though Middlebrook tried to explain what had happened, the officer refused to change them.

As they were arguing, a wave of Japanese aircraft flew over and dropped a stick of bombs, killing several people in the crowd. Men were shouting and yelling that they had passes and should be let through. Children and their mothers who *had* passed through the gates were sobbing because their husbands who could be seen waving *their* passes were being refused admittance. Whenever the gates were opened, there was a concerted surge towards them, and only with the utmost difficulty were the police able to close them again. The psychological effect of having got a permit and then being refused permission to leave was too much for many of the desperate men. Some of them, Middlebrook noted, were crying and sobbing. Others tore at the gates in vain, trying to force them open. Still others, waving their passes, screamed abuse at the police who stood there stoically silent, while the young lieutenant sat on the table with his tommy-gun. Finally, when fighting broke out, the lieutenant jumped off the table and ordered the police to fire a few rounds over the heads of the crowd. This calmed the crowd a little—and by then word had reached Brigadier Simson that all was not well. He drove down to Telok Ayer, and soon 'Simson passes' were recognised. Simson remained by the gates until the last passenger was aboard, carefully examining the passes.

Soon after five p.m. the Japanese planes struck again. Simson's car—less than a hundred yards away—was obliterated in a direct hit. But the most tragic death of all occurred as a young couple with their baby in arms stood waiting for their turn to pass through the gate. Their passes were in order. As the fighter-bombers swooped low over the crowd the wife was hit by a piece of shrapnel and killed instantly. Her dazed husband—standing next to her and still clutching the baby—was unharmed. At his side lay the body of his wife. In front of him was the ship that was the child's sole hope of freedom. Buck Buckeridge, who had been fighting a fire on the wharf, saw it all, and wrote 'Never have I seen a look of such agony on a man's face'. Buckeridge watched as the husband, dazed and crying, hesitated. A sailor yelled at him to come aboard. He looked back—one last glance at the body on the pavement—and then, blinded with tears, took the only decision he could take for the sake of the baby. Stumbling, he passed through the gate, leaving the mother's unburied body on the wharf.

After that, the Japanese bombers left the docks alone and by 6.30 p.m. the last passenger was on board and the gates were shut for the last time. That night an armada of 44 ships—ranging from naval sloops (of a kind) to outboard motor launches—sailed south for Java. Admiral Spooner was on board. So was Group Captain Nunn. So was Air Vice-Marshal Pulford, whose last words to Percival, as he said good-bye, had been, 'I suppose you and I will be blamed for this, but God knows we've done our best with what we've been given'.

There was another—though less spectacular—evacuation that evening, this time from Government House, which by now had the air of an enormous white ghost villa. Its empty corridors and salons—the only word, really, to describe the splendid but pretentious rooms—echoed with the crump of bombs, the swish of shells and the bark of guns surrounding the building. By now the shelling was so severe that people hardly dared to climb the handsome staircase to the first floor. The last telephone link with the city had been cut. Many of the servants had either been killed or had fled, and though the Governor had been determined that the Japanese should not drive him from his home, he now had no alternative but to go.

The few remaining servants hurriedly packed one suitcase for Lady Thomas who was still ill in bed. Because of the shelling, Sir Shenton refused to allow any servant to go upstairs to get his clothes, but insisted on going himself to pack a suitcase. His ADC ran to the deserted kitchens and quickly shovelled any tinned food he could find into a hold-all. There was not much—a few tins of biscuits, milk, meat and fish and processed cheese—but they would be useful later on. At half past six an ambulance left with Lady Thomas while the Governor remained behind for a few minutes longer. Only his ADC was with him as he stood for the last time on the spacious green lawns, now pitted with craters, in front of the palace that was at once the symbol of his prestige and power and yet, in some curious fashion, the symbol, too, of Whitehall's outmoded preoccupation with impressing 'the natives' rather than taking adequate measures to defend them. Then, with a sigh, the Governor stepped into his car and drove for the last time in his life down the long, winding road to the ornate gates. For the last time the sentry presented arms as Sir Shenton set off for his new home—the Singapore Club in Fullerton Building.

Here, two of the members' bedrooms had been made ready for him—one to be shared by the Governor and Lady Thomas, the other for his small remaining staff. They enjoyed the doubtful luxury of a small shower room—doubtful because the tap only worked intermittently, and already most of the water had to be carried from a standpipe in the street. That evening the Governor had his first 'club' dinner—bully beef and tinned potato salad, washed down with tea and tinned milk—which he ate perched on the edge of his bed. Lady Thomas was too ill to take food.

Nearly a hundred VIP's were now crowding into the few bedrooms usually reserved for up-country members. Some had brought their own camp beds. Rooms normally occupied by one man now held four or five. Apart from the Governor —who took his meals in his room—everyone had to queue up for what scratch meals were available in the makeshift cafeteria.

Their plight, however, was nothing compared with the

199

wounded on the lower floor which had been turned into a make-shift hospital. 'The conditions were appalling,' the Governor wrote. 'Civilian doctors and sisters and MAS workers will bear me out [that] there was practically no nursing staff and men lay for hours with their wounds unattended.' Using the standpipe in the street, two MAS girls started a canteen and between them kept a supply of tea going day and night for the wounded.

Amidst all the tragedy and bitterness of Black Friday, there was one moment of extraordinary serio-comedy. At almost the same time as the Governor was settling in at his new temporary headquarters, Tim Hudson was experiencing the most bizarre event of his life. Indeed, it was so wildly improbable that had it been included in a work of fiction, it would have been ridiculed as an implausible travesty of the truth. Yet it did happen, and as Hudson was later to recall, 'Friday the thirteenth certainly was my day. First I was damn nearly killed—and then out of the blue I was offered a fortune.'

Dusk had just fallen when Hudson, after a meal of sardines and baked beans and a stiff brandy (from the 'medical supplies') set off from the General Hospital in his Hillman for Dunlop's godown. This was a nightly chore, for early on in the bombing he had arranged for the European on duty during the day to leave him a report each evening so that he could keep track of what was happening when he couldn't get in during the day.

Keppel Road, by the docks, was by now an appalling jumble of potholes, craters, twisted wires and smashed trees. Passing the bombed-out *Tribune* offices, he drew up outside his godown in the deserted street. The coolies had gone, and he knew the office would be empty. As he looked round, he noticed a large American car drawn up by the side of the road about a hundred yards away—though his mind hardly registered the fact (until later) for the streets of Singapore were littered with abandoned cars.

With the aid of his torch he entered, closed the big sliding godown door behind him, and once in his blacked-out office, switched on the light and sat down.

The report was on his desk. There had been no shipments. Hudson noted that stocks of rubber totalled just over a thousand tons. He remembers thinking 'the Japs are going to get

200

the lot'. But there was nothing he could do about it. There were one or two minor points to be noted in the report. The coolie labour force had fallen off. One of the clerks had been killed in a raid. And that was about as far as he had got when he was suddenly startled by violent banging on the big door of the godown.

His first instinctive thought was burglars—but that of course was laughable. What would anybody do with a thousand tons of rubber? The office equipment and furniture? Nothing had any value any more. If there were thieves abroad they would be making for those godowns containing food—food that would always fetch a price on the black market.

The banging was repeated. Picking up his torch ('I was quite unafraid, I thought it must be somebody who wanted help') he crossed the godown, passed his rubber air raid shelter, and cautiously slid the door open an inch or two.

Outside stood four Chinese. As he shone the torch briefly he could see they were well-dressed and two of them carried bulging briefcases. Before he could speak, one said in the polite, undulating tones of his race, 'Please do not be afraid, Mr. Hudson. May we come in and talk to you?'

Mystified, Hudson opened the big sliding door a little further, and one by one the four men squeezed into the big airless cavern and followed him into his office. One offered him a cigarette. Another courteously held out a match. For the first time Hudson was able to take a good look at the mysterious quartet. They *seemed* to be all right. In fact they looked like four prosperous Chinese businessmen, neatly dressed in European white suits, with collars and ties.

'Forgive us, Mr. Hudson,' said one who was obviously the spokesman, and as Tim started to speak, he held up his hand and added, 'Please—may we show you something?' He clicked his fingers. The two men with briefcases stepped up to the desk, stood in front of Hudson, and when the leader gave the slightest of nods they opened the briefcases and tipped out the contents.

Suddenly, the whole of Hudson's flat-topped desk seemed to be covered with a miniature mountain of money—hundreds of bundles in rubber bands. 'I was now beginning to get mad,' Hudson remembered, but before he could speak, the leading Chinese said smoothly, 'You see, Mr. Hudson, we are not thieves. There are half a million dollars on your desk. They can be yours if you wish.'

Angrily—for this seemed to be a joke in the worst possible taste—Hudson asked them who the hell they were, and what sort of a trick was this, and why the devil did they come in at this time of night?

Their gesture might have been theatrical, the spokesman apologised, but they had hoped that in this way they could establish their good faith. Their names didn't matter. The object of their visit was very simple. They wanted to buy his rubber—for half a million dollars.

'But you must be crazy—it's not my rubber to sell,' cried Hudson, his eyes goggling at the fortune on his desk.

'Does it matter any more?' asked the spokesman. He knew exactly how much rubber there was—down to the last pound. The war would be over in a matter of days and Hudson, as he pointed out, had no means of getting rid of his rubber. It would all go to the hated Japanese. But they had a boat provisioned to leave for Java, and if Hudson only gave the order, they could get the rubber away, instead of leaving it for the Japanese—'and you, Mr. Hudson, could pocket half a million'.

For a moment Hudson was sorely tempted. He would hardly have been human had his reactions been otherwise. For he knew that there wasn't another cargo ship left in the harbour. He knew he could never get the rubber away. He knew the Japs would take it all. The trouble was—the rubber wasn't his. It didn't even belong to Dunlop's. Weeks ago the government had asked him to help in centralising stocks of rubber saved from various plantations up-country. He didn't really know to whom it belonged—and yet, the Japs *would* surely grab the lot. 'I don't *think* I ever thought seriously of keeping the money for myself,' Hudson wrote later. 'The whole business had a nasty taste about it.'

The final moments degenerated almost into an anti-climax. 'I decided I couldn't do it, but they had been so polite that unconsciously I said, with some formality, "I'm sorry, gentlemen. I'd like to accommodate you, but I'm afraid it's impossible." We had already talked a bit, of course, so they realised I meant what I said. The big fellow gave a nod, the two men with the briefcases started shovelling the notes in, and then I saw them to the door—and that's all there was to it.'

All day, when so much was happening, an extreme tension

prevailed at Fort Canning. The British perimeter, which was clearly defined, stretched for twenty-eight miles, and at one point where it crossed Bukit Timah Road, was less than three thousand yards from Orchard Road. It was not in this direction, however, that the enemy launched the full weight of its armour on the Friday. This was reserved for the coastal area to the west, a ridge by the fishing village of Pasir Panjang, which was being stubbornly defended by the 1st Malay Brigade against violent attacks by the Japanese Chrysanthemum Division. Behind the ridge lay the Alexandra area containing the island's largest ammunition dump and a big military hospital.

For two days the Malay Brigade had held out until it was 'almost obliterated'. A regular, locally-raised unit commanded mostly by Malay-speaking British officers, it was a living and dying illustration of the folly of not having raised more such local forces before the war in which men could defend what was their homeland, for, as Percival noted, the Malay Brigade 'showed what *esprit de corps* and discipline can achieve. Garrisons of posts held their ground and many of them were wiped out almost to a man.'

Here was direct fighting—a battle that could be joined against an enemy which could be seen—and the Malay Brigade fought as hard as any in the campaign. In other parts of the line, however, Allied troops were becoming more and more jittery, for now it had become a war of nerves against the dog-tired British and Australians who had rarely been able to snatch more than an occasional hour of sleep in the racket of screaming shells and crumping bombs. And even if they had slept, it had never been a real rest. In the thick, luxuriant jungle outside their perimeter, the Japanese waited hidden and unmolested.

To the Allied soldiers, whose morale was crumbling, the spectre of certain defeat was linked with a strange sense of frustration, a deep-seated feeling that by rights they ought to have been winning, not losing. As they lay in the coarse lalang round the Dairy Farm or crouched in the sandy bunkers of the golf course, often in the same sweat-soaked clothes they had worn for weeks, all they could feel was that this could never have happened if the brass hats in their armchairs back home hadn't let them down. It was a deep, bitter feeling that contributed much to lowering morale, and it was hard for them to understand—and even more difficult for officers to explain—that in Russia and North Africa events of such magnitude were being enacted that the siege of Singapore could never become more than a footnote in the momentous history now being written. The one thing they did know, however, was that the fight was as good as lost —and inevitably morale sagged still more. Officers as well as men 'had developed a withdrawal complex' and were already thinking of plans to escape. The number of desertions increased. So did the ugly scenes on the docks where in some cases armed deserters tried to force women off escape launches.

By lunch-time on Friday the position was so grave that Percival called a conference at Fort Canning for two o'clock. All the area divisional commanders, together with principal staff officers, were ordered to attend. Gloomily they discussed future operations, particularly the possibilities of staging a counter-attack. All the generals were against it. One after another they emphasised 'the effect on their troops of continuous day and night operations with no hope of relief'. They had to take into account the plight of the civilians, which was by now hopeless. Gordon Bennett remembered that 'it was unanimously considered that new enemy attacks would succeed and that sooner or later the enemy would reach the streets of the city'. He noted that 'it was decided to send a message to General Wavell urging him to agree to immediate capitulation'.

In fact Bennett's memory was at fault, for though he had advocated immediate capitulation, Percival still believed that it was possible to fight on for a little while longer. Even he, however, realised that there 'must come a stage when in the interests of the troops and the civil population further bloodshed will serve no useful purpose.' When the conference had ended he cabled a candid appraisal of the situation to Wavell. Though he did not suggest an immediate capitulation, he did ask that he might be granted wider discretionary powers to be used when the right moment arrived.

Wavell's reply was brief and uncompromising. 'You must continue to inflict maximum damage on enemy for as long as possible by house-to-house fighting if necessary,' he cabled. 'Your action in tying down enemy and inflicting casualties may have vital influences in other theatres. Fully appreciate your situation but continued action essential.'

Gordon Bennett had fought hard at the conferences for an immediate surrender, and possibly his lack of success contributed to an extraordinary action which he now took behind his commanding officer's back. Without reference to anybody, the aggressive red-haired Australian cabled his Prime Minister in Canberra that 'in the event of other formations falling back and allowing the enemy to enter the city behind us' it was his 'intention to surrender to avoid further needless loss of life'. This decision was, of course, contrary to Percival's orders to fight on, which was perhaps why Bennett did not take the trouble to inform him.

Gordon Bennett was also 'giving close consideration' to another significant and private matter—a plan to escape, for he had no intention of languishing in a Japanese prison camp. It was not a sudden impulse, brought about by the emotional stress of heavy fighting. The idea had been long in his mind, and in fact he had discussed it with the Sultan of Johore before crossing the causeway. Bennett's forces had been stationed in Johore and it seems that the Australian general had got on famously with the colourful Sultan. Possibly he was impressed with the pomp and ceremony, the Oriental trappings of a life he could hardly have envisaged before. In any event, the Sultan entertained him lavishly, heaped gifts upon the Australian (which he certainly did not refuse) and almost on their last evening together, the Sultan invited him to dinner, when Bennett was emboldened to ask the ruler if he could perhaps provide a boat in the event of his escaping.

This plan he had of course kept to himself and a few close friends. Now, however, that dinner party and conversation must have seemed a world away in time, and the original vague idea had to be crystallised into something approaching action. He had now only a matter of hours, not days, if he wanted to get away. He set about getting a boat. He did not, however, acquaint his Prime Minister (or Percival) with this news—possibly because he must have known that in no circumstances would approval have been given for a general to leave the men under his command.

The fact that Gordon Bennett kept his escape plans secret has an intriguing significance because another Australian, Mr. Bowden, the civil government representative in Malaya, *did* ask for permission to escape, and even though he was a civilian of 52 he was met with a firm refusal. Bowden, a typical 'no nonsense' Australian, had produced a stream of invaluable reports enabling the Australian prime minister

205

to face Churchill with the authority of local knowledge, but the government denied his request because amongst other reasons, the 'effect on morale could be bad'. The Australian government must have wondered whether it had been too hard on Bowden for it tried to reassure him in a second cable promising him that 'if worst comes, you and your staff are to insist on receiving full diplomatic immunities. . . . Through Protecting Power we shall insist on you and your staff being included in any evacuation scheme agreed on with the Japanese government.'

The Malay Brigade had been desperately trying to hold the vital Pasir Panjang ridge but at last—after a heroic and stubborn defence—the first wave of the Japanese troops was pushing through into the vital Alexandra area—and making straight for the Alexandra hospital.

The advance enemy troops were sighted behind the hospital, which was crammed with wounded, just before two o'clock. After a hurried conference it was decided that there was no alternative but to surrender. As the Japanese reached the grounds at the back of the building, a young lieutenant called Weston was deputed to go from the reception room to the back entrance. He carried a white flag, and stood there, unsuspecting and unflinching, as the first few Japanese reached the porch. Without a second's hesitation the soldiers charged in and bayoneted him repeatedly. As Weston lay dying, more and more troops surged in over him. One party made for the operating theatre block. In the corridor outside the main theatre, patients were being prepared for operations. As they lay there on stretchers, puzzled by the noise of fighting and screams they could not comprehend, several Japanese faces appeared at the windows above them. Some scrambled through. Others barged in through the corridor door. All the Royal Army Medical Corps personnel put up their hands, and Captain Smiley, who was in charge, stepped forward and pointed to the Red Cross brassards on their arms. With a flick of his gun, the leading Japanese motioned the handful of British to move along into one corner of the corridor. As the unarmed men obediently did so the Japanese, for no apparent reason, set upon them with bayonets. The first man to go down was Lieutenant Rogers who was bayoneted twice through the throat and died immediately. Captain Parkinson, standing next to him, was also killed, together with two orderlies. Awaiting an operation—and actually on the table—was Corporal Bill Holden of the 2nd Loyals. Before he could do anything, he too was bayoneted to death. Two Japanese now lunged at Captain Smiley. Somehow he managed to deflect the first bayonet thrust and the blade hit his cigarette case in his left breast pocket, wounding his left arm. When the second Japanese wounded him in the groin, he fell over and owed his life to the fact that he feigned death as the Japanese ran from the corridor.

While this was happening, other Japanese troops were forcing all the patients to get out of the wards. The men who could not move were bayoneted. In the broiling heat, two hundred patients—together with a few RAMC personnel —were paraded in the grounds. All the patients were desperately ill. Some could barely hobble. Many collapsed. It made no difference. Herding them into groups of four or five, the Japanese roped them together with their hands behind their backs. They were then marched to the old servants' quarters behind the hospital—a building consisting of several small rooms, ranging in size from nine feet by nine to ten by twelve. Between fifty and seventy patients were jammed into each room. Wedged together, it was impossible for them to sit down and it took several minutes for some patients to get their arms above their heads and make a little more room in this modern version of the Black Hole of Calcutta. There they were left for the night. Water was promised but none arrived—though those nearest the open windows could watch the Japanese soldiers sitting down on the grass, eating tinned fruit. From time to time during the night the intolerable pressure of bodies wedged tightly against each other was eased in a fearful manner when the Japanese would take a small party out and lead it away. Those left behind could hear screams—then a Japanese soldier would return wiping blood from his bayonet. Only three men escaped when a shell scored a direct hit on the building, blowing off doors and windows. Though it killed several of the patients, the confusion did give a handful of men their only chance. Eight made a dash for it, and though five were gunned down, three men got away. They were the only survivors of this night of horror.

The speed of the Japanese thrust was being studied with jubilation at Berchtesgaden in Germany. As allies, the Germans and Japanese might have been uneasy bedfellows, but Hitler had been watching every move of the war in Asia, merely because it had succeeded in drawing off such substantial forces from Europe, and he had ordered Admiral Raeder, head of the German Navy, to prepare a report on the 'prospects' in the Far East. In his report to the Fuehrer on Friday the 13th, the German admiral made an elated assessment of the future, saying,

'Rangoon, Singapore and, most likely, also Port Darwin will be in Japanese hands within a few weeks. Only weak resistance is expected on Sumatra, while Java will be able to hold out longer. Japan plans to protect this front in the Indian Ocean by capturing the key position of Ceylon, and she also plans to gain control of the sea in that area by means of superior naval forces. Fifteen Japanese submarines are at the moment operating in the Bay of Bengal, in the waters off Ceylon, and in the straits on both sides of Sumatra and Java. With Rangoon, Sumatra, and Java gone, the last oil wells between Bahrein and the American continent will be lost. Oil supplies for Australia and New Zealand will have to come from either the Persian Gulf or from America. Once Japanese battleships, aircraft carriers, submarines, and the Japanese naval air force are based on Ceylon, Britain will be forced to resort to heavily-escorted convoys if she desires to maintain communications with India and the Near East. Only Alexandria, Durban, and Simonstown will be available as repair bases for large British naval vessels in that part of the world.'[1]

As Hitler was reading this, Churchill, across the water in Downing Street, was reading a very different assessment, of the problems of this vast area. It had arrived in a gloomy cable from Wavell who reported to his Prime Minister that,

'. . . The unexpectedly rapid advance of enemy on Singapore and approach of an escorted enemy convoy towards southern Sumatra necessitates review of our plans for the defence of the Netherlands East Indies, in which southern Sumatra plays a most important part.

[1] Fuehrer Conferences on Naval Affairs.

With more time . . . strong defence could be built up. But ground not yet fully prepared . . .'

It was clear now to Churchill that the end was approaching, yet he was loath to give up the struggle. Ever since he had made the decision not to divert the 18th Division to Burma—a decision made much against his will and partly to mollify the Australians—Churchill had exerted all the pressure possible on Wavell to delay the capitulation. He had realised that Singapore could not resist indefinitely. There was no longer any possibility of holding out until naval relief arrived. It was a question of time, but until now Churchill had believed that 'the only chance . . . of gaining time, which was all we could hope for, was to give imperative orders to fight in desperation to the end.'

Churchill had felt strongly that, despite all the doubts 'and fears entertained in Whitehall, 'it is always right that whatever may be the doubts at the summit of war direction the general on the spot should have no knowledge of them and should receive instructions which are simple and plain'.

Now, however, the Prime Minister received a second cable from Wavell—which had been despatched at the same time as his 'carry on fighting' cable to Percival—warning Churchill that the Japanese were close to the city, that the Allied troops were incapable of launching a counter-attack, and that he feared resistance was 'not likely to be very prolonged'.

Wavell had not asked the Prime Minister for powers to capitulate. Indeed, he told him that he had ordered Percival to fight it out house by house. Nonetheless, the implication of the message was clear and Churchill now had to make the ultimate decision whether or not to continue the struggle, knowing that if he insisted on fighting for much longer, he would have to bear the responsibility for thousands of civilian deaths.

It was possible to argue that, in terms of power politics and global war strategy, the sufferings of prolonged resistance in Singapore would be negligible if they contributed to a great surge in the British fighting 'image' comparable to that inspired by the heroic American defenders in the Philippines. Though the terrain and the conditions were vastly different, Churchill must have been sorely tempted, but he cast the temptation aside, for he 'was sure it would be wrong to enforce needless slaughter, and without hope of victory to inflict the horrors of street fighting' on the civilians. He asked General Brooke, Chief of the Imperial General Staff, to come and see him in Downing Street, and told him 'where I stood'. Brooke agreed, and Churchill prepared to send a cable to Wavell, telling him, 'You are of course sole judge of the moment when no further result can be gained at Singapore, and should instruct Percival accordingly'.

That cable marked the end of Churchill's dreams and hopes—hopes that by a heroic defence against inevitable defeat, Singapore would rank in military history with Warsaw; that instead of handing over intact this glittering symbol of Britain's colonial power, the ashes of certain defeat would provide history with a matchless epic of unyielding British courage that would echo around the world.

CHAPTER TEN

THE DYING CITY

Saturday, February 14—Sunday, February 15

To all who now remained, the Saturday and the Sunday became blurred into one long, agonising spell of time. Men and women worked and ate, even slept a little, but, with rare exceptions, none who lived through these two days could distinguish one from the next in the hazy outlines of their personal nightmares. As they struggled on like automatons, total war viciously attacked each and every one of their senses. If a woman held her hands to her ears to blot out the sound of shells or bombs, her eyes still took in the mangled flesh of the wounded. If she covered her eyes, the smell of corpses assailed her nostrils. But worst of all was the sense of shame, for in the once-beautiful city—now clothed in filth from burning oil—the sense of humiliation was hurting physically, like the mounting throb in a deep wound. 'It sounds silly,' wrote Hudson, 'but when I saw an old friend in the hospital, I nipped down a corridor—I didn't want to meet him—I didn't want to talk to anybody.' Freddy Bloom felt it. MAS women who, because of long friendships in happier times had stuck together, now tended to avoid each other when off duty.

In the streets and squares thousands of dejected soldiers wandered about aimlessly. Some were bitter, like the brick-red Tommy stripped to the waist outside Fullerton Building, who was haranguing a crowd of troops, 'It's time to surrender—we're fighting for a way of life that's finished anyway.' But most of the leaderless, listless troops were, like the civilians, conscious of a vague feeling of shame, not only at what happened, but at their dirt and squalor. In a country where the heat demanded two or three clean shirts a day, soldiers were still wearing stinking clothes they had not changed for many days. Some washed—and did their laundry —by the side of busy roads where the water gushed from broken mains, Others made for the Singapore River or the small creeks leading to the Chinese timber yards. The water was filthy—but it didn't matter, it was wet.

For water, even more than bravery, had become the most critical factor in holding out since the moment when the enemy had captured McRitchie, the last remaining reservoir on the island. Now the only water to reach the city came from one solitary pumping station called Woodleigh, within 800 yards of the Japanese front lines. Here an unnamed civilian engineer and his wife heroically kept the pumps working while the bullets flew around them. Who they were nobody seems to know. The few water engineers of that time who are still alive are uncertain because the handful of engineers was constantly being rushed from one key post to another. Brigadier Simson managed to telephone the engineer at Woodleigh urging him to carry on, but noted in his report, 'I regret I have no record of his name.' There seems little doubt that the Japanese—already thinking in terms of occupational problems—refrained from bombing Woodleigh, for the engineer and his wife were allowed to continue pumping after the Japanese had overrun the station.

By now the water problem was simple: two-thirds of the 'Woodleigh supply' was running to waste. Due to broken mains, water had already failed in the high parts of the city. Most of the Asian staff had vanished, and though Percival had given Simson a party of Royal Engineers to help with repairs, the obstacles were insuperable. And now, inevitably, the water shortage brought its concomitant of disease. There were reports of bodies in the reservoirs. Many Asians in bombed buildings were carelessly drinking contaminated water. More and more people—children particularly—were in danger of typhoid.

Just before ten o'clock on Saturday, Brigadier Simson reported to Percival that the failure of the water supply seemed imminent, and Percival immediately drove round to the Municipal offices for a conference with Simson and the Municipal Engineer. It seemed that with luck the supply might last for forty-eight hours, but the mains were more likely to run dry in half that time.

'While there's water,' announced Percival grimly, 'we fight on.' Then he left to tell the Governor at the Singapore Club of his decision.

Though every corner of the club had by now been filled with VIP's, the harassed secretary managed to find a small luggage room where Percival and the Governor could talk privately. Shenton Thomas was haunted by one dread— the danger of an epidemic. He told Percival so frankly, after the General had said that he must fight on for as long as possible, and when the two leaders had parted, Shenton Thomas felt he was duty bound to acquaint the Colonial Office with his fears. He cabled them:

'General Officer Commanding informs me that Singapore City now closely invested. There are now one million people within radius of three miles. Water-supplies very badly damaged and unlikely to last more than twenty-four hours. Many dead lying in the streets and burial impossible. We are faced with total deprivation of water, which must result in pestilence. I have felt that it is my duty to bring this to notice of General Officer Commanding.'

Percival was also sending off a signal—to Wavell in Java, asking him for wider discretionary powers to capitulate. Once again Wavell—not having yet received Churchill's cable —had to reply, 'In all places where sufficiency of water exists for troops they must go on fighting. Your gallant stand is serving purpose and must be continued to limit of endurance.'

To the weary troops and the million civilians, the Japanese must have seemed all-powerful, and yet, unknown to the defenders, there was an element of bluff in the enemy attacks

212

on the outskirts of the city, for the Japanese had nearly exhausted their ammunition. As Colonel Tsuji, their Chief of Operations, later admitted, they were down to a hundred rounds for each field gun, 'and less for our heavy guns. . . . The divisional Chief of Staff . . . came reluctantly to the conclusion that it was a sheer impossibility to proceed with [the attack] . . . troops were exhausted by the violent bombardment of the enemy. Arms and legs were flying through the air and heads scattered everywhere.'[1] With supreme irony, it was not only the soldiers of the Empire, but the soldiers of the Emperor who had all but reached Wavell's 'limit of endurance'.

On the other hand, though Japanese ammunition was running short, there were bombs to spare (some captured from the British up-country), and it seemed that the city was never free from raids. At least five hundred civilians were killed on the Saturday, and by now the raging fires had become the city's greatest problem, after water, for here, too, water was at a premium. The Central Fire station had been hit several times and the water supply was so limited that on Saturday Buckeridge had his first bath for three days, washing his uniforms in the water afterwards, and keeping it for the next bath.

The fires seemed to follow a particular pattern. In his diary Buckeridge described a big one in Old Road from his own specialised, technical viewpoint. It had spread over five or six godowns on the Singapore River, all filled with combustibles like rubber, shellac and soya beans. 'It was typical of air raid jobs. Buildings collapsed by bomb explosions, cargo well involved, upper floor contents piled on ground floors to make a bonfire sixteen feet high.' This fire was near the Singapore ice works, and Buckeridge was gasping with the heat when the factory manager brought him a bucket of icy water to sluice over his head. Another time, when a row of shophouses had been set alight, Buckeridge's men had just extinguished the blaze when an old Chinese lady emerged from an untouched shop with half a dozen cups of tea on a tin tray. 'She thanked me very politely for saving her home.'

There were other moments of welcome relief—even the occasional opportunity to grin, if only at the futility of it all. On one occasion a British sergeant drove up in a military truck, jumped out of the cab, tapped Buckeridge on the shoul-

[1] *Singapore: The Japanese Version.*

der, and yelled, 'I've been told to destroy this lorry. Mind if I drive it into your fire, mate?'

'Good God!' cried Buckeridge. 'I'm trying to put this bloody fire *out*!'

'Okay mate—no offence,' replied the sergeant cheerfully, and drove the lorry fifty yards down the road before setting fire to it himself.

No historian has ever come close to recording the details of the great fires of those final days in Singapore. Almost all records—apart from personal ones like Buckeridge's—were lost in the confusion. The searing flames started up in every part, almost every street of the city. They ranged from one in the car park in Collyer Quay, in which hundreds of abandoned vehicles were burned out after a Japanese incendiary attack, to one in a godown filled with cases of fire crackers (popular on Chinese New Year) which exploded and jumped in all directions. Not until nearly the end, however, was Singapore faced with a new and menacing kind of conflagration—the 'river fires' which culminated (in Buckeridge's colourful language) 'in a bloody great fire where no fire could possibly be'. This was the fire of Pulo Saigon Bridge which crossed the Singapore River, and the sight was so extraordinary and unbelievable that scores of people rushed to the river bank and stood gaping at a sight never to be forgotten. For the bridge was constructed entirely of steel girders, and it was ablaze from end to end.

The fire had started in a bizarre fashion. A huge patch of blazing oil from a bombed vessel at the mouth of the river had floated up river with the turn of the tide. 'It was a sneak-thief kind of enemy, this floating, blazing scum,' wrote Buckeridge. As the thick, black, burning pool—forced along relentlessly by the incoming tide—reached the crowded sampans in the heart of the city, the oil and the flames twisted and writhed between junks, lighters, sampans packed so closely a child could have scrambled across them. Scores were set alight, and tongues of flames even reached buildings on the banks. Finally the blazing pool reached the steel 'trellis work' of the Pulo Saigon Bridge, one of the oldest in Singapore. At least it did not seem possible that this ancient Meccano-like structure could be set on fire. Nor would it have been but for an unlucky chance. A Japanese attempt to bomb the bridge resulted in a near miss—but the blast

214

burst an oil pipe running along the side of the bridge, and immediately a stream of oil was spurting down to meet the blazing oil below. The flames leapt towards each other at incredible speed, and long before the bridge stop-cock could be turned off, the asphalt roadway on the Pulo Saigon Bridge and the lacy ironwork were blazing. Only when the tide started to go out did the oil patch below the bridge begin drifting down river, and the red-hot, twisted girders of the bridge start to cool off. By ten p.m. the strangest fire in Singapore had burned itself out, and Buckeridge was able to return to Central for a supper of cold ham, biscuits, coffee 'and a quiet whisky salvaged from destroyed stocks'.

Inevitably the fires and bomb-damaged buildings created more and more opportunities for looting, which was now beginning to assume dangerous proportions. When Buckeridge was called to a fire in a food godown in Havelock Road, 'I managed to keep the fire under control and saved the godown—but I couldn't stop the looters'. Hordes of them arrived. Some were in cars. Unashamedly they loaded them up as swiftly as they could and drove off. Others came trundling carts or pulling rickshaws. In a few minutes 'the godown was a naked shell'.

The worst looting, however, occurred in the teeming sections of the city behind 'white' Singapore, where the public markets, normally selling fish, meat, fruit, and eggs, had either been hit or left unattended, and where now gangs of men were systematically stripping the stalls and shops until it looked as though locusts had passed by, leaving them naked and empty. Next the looters turned to the big warehouses, smashing doors and barricaded windows in search of clothing, merchandise—anything from bicycles to radios and cameras—treasures beyond price which until now had only been admired longingly behind the barrier of a plate glass window.

Even the Rev. Bennitt (to say nothing of the Bishop of Singapore) admitted to a little 'looting'—of a sort. According to 'The Rev.'s' diary, 'I went with the Bishop to scrounge a wheel for his car'. For the Bishop had a puncture in his car and nobody could find the time to repair it. Bennitt, however, had seen an abandoned car similar to the Bishop's near Yoch Eng aid post. They found it and pinched the wheel.

Things were quiet at Yoch Eng, so the Bishop and 'The

Rev.' decided to visit the village of Siglap a mile or so
farther along the east coast road. Bennitt had made a good
friend of the village baker and was certain he could get
some fresh bread there. It did not seem to have occurred to
either of them that Siglap was outside the perimeter and
therefore theoretically occupied by the Japanese. Yet when
the Bishop and Bennitt reached the village they found all
the small Chinese shops open. Outside one a man was
having his hair cut, and 'everything was completely peaceful and quiet.' Having penetrated enemy territory, one can
understand 'The Rev.'s' rather pained reaction, 'When we got
back, people would not believe we had been there'.

And yet everything was so confused that anything was
understandable—even stupidity. Tommy Kitching, who on
the previous day had been ordered to destroy all his maps of
the island, received an urgent phone call from Fort Canning.
Malaya Command now urgently *wanted* all the maps of
Singapore he could lay his hands on—the very maps he had
been warned must be destroyed. Kitching noted the following conversation in his diary:

'But damn it all, man, they gave me orders yesterday to
destroy every single copy!'

'Yes, but now they think they might want them.'

'Well, I haven't got any—haven't you any at Fort Canning?'

'No, they're all destroyed too.'

Kitching had turned his office into a bomb and shell-proof
shelter ready to withstand a prolonged siege. He had bought
enough tinned food to last two months, an oil stove and a
good supply of kerosene. He had also filled kerosene tins and
bottles with a reserve supply of twenty gallons of water for
the five colleagues who slept and ate in his offices.

People now slept anywhere they could. Cicely Williams,
exhausted by her brood of children, had not slept for three
nights, and had to get away to rest and recover her energy.
Leaving the children in charge of her Asian nurses, she
sank gratefully on to a camp bed where she had the best
night's sleep of the war, finding that 'the noise of shells
was positively pleasant as heard from the relative security
of thick walls'. But then, her bedroom was a cell in Outram
Road jail.

Surprisingly, there were few suicides. A few Chinese who
knew they were on the Japanese death list and had been unable
216

(or unwilling) to get away, quietly took their lives. Among the Europeans there was only one recorded case of a suicide pact—between a young English planter called Colin Johns who had fallen in love with a beautiful Chinese girl. Nobody ever really got to the bottom of their story, though it was known that Johns, who had been evacuated from up-country, had become hopelessly infatuated, had resigned all his clubs, and had set 'up house with the girl in a flat in a converted old mansion on Nassim Hill. It was obvious, too, that she was desperately in love with him—anyone who had caught the occasional glimpse of them dancing together had been able to see that for themselves. She obviously came from a good family and one rumour had it that her father refused to let her marry Johns. Another said that Johns had a wife conveniently tucked away in England. No one knew—for the very simple reason that nobody bothered to find out.

On the Saturday—or perhaps during the night of Friday-Saturday—the couple apparently realised the end was inevitable and agreed to die together by sealing up their garage door and gassing themselves with their car fumes. There they were discovered when their amah arrived earlier than expected and forced open the garage door. Terrified at what she had discovered, she ran down Nassim Hill towards Tanglin Circus, wailing, 'Tuan and mem both dead!'

By the time the ambulance reached the garage, Johns was dead. The girl seemed to show a faint sign of life and was rushed to the General.

The Rev. Bennitt was not only a highly respected and well-known figure, he was a man without an enemy in the world. Everybody in Singapore liked 'The Rev.' and admired the sterling work he had done, particularly among the Chinese at Yoch Eng. But now, in the Raffles Place area, Tim Hudson found his conduct intriguing, to say the least of it. For 'The Rev.' would go into a shop, come out with a tiny purchase, go into another, and buy an equally small, mysterious packet. Finally, after this had happened half a dozen times, Hudson, who knew him slightly, could contain his curiosity no longer, and asked him point-blank what he was buying.

'Buying?' asked 'The Rev.' 'Oh! These? Razor blades, my dear fellow.'

In fact, 'The Rev.', like thousands of others, was already thinking ahead to the grim days of internment, and he had

217

one pet aversion—growing a beard. It would, he felt, be a sign of 'giving in', of 'letting yourself go'. So, since razor blades were getting scarce, he was going from shop to shop buying a few at a time—in all, enough to give him a shave every other day for several years.

There was not only a run on razor blades. There was an unprecedented rush to the dentist's. Stamford Road, where Radcliffe, one of the dentists, had his consulting rooms, was being constantly shelled, but even that did not deter the queue of people who felt, like Tim Hudson, that 'If I had to be interned, at least I didn't want toothache as well'. In some indefinable way the fear of toothache had become a minor obsession, worrying able-bodied men more than the prospect of the dysentery or beri-beri that was to kill hundreds.

There was a rush, too, on Kelly and Walsh, the booksellers in Raffles Place. When Tim Hudson arrived there half the shelves were empty, and the big airy shop he knew so well had the bleak, unwelcome look of a 'going out of business' sale. Despite the heat, a milling throng scrambled for the few books that were left, while a smiling, unfrightened Chinese girl took the money, counted change, and apologised because wrapping paper had run out. When the manager saw Hudson, who was an old customer, he beckoned him to the inside office and whispered, 'I've kept a few back—pick any couple of books you'd like, Tim—no charge, of course.' Hudson managed to find a Shakespeare and a volume of Somerset Maugham's short stories.

Most shopkeepers refused money from their old and trusted customers. When Freddy Bloom went into Maynards the chemists, the manager insisted on thrusting upon her three toothbrushes, three tubes of paste and a box of soap tablets, and then unconsciously relapsing into the words he had used daily for twenty years, asked brightly, 'Will that be all, Mrs. Bloom?'

Curiously, few people bothered about buying tinned food. Perhaps instinctively they felt as Buckeridge did, 'It's going to be a bloody long stay'. And so it cannot have seemed worthwhile buying a 'luxury' that would have lasted only a few days. On the other hand, there *was* a run on one luxury—cigarettes. Even the most philosophical were dismayed at the prospect of facing up to the rigours of internment without cigarettes or a pipe to tide them over the first few days.

'Booze somehow didn't matter,' Hudson remembers, 'but cigarettes became a must.'

Others invested in cases of pipe tobacco and a dozen new pipes. Overnight, pipe cleaners vanished too. As the tobacco stocks began to dwindle alarmingly, shopkeepers tried to limit supplies to individuals, though not always successfully. In the 'smokers' shop' at Gian Singh, the big food store in Battery Road, three Europeans had to be taken to hospital after a free-for-all when one man demanded ten cartons of cigarettes and those queueing up behind shouted, 'Share 'em out!' The man at the head of the queue tried to grab the cigarettes. Immediately the others fell on him with the tigerish ferocity of a rugby scrum. The counter was wrecked, precious stocks were trampled underfoot. Nobody knew who was fighting whom. The tearful manager tried to get the police but there were no police. In the end he left the scrum to fight itself out, while in the adjoining departments of the big store assistants and customers tried to ignore the unedifying spectacle of white men fighting like animals.

But without doubt those in the most pitiful plight were the mothers with young children. For weeks now the pathetic groups of women, mostly young, living out of one suitcase, with their children tugging at their soiled dresses, had been a daily spectacle in Singapore. Some had obstinately (and stupidly) refused to leave without their husbands, taking heart from the spurious military communiqués. Others, who were penniless, had not realised in time that the government was ready to stake their passage money.

Now this unhappy band faced one common problem. Not for them the mad rush to buy cigarettes or toothbrushes or books. Now that internment was all but a reality, only one thing mattered: the welfare of the children. Clothes, shoes, hats against the sun, baby foods—all these had now become dire necessities. The mothers knew they could—and would—have to go without themselves. But the children—often deprived of milk and special foods—were different. And yet there was no official body to whom they could turn for help, not even a charitable organisation with a 'treasure chest' able to dole out the reach-me-downs of other, luckier children who had left.

Then, in the last hours, something very close to a miracle happened. How the word got round—how it by-passed shelled roads, torn buildings, smashed telephones—will never be known, but it did, and while the shells whizzed overhead and the fires raged round the corner, Raffles Place unaccountably became filled with excited, laughing children suddenly decked out in their 'Sunday best'. It was an astonishing sight. Little girls pirouetted as they showed off spotless, cool, pretty white dresses. Boys proudly displayed trim shorts and white shirts. There were floppy hats and shining new sandals for everyone. In addition, each child—or its mother—carried a parcel containing a duplicate outfit—everything from underpants or panties to a spare pair of shoes. Even the mothers —still in their old, unpressed clothes—seemed to throw back their shoulders with a new surge of pride and thankfulness.

'I'm not sentimental,' said Tim Hudson, 'but when I saw them—as excited as if it was Christmas Day—I couldn't help thinking there must be a God somewhere who looks after kiddies.'

For the 'miracle' had been performed by Robinson's in Raffles Place, whose manager, Mr. L. C. Hutchings, had, to his eternal credit, decided that every European mother now facing internment could come to the store and get two free outfits for each of her children. The cost? 'Let's talk about that later,' said Mr. Hutchings.[2]

Around this time Brigadier Simson heard that one of his staff officers, Major George Coode, was planning to escape if the city capitulated. The Major—who happened to be an extremely fine sailor—had managed to acquire and provision a motor launch, but Simson had been so occupied with his denial schemes that he and Coode had hardly seen each other for several days. The Major had asked Percival for permission to escape, and Percival had agreed, on the understanding that if the British had to capitulate any escape would be during the vital period between the arrangements and the time the capitulation came into force. There was bound to be a few hours' delay and Percival was sure the Japanese would insist on a promise that no attempts to escape would be permitted. Percival would have to honour this pledge while his troops were still at large.

[2] Though most Asians would not be interned, the offer did apply to those—such as the Asian wives of Britishers—who would go into internment. Most Asian mothers, however, did not face the same problems as the European women, who had often been evacuated from up-country and did not have any friends in Singapore.

By chance Simson ran into Coode, who told him of his plans. Simson immediately asked, 'Can I book a seat?'

'Why, of course,' replied Coode. So Simson also asked Percival for permission to escape in the event of surrender. He wanted, he told the General, 'to carry on the fight'. Percival made no objection—apart from the same understandable conditions he had imposed on Coode. Simson thanked him, and from that moment until the following evening did not give the matter another thought. After all, there was still plenty of work to be done.

Another man was suddenly offered the opportunity to escape—none other than Mr. Bowden, the Australian government representative, who had been refused permission to leave the island. General Percival felt that—perhaps because he was a civilian of 52—he should go. Though he had been an invaluable link between the island and his government, the War Council no longer functioned, and civilian administration was grinding to a halt. Bowden was offered a place on the *Osprey*, a launch designed to seat ten people, which was due to leave late on the Saturday night. Bowden—an extremely honest as well as likeable man—at first demurred, but when he was told categorically that capitulation was 'very close', he made up his mind to go, together with his two assistants. But, he insisted, he must let his government know. This was none too easy for by now there was only one way to get a wireless message out of the island. All communications had been reduced to a single small hand set operated within a few feet of the edge of the lapping fringe of the harbour where the cable actually entered the dirty water. Somehow Bowden's last message was tapped out: 'Our work completed. We will telegraph from another place at present unknown.' Then at 6.30 p.m. Bowden and the others met by the launch.

The 'small party' had swollen to 38. As they tried to get aboard, their passage was barred by deserting troops seeking to escape. Some were armed with hand grenades. Others carried tommy-guns. The uglier elements threatened to open fire on the launch unless they too were taken aboard, and indeed, as the *Osprey* moved out, rifle shots were fired at her. Nobody was hit, and in mid-harbour, and under cover of dark, the party transferred to a forty-foot diesel-engined vessel called the *Mary Rose*. Behind them, black smoke from the Naval Base still blotted out the sky. In the heart of the city a soap factory was blazing furiously. A shellac godown and timber sheds spurted flames scores of feet into the air. Across the water, the oil reserves in Pulau Bukum had been deliberately set alight, so that 'even the ocean seemed to be on fire'.

Back in the privacy of his bedroom at the Singapore Club, Sir Shenton Thomas was writing his daily diary, 'Much quieter night in the Club. Percival told me position no worse and therefore we will carry on.'

Sunday morning dawned without a breath of air. Gordon Bennett remembered it as 'a hopeless dawn of despair. There is no hope or help on the horizon. The tropical sun is sending its steamy heat on the dying city which is writhing in its agony.'

All over the city people, as though sensing that the moment of destiny was at hand, joined in Sunday-morning prayer. In the General Hospital, Freddy Bloom and the other nurses gathered in a bleak ante-room for a brief service. In the cathedral, which was still filled with wounded, 'The Rev.' had put back as many pews as possible in the choir. Every one was filled, and every inch of space was crowded with standing worshippers. Those who could not get inside stood in the green compound. They could not hear the service but, as if impelled by some primitive instinct, they stayed there silent and devout, until it was over and those inside filed out.

General Percival was also at church—in freshly starched uniform, attending communion at Fort Canning. But he at least knew one thing—that at long last the 'wider discretion' he had demanded had been granted, for in the early hours of the morning he had received a cable from Wavell, reading,

'So long as you are in a position to inflict losses and damage to enemy and your troops are physically capable of doing so, you must fight on. Time gained and damage to enemy are of vital importance at this juncture. When you are fully satisfied that this is no longer possible I give you discretion to cease resistance. Inform me of intentions. Whatever happens I thank you and all your troops for gallant efforts of last few days.'

Now the decision was up to Percival, and he lost no time

222

in calling a conference of all senior commanders, together with one civilian—'Dickie' Dickinson, the Inspector-General of Police, who had been phoned at his office at eight a.m. and told to present himself at Fort Canning at 9.30. Percival had not invited Shenton Thomas to the conference, but the ever-loyal Dickinson, a firm believer in protocol, had no intention of going to Fort Canning without the Governor's permission. He managed to get through to Shenton Thomas at the Club, and the Governor immediately said, 'Of course you must go.' (In fact, Dickinson had quite rightly been invited instead of the Governor because 'I was in effect one of Percival's Commanding Officers since the police had come under the Army, and this was a purely military conference.')

Simson of course was present, together with the three senior commanders and an RAF officer. Grimly they made their way to a small bomb-proof room under Fort Canning Hill. Percival sat at the head of the table and Dickinson remembers that the solemn occasion was marked by 'a considerable amount of spit and polish'. No aides were present as each commander gave his own gloomy recital of the crumbling defence. Simson repeated an early morning warning that the water situation had worsened since the previous evening, and then Percival announced briefly that Wavell had granted him the power to capitulate. From then on the discussion of any possible counter-attack was purely academic and pointless, for everyone present knew there was almost no water, that Army food reserves were only sufficient for a few days, and that the only petrol left was in the tanks of the vehicles. The conference lasted barely twenty minutes, ending when, as Gordon Bennett recorded in his diary, 'Silently and sadly we decided to surrender'.

As soon as the meeting had broken up, Percival sent for Hugh Fraser, the acting Colonial Secretary (who had replaced Stanley Jones) and Brigadier Newbiggin, his Chief Administrative Officer, and told them to drive up the Bukit Timah Road to meet the Japanese and try and arrange a truce for four p.m. when terms of capitulation could be discussed. That done, he issued his final military orders—for the destruction of all ciphers, codes, documents, secret equipment and guns.

Hugh Fraser had been a highly popular, cheerful Federal Secretary up-country before taking over the mantle of Stanley Jones, and he did not relish this 'distasteful task' and only

223

undertook it because Sir Shenton Thomas was adamant that in no circumstances would he parley with the Japanese.

This was the first meeting with the enemy, and it was a moment which should have been marked with gravity. Instead the journey and the meeting at times resembled a Marx Brothers film. Had not Fraser written a long, documented account of the episode, it would be difficult to believe what actually happened.

It will be remembered that in his 'airmail' letter, Yamashita had told Percival that, if he wished to surrender, he was to send a car with a Union Jack and a white flag as far as it could proceed along the Bukit Timah Road. At exactly 11.30 a.m. Fraser and Newbiggin, carrying a letter addressed to the Japanese High Commissioner, set off from Fort Canning in an open car, together with an interpreter. A second car followed in case of accidents. They had reckoned to be at the Japanese headquarters by noon, but were hopelessly wide of the mark, for it took them over two hours, instead of half an hour, to make contact with the enemy.

Right from the start everything seemed to go wrong—ironically on a mission whose main object was to speed the moment when lives would be saved. They had planned to drive to Newton Circus, a roundabout where they would turn up the Bukit Timah Road, but had to turn back twice because craters had made the roads impassable. Somehow they reached Newton Circus after winding their way along back roads and alleys. There they dismissed the second car and set off slowly along Dunearn Road.

Half-way towards the Japanese headquarters their car crossed the bridge over the canal into Bukit Timah Road. Their way was fairly clear until they reached a point where Adam Road, a major east-west highway, crossed Bukit Timah Road. Here they found the entire area heavily defended by a barbed wire barrier. The three Britishers scrambled out with the intention of removing enough of the obstacle to allow their car to get through. Just in time they discovered 'it was stiff' with anti-tank mines. There was nothing for it but to recross the canal into Dunearn Road—where to their chagrin they were held up at the point of a revolver by a British patrol. Laboriously they explained that they were not defecting to the Japanese. But not until the officer in charge was called did anybody realise who they were. The officer then warned them that the wide Adam Road, which

224

they would have to cross, was heavily mined, and it would be impossible to drive a car across, even if they could get the barrier down.

Now they had no alternative but to leave the car and set off on foot. They unfurled their flags and started walking—'picking our way carefully, very carefully, through the mined area'. All this time enemy planes were bombing and machine-gunning the British front line and 'the whine of shells passing overhead became almost monotonous'.

With the sweat pouring off them in the mid-day sun, they strode along until finally a party of Japanese troops, automatics at the ready, emerged cautiously from a rubber plantation. Through their interpreter, Fraser and Newbiggin pointed out the significance of the white flag they carried. Here, at the side of the long road, with its orchids growing on the canal bank and the sombre rubber trees behind, was a rare moment of history as the sweat-stained Britishers came face to face with the first Japanese to realise that the war in Malaya was as good as over. The British officers might have been forgiven for nervously wondering what their reception would be from the Japanese. It could have been anything—anything from jubilation to being gunned down in savage retribution. The one reaction they could not possibly have expected was what in fact did happen. Excitedly the Japanese crowded round the three men, politely pushing them, and arranging them for a group photograph. The war might not have existed. All they wanted to do was to take pictures. All the Japanese seemed to be festooned with cameras slung around their necks. They begged the Britishers to line up—they squeezed them a little closer to make a better photographic composition, they turned them so they faced the sun—and flatly refused to send for their officer until they had shot the last spool of film. Only then, as the dazed Britishers wondered if their senses had left them, did the Japanese soldiers deign to send for two senior officers who arrived quickly from Japanese headquarters. It was now two o'clock.

In his letter Percival suggested that a cease-fire should be ordered on both sides at four o'clock, giving the two opposing commanders the opportunity to discuss terms of capitulation. To Yamashita, however, the idea of 'discussion' was preposterous. He would have nothing to do with such a proposal. He would not order a cease-fire, he said, until Percival had 'signed on the dotted line'. And he would treat with

225

nobody but Percival in person. Meanwhile the shelling would go on.

Yamashita had drafted out a letter for the two envoys to carry to Percival. It set out in general terms the Japanese conditions for a cease-fire, and a demand that Percival should present himself at the Japanese headquarters in the Ford factory at Bukit Timah that evening. Yamashita guaranteed him a safe conduct, and volunteered to send a car to await him near the mined barrier at Adam Road.

This was all Fraser and Newbiggin could achieve, though their eventful afternoon was by no means ended. Despite the fact that they were retracing the very same steps they had taken barely an hour or two previously, the Japanese now unaccountably insisted on blindfolding them for the trip back to Adam Road. Since they were properly led, this absurd procedure might have seemed more childish than irritating. But instead the journey was terrifying, for it coincided with a time when British gunners were laying down a heavy barrage over this area, and the shells whined uncomfortably close to the men who were temporarily 'blinded'.

Eventually they reached Adam Road and their car, and only one more adventure lay ahead of them. At the junction of Bukit Timah and Stevens Road, a British sergeant who, as Fraser noted, 'had quite obviously not destroyed his private stock of liquor' fired a revolver at the British party, missing them by a miracle. Then he ordered his platoon to surround the car. The sergeant was itching to fire again, but must have had second thoughts, though the danger remained acute until two officers arrived and, 'at the point of their revolvers, persuaded the sergeant of his error'.

Tired, dispirited, drenched with sweat, the little party reached Fort Canning just before four a.m. It gave Percival little more than half an hour to prepare for the most humiliating moment of his military career.

Together with three staff officers, General Percival set off to retrace the journey taken by Fraser and Newbiggin. At the approaches to the village of Bukit Timah they got out of their car, unfurled the Union Jack and the white flag, and marched under enemy escort to the Japanese headquarters—the bleak, functional Ford Motor factory. Perhaps understandably, British records have been reticent about this meeting, though Japanese documents and verbatim reports give a detailed picture of what happened, together with photographs of the two generals face to face at last—Percival, thin, tired and dispirited; Yamashita like a heavy, thickset bulldog, with his clenched right fist on the table ready to pound it as he emphasised a point.

Yamashita arrived several minutes late—and from the outset any hopes which Percival might have entertained for getting conciliatory terms vanished. 'Pale, and with bloodshot eyes,' Percival listened dumbly as Yamashita announced, 'The Japanese army will consider nothing but unconditional surrender at 10 p.m. Nippon time.' (8.30 p.m. Singapore time.)

'But I can't guarantee it,' blurted out Percival. 'We just can't submit our final reply before midnight.'

Yamashita raised his voice and thumped the table. 'Are our terms acceptable or not? Things have to be done quickly. We are ready to resume firing.'

As Percival hesitated, one of Yamashita's aides pushed in front of him a list of questions in English. Percival looked at the first one: 'Does the British army surrender unconditionally?'

Again Percival cried, 'Please, wait until tomorrow morning for the final answer.' And again Yamashita, leaning forward, retorted, 'In that case we will continue the attack until tomorrow morning. Is that all right, or do you consent immediately to unconditional surrender?'

With 'bowed head and in a faint voice,' Percival gave his consent. The surrender would take place at 8.30 that night.

Yamashita briskly picked up his pile of papers and told Percival that the British troops should be immediately disarmed except for a thousand who would maintain order during the night. He agreed that, in order to prevent incidents, Japanese troops would be forbidden to enter the city until the following morning. 'But,' he warned Percival, 'if there is any violation of these terms, a full-scale attack on Singapore will immediately commence.'

Percival had one last request to make. 'Will the Imperial Army protect the women and children and the British civilians?'

'Please rest assured,' replied Yamashita in a more conciliatory tone, 'I shall positively guarantee it.'

Then, pushing a slip across the table, he urged Percival,

'Please sign this.' Percival signed—and then standing straight as a ramrod, turned on his heel. It was 6.10 p.m. on February 15.

Back at Fort Canning, Percival drafted his final signal to Wavell: 'Owing to losses from enemy action, water, petrol, food and ammunition practically finished. Unable therefore to continue the fight any longer. All ranks have done their best and grateful for your help.'

It was the last message out of Singapore.

Meanwhile, Brigadier Simson had been making his final preparations to escape. Secure in the knowledge that Percival had given him permission, the Brigadier drove for what he thought would be the last tour of the city. 'I saw that all my scorched earth responsibilities would be completed by six p.m.' Coode—in whose boat he was going—had warned the Brigadier that he planned to sail soon after seven p.m., and when Simson was satisfied that he could do no more, he drove to Fort Canning to say good-bye to Percival.

Percival was sitting at his desk looking utterly dejected. He hardly seemed to realise that Simson had entered the room, that the Brigadier was holding out his hand to say good-bye.

One will never know what passed through Percival's mind at that moment. Was he envious because Simson had been right about defences? Was he so depressed that he could not 'think straight'? In any event, he looked up at the Brigadier, and to Simson's astonishment refused point-blank to permit him to leave.

For a moment Simson was too flabbergasted to reply. Then he blurted out, 'But sir, you've already given me permission. And, what's more, it's the duty of every soldier to escape if he can.'

Percival did not agree. 'Officers,' he insisted, 'should stay and look after their units.' It .did not seem to make any difference when Simson pointed out that he *had* no units. He had been attached to the staff. 'And anyway,' added Simson, 'for the last six weeks I've only been Chief Engineer in name —and as Director-General of Civil Defence I've no ties of any sort to prevent me from going.'

'I'm sorry, Simson.' Percival abruptly turned to the papers on his desk as though to indicate that he did not wish to discuss the subject further. Without another word Simson
228

walked out of the room, drove straight to Major Coode and told him to cancel his place. Then he started to prepare for internment.

Around the same time, Gordon Bennett—unhampered by such niceties as obtaining permission—was preparing to leave for the docks. Originally his escape party had grown to six, but three had fallen out, including a Captain Curlewis, 'who expressed doubts about the propriety of leaving the men'. Gordon Bennett had no such doubts. Instead he entertained a feeling 'that I must at all costs return to Australia and tell our people the story of our conflict with the Japanese'.

Bennett's escape has been a source of controversy for 25 years, and since it is accepted that part of a soldier's duty is to escape, one might wonder what all the fuss has been about, and why (as we shall see later) the escape did in fact ruin Bennett's army career. The answer lies not only in the devious manner in which he concocted his plans without informing Percival, but also in the fact that when he did go, he left thousands of Australians behind, and practically his last order to them was a strict injunction *not* to escape. For on this last night, while he was itching to be gone, other Australians were also discussing the chances of escape. After talks with his senior officers, Bennett came to the conclusion that 'to allow any large scale unorganised attempts to escape would result in confusion and slaughter'. This was an incredible decision considering that Bennett was almost on his way. Bennett now issued an order that all Australian units were to remain at their posts until 8.30 the following morning. A copy of the order (which aroused great bitterness) was preserved during captivity and included the unequivocal sentence, 'All precautions must be taken to ensure that the spirit of the cease-fire is not destroyed by foolish action.' Having drafted the order, Bennett arranged for all troops to be issued with new clothing and two days' rations, handed over command to his artillery commander, and set off for the docks.

At 8.30 p.m. an uncanny, eerie silence fell across the burning city. Almost from one moment to the next, the din—the shelling, the bombing, the bark of guns which had been a part of everyone's lives, was abruptly stilled. It was the silence of death. Only one kind of local noise, the crackling flames and falling timbers of uncontrolled fires, remained to provide a

229

grim reminder that war does not end with the breeching of the guns.

To many the news of the cease-fire came as an astonishing shock. Dr. Cicely Williams, having had a good night's rest in the local jail, had returned to her children in the Dental Department, and was snatching an hour's sleep on the floor when a doctor poked his head round the door and cried, 'There's an armistice!'

'Why?' asked Cicely Williams. 'Who's given in?'

'We have,' said the doctor abruptly.

Tim Hudson was awakened by the silence. He had dropped off on the floor of the Medical College and suddenly, for no apparent reason, found himself wide awake in the dark, surrounded by recumbent, snoring men. Something 'was uncanny and at first I couldn't understand what it was'. He lit a cigarette and for some moments lay there, puzzled, unconsciously waiting for the shriek of a shell or the crump of a bomb. When none came he jumped up and ran out across the lawns to the hospital proper.

'What's happened?' he yelled, grabbing the first man he saw.

'Haven't you heard? We've surrendered!'

'Are you sure?'

'Of course.' And then the man added good-humouredly, 'No need to shout, old man.' For the first time Hudson realised that for days he had been shouting, as though talking to deaf men, in order to be heard above the unending pandemonium.

Hudson made his way towards the central ward. Every nook and cranny was overflowing with wounded, and as he picked his way carefully between the stretchers, he came to the junction of two long corridors stretching away. A pretty young nurse in a soiled, blood-stained uniform was weeping quietly. Tim knew her only by sight, though more than once she had helped to receive patients he had brought in.

'Isn't it awful?' she said.

As Tim tried to console her, she looked up, wiped her tears, forced a smile, and then without warning, asked quietly, 'Will you please give me a kiss? We don't know what's going to happen now.'

Tim remembered that 'the idea gave me an awful shock. What an awful thing to kiss a nurse in uniform.' He hesitated and said, 'Do you think I should, with you in uniform?' He kissed her gently. He never did discover who she was, and he never saw her again.

At first 'The Rev.' believed the truce was the work of fifth columnists. He had spent a busy day, starting with a communion service (but managing nonetheless to play a rubber of bridge after lunch) and now he could not believe the 'uncanny quiet'. Finally someone told him it was official and, as he noted in his diary, 'I wandered around a bit'. He had an objective in mind, for he 'had a wash at the Adelphi Hotel, one of the few places where there is still some water'. The city was still ringed with flames and the very last entry in his war diary (in which he had kept a meticulous daily note of the weather) ended with the dry remark, 'Weather fine for fires'.

Buck Buckeridge also 'celebrated' with a wash—or rather, a bath at the Central Fire Station, in the same dirty water he had used to wash his uniform. And that night he wrote, 'So, that was it. We'd given up. Or someone had. The gang of men round the table was as weary as I was, but I'm sure that every single one was willing and eager to carry on the struggle. But there was no struggle. It was over. We talked as though we shared a dreadful secret. Dreadful it was, but secret, no. We didn't know what the hell had gone wrong. We were damn sure it wasn't us.'

Some people never knew until later that the war was over. When McAlister's closed its doors—and the Observer Corps had been disbanded—Willie Watt had decided to move out from his Singapore headquarters to his house 'San Remo', eight miles east of Singapore on the coast near Changi. Though no Japanese troops had yet penetrated this area, Watt was several miles outside the British perimeter, and was going to find it extremely difficult to surrender when he tried to.

In one of the Asian wards at the General the beautiful Chinese lover of Colin Johns, the planter who had committed suicide, had regained consciousness and was off the danger list. Over and over she kept wailing in Chinese, 'Let me die, let me die'. As so often happens, while so many people who had wanted to live were dying, the doctors had been able to save the one person who had only wanted to die.

That night the Bishop of Singapore, the Rt. Reverend John Leonard Wilson, held a service in the cathedral. The stone floor of the nave was still crowded with rows of wounded, some on camp beds, others lying on blankets, but the pews still remained in the choir, and hundreds of men and women—many of them Asian—crowded inside as the congregation sang 'Praise, my soul, the King of Heaven'.

While the Bishop offered up prayers for the morrow, 'Dickie' Dickinson was standing on the balcony of his police station in New Bridge Road with his chief assistant. Dickinson had just returned from a visit to the Governor—'a miserable meeting. The shame of it was the worst.' The city was dark except for the fires. The two men hardly talked. Dickinson was wondering how Bunny, his wife, was coping at the Blood Transfusion. The street below seemed fairly crowded with people suddenly free to walk about without fear, but Dickinson hardly noticed, for his mind was on other things. He was thinking, he remembers, that, despite the shame of it all, at least the dangers were over—it was the end of blood and death and bombs.

Then, unaccountably, it happened. From the dark anonymity of the crowd below someone—perhaps with an old score to avenge—celebrated the end of the war by tossing a Mills bomb up on to the ten-foot-wide balcony. It landed at the feet of the two men. Dickinson remembers his number two 'hurling himself in front of me' but it was too late. The full force of the bomb caught Dickinson, one fragment going through his jaw. He had a vague recollection of falling—but that was all, as blackness engulfed 'the gentle policeman'.

In his Japanese version of the fall of Singapore, Colonel Tsuji makes the fascinating point that he found among the conquered British 'an expression of resignation such as is shown by the losers in fierce sporting contests' and though it is doubtful if a Japanese could penetrate and analyse the thoughts of the defeated British, it is a curious fact that on this last night of 'freedom'—the unreal interval of suspended time between war and captivity—all feelings of apprehension seem to have been absent. Perhaps the dismaying shock of defeat—or for some the temporary feeling of relief—had anaesthetised all thoughts of the perils that lay ahead, so that many diaries and papers indicate (especially when reading between the lines) a naïve belief that since the war had been lost honourably, the victors would treat the vanquished in an equally honourable fashion.

George Wade, a member of the MAS—and in civilian life

an expert on controlling Singapore's voracious white ants —noted in his diary, 'That night we had a steak and kidney pie, Christmas pudding and strawberries and cream, all out of a tin for our Surrender Dinner'. Leslie Hoffman—secure for the moment in his father's house at Serangoon—was surrounded by British troops who pressed on him vast stocks of tinned food—and a black Scottie dog called 'Whisky' which one of the soldiers asked him to look after—almost as though he would be returning soon to collect it.

Everyone was busy preparing their 'internment kits'—some bulky and unwieldy, since many people innocently assumed that in a climate as hot and humid as Singapore's the Japanese would obviously have to provide transport. 'If they put us in Changi,' Freddy heard one MAS woman say briskly, 'I'm not *walking* the nine miles. And if I refuse to walk, they'll *have* to transport me or leave me free.' It never seemed to enter the heads of many people that if they started getting 'cheeky', the Japanese soldiers would have as little compunction in killing them as in swatting an irritating bluebottle. In the first flush of 'peace' the rape of Hong Kong, which had been imprinted starkly on their minds earlier in the year, seems to have been forgotten. Nor did it enter the heads of many men and women that correct behaviour on their part would not necessarily be a passport to correct treatment by their jailers.

Tim Hudson was not of this school of thought. He packed a small bag, soberly prepared for the worst, above all thankful once again that Marjorie had got away. His only real concern was that he had promised Marjorie that if the city fell he would do all he could to help Mei Ling—but now on this last night he found it impossible to get through to Stevens Road. It was not his fault for the Army refused to let him pass, but he would have liked to give her all the Malay money still in his pocket. He would have no use for it, anyway.

Tim remembers that as the night wore on he felt 'fed up and anxious to do something'. There was no ARP post left. Everyone had gone to make some new start in life. The Chinese who had worked so courageously had vanished, probably to their kampongs. And above all, Tim wanted a bath. He had spent most of the day helping to bury the dead —and in order to place the bodies close to each other, he had had to stand in the pits where 'the yielding feeling of the lower bodies was appalling'. He felt he wanted to throw away every stitch of clothing, luxuriate under a shower, and come out a new man, divorced from the reek of death.

On an impulse he set off in the Hillman from the General Hospital for the Central Fire Station on the off-chance of finding Buckeridge. Half-way there his car stuttered to a stop, out of petrol. It was symptomatic of those final hours that Tim got out with his small suitcase, banged the door behind him, and set off walking without ever again sparing a thought for the sturdy little car.

He arrived at Central just as Buckeridge was on the point of leaving. 'Come on,' he said to Tim mysteriously, 'I'm going somewhere that might interest you.'

'All I want,' replied Tim, 'is a bath.'

'Might be able to fix that,' Buckeridge grinned. 'But can *you* fix me up with a drink?'

Hudson suddenly remembered the two bottles of whisky hidden in Dunlop's godown. 'Well, I *might* be able to.' He explained what he had in mind.

Buckeridge still had plenty of petrol so the two old friends set off for Keppel Road. A few lights were appearing now —not street lamps but friendly square patches shining here and there out of buildings. They had to make several detours round bombed streets but Dunlop's godown was still standing, and Buck waited outside in the car while Tim ran in, and found his two bottles of whisky.

As he came out, a small figure emerged from the surrounding shadows. It was a woman, carrying a parcel wrapped in brown paper.

'Mei Ling!' cried Tim.

Hesitatingly, Mei Ling—who had somehow never seemed very interested in her job or her employers—told Hudson that she had been waiting since six o'clock. She had felt sure the tuan would come to his office sooner or later. Tim and Buckeridge pooled all the dollars they had and gave them to her. She accepted the money politely, then held out the paper parcel.

'What's that?' asked Tim Hudson.

'The tuan's dhobi,' answered Mei Ling and opened up the parcel—two spotless shirts, two freshly starched pairs of khaki drill trousers, socks, a lightweight jacket. And on top of the clean-smelling pile was a photo of Marjorie which Mei Ling had taken from Tim's desk. 'It was one of the few times I damn nearly cried,' Hudson admitted later.

234

'Come on,' said Buckeridge—gruffly for him. 'I'll take you for a nice cold bath before you ruin those clothes.'

There was nothing they could do for Mei Ling except drop her in the middle of town. Her family lived somewhere along the east coast, and she was confident she would make her way there unharmed.

'I don't suppose I'll ever see her again,' Tim sighed. 'What a bloody thing war is.' Then he turned to Buckeridge and asked, more cheerfully, 'What's this about a bath?'

Almost gleefully Buckeridge explained. Among the few treasures Lucy had left behind was a small key to the private entrance used by the senior staff at Robinson's. Almost the last advice Lucy had given him was to go to Robinson's 'if the city folds up' in case he needed anything to take into internment. And only a couple of days previously one of Robinson's men had casually passed on the information that as soon as the water supply had been threatened, all the baths on sale in Robinson's plumbing department had been filled to the brim—just in case.

They parked the car behind Raffles Place—now filled with people—and Buckeridge led the way through the courtyard where he had helped to smash up the hundreds of bottles of whisky. They had barely entered the vast, deserted department store when a cheerful woman's voice hailed them, 'Who's there? Come on up!'

The stairs to the upper floor were set at the back of the store—a handsome, wide staircase that split left and right so shoppers could go up one side and down the other. A light was shining—and instinctively they took the left staircase, simply because it was marked 'Up'. At the top stood Mrs. Hutchings, wife of the manager. 'Why! It's Lucy's husband,' she cried, 'I recognise the beard. Don't be alarmed—there's half a dozen more upstairs—though we don't want a crowd. How about a nice cuppa tea?'

In the furniture department a couple of electric bulbs glowed brightly. A dozen or so men sat lounging in the deep armchairs and sofas that nobody would ever buy now. Busily Mrs. Hutchings bustled from one to another with a big tea-pot. Almost guiltily—because it was, after all, against the law—Hudson opened his suitcase and produced his two bottles of whisky. He was about to take a swig before passing the bottles round when Mrs. Hutchings said in shocked tones, 'Oh no! I'll get some glasses and soda from the restaurant!'

235

And this remarkable woman called for volunteers who accompanied her to the basement restaurant, returning with plates and glasses, while two men struggled up the stairs laden with cartons of tinned meat and pineapple. Then, before they started supper, every man raised his stengah and the toast was 'Absent Friends'.

Tim got his bath. In fact he had two, for he had the choice of a dozen baths filled with water. In the ladies' hairdressing department he found some soap, then lay in the first bath, scrubbing himself until the water was black, after which he washed the rest of the dirt off in a second bath. Then he returned to the ladies' hairdressing, found some toilet water and rubbed himself all over. Only when he was finally satisfied that he was clean did he put on the freshly laundered clothes Mei Ling had brought him.

Like the others in Robinson's, Tim Hudson spent his last night of freedom in the luxury of the most expensive and comfortable beds that Singapore had to offer, taking his choice from dozens lined up in the furniture department. He was asleep almost before his head touched the pillow.

Down by the docks Gordon Bennett was in trouble, and it looked as though his plan to escape would get him no further than the edge of the harbour. Various accounts of his bid for freedom (including his own) have told how he 'gave a lift' to a party of planters who had joined the Volunteers and were also bent on escaping. In truth it was the Volunteers who made Gordon Bennett's escape possible, and by a remarkable coincidence they were led by Lance-Bombardier M. C. Hay—none other than the husband of Marjorie Hay, who gave us such a vivid description of the dismissal of Stanley Jones. Hay had thrown up his important job as Inspector of Mines to join the Volunteers, and had fought his way from Kuala Lumpur to the island. On this last night, with a bunch of friends, he had received permission to escape, and they had set off for the docks. Hay happened to be a brilliant linguist, who spoke amongst other languages Hindustani and Chinese—and like Marjorie, his wife, he kept an excellent, detailed diary.

Deciding to go on foot, the grimy, tired men made their way through the city to the docks 'waving lighted cigarettes about to show we were not Japs'. They were repeatedly challenged by sentries, but as most of them were Indians Hay

236

was able to answer in Hindustani. Eventually they reached a landing stage where 'we met General Gordon Bennett and two other Australian officers. They had found a sampan, but could not find the oars, and appeared to have no idea of how to row it.' Bennett told Hay that he planned to make for Malacca, on the west coast of Malaya, in the hope of finding a large boat. (Since Malacca was near Johore, Bennett was possibly banking on help from the Sultan.) Hay, however, said firmly that he had heard that some junks were anchored in the outer roads, and planned to find one and make straight for Sumatra. It was obviously a far better plan than Bennett's, and it did not take the Australians long to agree that the two parties should join forces.

Hay—a man of infinite resource—quickly found the missing oars for the sampan. As it was not big enough for them all, Hay agreed to take along the Australians, leaving his own comrades on the dockside for the moment. He wanted to find a boat capable of taking all of them into the harbour to search for the junks. He soon found one—a *twakow* with better oars, lying offshore. Then he started to return to pick up his friends. At this point, 'the general said he wanted to start out to sea at once. I pointed out that the object of coming to find a larger boat was so the parties should proceed together, and that I did not propose to leave my friends.' Slightly disgusted, Hay offered to give the General the *twakow* and find another one for his party, whereupon the general's ADC—obviously realising the value of keeping Hay —hurriedly said they should all stick together.

Eventually they did find three junks. They boarded one which had a Chinese crew on board, only to find that the *taikong* (master) 'was just settling down to a pipe of opium', and flatly refused to sail until the following morning. Hay was not the sort of man to be put off. For years he had been used to dealing with recalcitrant Chinese in the tin mines. Without a moment's hesitation he jerked the skipper's pipe out of the man's mouth and 'confiscated' his opium, telling him in forceful, fluent Chinese that there would be no smoking until the junk was under way. Then—having established his authority and knowing his Chinese—Hay suggested to Gordon Bennett that he should give the *taikong* a present, at which the Australian handed over a hundred dollars.

Ten minutes later the old junk slipped her moorings and they were heading south.

Barely a mile away from the escaping junk—and separated only by the brief stretch of Battery Road from Hudson in Robinson's—the hundred or so leading civilians of Singapore were also preparing for their last night of freedom before the Japanese troops made their triumphal entry into the city on the following morning. The first vague rumours were beginning to circulate. Some said all civilians would be lined up on the Cricket Club padang. Others that 'senior officers will be allowed to remain at large—we'll be needed to run the city for the Japs'.

The Governor's wife was responding to treatment for her dysentery, but she was still too weak to leave her bed. Sir Shenton Thomas, however, left their small room after a makeshift supper, and late that night stood with Hugh Fraser looking out of Fullerton Building at the light of a watery moon dancing on the sea, the pale gold mingling with the scarlet of the flames down by the docks. The Governor had just heard that 'Dickie' Dickinson had had a major operation, but had not recovered consciousness. It would be touch and go whether he lived. For half an hour the two men stood there, alone and busy with their thoughts. The time was almost midnight. After just seventy days of war—was it really only seventy days since the first Japanese air raid on Singapore? —the city was quiet. Fraser recalled afterwards that they hardly exchanged a word, except when the Governor turned to him and—not really speaking, but thinking aloud—said in a voice that echoed everything he most passionately believed in, 'It doesn't matter about us. It's the people I'm sorry for. It's *their* country—and somehow we've let them down.'

It was the end of the siege of Singapore. It was the end of the war in Malaya. But for many thousands the real killing was yet to come.

PART THREE

AFTER

CHAPTER ELEVEN

THE ROAD TO CHANGI

Monday, February 16—Monday, March 9

Soon after dawn on Monday the first Japanese troops entered the city. With an irony hard to match, almost the first step the victors took was to ask the British officials in key posts to carry on as usual. For now the Japanese unexpectedly faced overwhelming administrative problems. They had advanced 650 miles from Singora in Siam to the harbour in Singapore in seventy days—a remarkable average of nine miles a day. As a result they had so overstretched themselves that not even the most sanguine Japanese staff officers had been prepared for victory so soon. The Japanese High Command had estimated it would take a hundred days to reach and storm Singapore. They had expected the 'fortress' to fight to the last man. Instead, their forces had taken the city with a month to spare —a city now crowded with a population of a million civilians, and over eighty thousand hungry troops. Japanese civil government officers—their plans for running Singapore still unfinished—were at the moment of capitulation enjoying life in Bangkok, over a thousand miles to the north.

There was only one thing to be done. The Japanese appealed to the British to help. British firemen, doctors, nurses, water engineers, health and sanitary workers were asked to remain at their posts until their Japanese counterparts arrived. Fires were still burning, wounded were still dying, water was still running to waste. And the only people in a position to restore some semblance of order were the conquered British.

The city was in a fantastic state. When Tim Hudson walked out of Robinson's into Raffles Place, after his night's sleep in the furniture department, he found it crowded with hundreds of British, Australian and Indian soldiers, squatting quietly on the pavements, smoking as they philosophically awaited their future. One group of noisy Australians was dominated by the figure of a soldier wearing a top hat. As though unable to realise the significance of what had happened,[1] many soldiers were laughing and joking—especially those whose shirts bulged with tins of looted cigarettes. Round the corner in narrow Battery Road, Hudson could not walk along the path, which was barred by half a dozen kneeling soldiers, intent on a game of solo, and with a huge pile of loose cash in 'the kitty'. Above them the first signs of defeat met Tim's eyes—a couple of white sheets hanging from an upstairs window. Already small Japanese flags were fluttering from scores of shops, almost as though they had been furtively hidden for weeks for just such an occasion. Some Indian soldiers boasted Japanese flags hurriedly sewn or pinned on their tunics. Others had tied strips of white cloth round their helmets.

On Collyer Quay he came across the extraordinary sight of an Indian soldier in an abandoned car discarding his uniform for a suit of civilian white drill. All the Asian shops had been boarded up, and in the main streets hardly a Chinese or Malay was to be seen. Even Change Alley was silent except for a few scavenging coolies. The area was like a ghost town in which a million men, women and children hid behind the shutters of their houses and shops—a curious contrast to the tens of thousands of soldiers aimlessly thronging the streets.

Soon Hudson caught his first glimpse of the conquerors—short, tough sentries at most corners and bridges 'lugging rifles with bayonets that were bigger than they were'. More and more Japanese staff cars started to screech and blare through the city, recklessly dodging fallen cables, potholes, or corpses. A thousand Britishers, armed with staves, patrolled the centre of the city trying to prevent looting or disorder; for the most part the Japanese sentries seemed uninterested in their activities. In River Valley Road, Hudson came across a free-for-all between British and Indian troops wrangling over the contents of three abandoned army trucks. Half a dozen Japanese sentries idly watched without making any attempt to stop the fight.

On the other hand Japanese officers had no compunction about forcibly illustrating that they were the masters, as Brigadier Simson discovered when, for no apparent reason, he was taken for a two-hour ride round the city sitting in the

[1] Empire military casualties for the entire campaign totalled 138,708, of whom more than 130,000 troops became prisoners of war. Japanese battle casualties totalled 9,824.

242

back seat of a car between two young Japanese officers. It gave him 'an early demonstration of Japanese medieval culture' for as they approached the docks, Simson saw about fifteen coolies, their arms cruelly trussed behind their backs with barbed wire. They had been caught in the act of looting. Eight were Chinese, who, as the horrified brigadier watched, were pushed forward. An executioner with a two-handed Samurai sword appeared and promptly beheaded them in front of the crowd. The others—Indians and Malays—were released with a caution, for they were part of the new Co-Prosperity Sphere, while the Chinese were sworn enemies.

Even though the Japanese ruthlessly beheaded Chinese looters—for they reserved a special vengeance for the Chinese—many Japanese and British soldiers seemed to be on almost friendly terms. Men who would later be brutally beaten merely for some technical offence of manners now replied as equals to those Japanese who spoke to them in English. Colonel Tsuji[2] was so astonished at the number of vital installations still undamaged that he asked a young British officer, 'Why didn't you destroy Singapore?' Spiritedly the officer retorted, 'Because we will return again!' Unperturbed, Tsuji persisted, 'But don't you believe Britain is beaten in this war?' 'We may be defeated ninety-nine times,' replied the officer, 'but in the final round we'll win.'

Amongst the other ranks a similar tolerance sometimes prevailed. One British platoon was loading its luggage on a truck before setting off for prisoner of war camp in Changi barracks when a Japanese soldier beckoned the sergeant to follow him into a nearby house. Neither could speak the other's language, but with excited signs the Japanese pointed to an old upright piano in the abandoned house, urging the British soldiers to take it along. They did—and it survived three and a half years.

Though the Japanese had announced on the radio that those in 'essential occupations' would not be immediately interned, Hudson had no delusions that he would fall into this category. Some, however, were not sure. Tommy Kitching sought out the Governor—still in his room at the Club—and asked him hopefully if he could stay out. Sir Shenton thanked him for all the work he had put in, but told him, 'Kitching—if the Japanese ask me why the Chief Surveyor is essential, I'd find it very hard to say why.' Kitching didn't argue. The

[2] Author of *Singapore: The Japanese Version.*

243

two men shook hands and parted, after which Kitching returned to Fullerton Building, where his Chinese clerk, waiting to say good-bye, asked him for a personal souvenir. Kitching gave him a serviette ring, and 'after expressing his sorrow and sympathy, he departed immensely pleased with it.'

As befits a surveyor Kitching was an extremely methodical man, and he had long since prepared what he considered to be the bare essentials for his 'internment kit'. Now he made a note in his diary of every item as he packed his small suitcase. It makes a fascinating—and highly practical—list:

'Iodine, Dettol, Andrews Liver Salts, Elastoplast, toilet soap, 2 prs. shorts, 3 sweat shirts, 2 prs. stockings, 1 pr. shoes, a sheet, my dark blue blazer, 1 pr. flannels, 2 handkerchiefs, 2 sweat rags, shaving tackle, pencil, paper, hair brush, comb, aspirin, vitamin pills, plate, mug, knife, fork, spoon, towel, 2 face towels, serviette (as dish cloth), Asepso soap, scissors, electric torch.'

A couple of floors below, in his bedroom, the Governor was receiving another visitor—this time a Japanese intelligence officer who told Shenton Thomas that all civilians should assemble at the Cricket Club padang the following morning. This, however, was not the only object of his visit. As Sir Shenton listened coldly, the Japanese said he had been instructed to ask the Governor one specific question: How had Britain and the United States divided their spheres of influence in the Pacific? Though obviously he must have known the answer, Sir Shenton retorted that he had not the slightest intention of divulging the information. 'It's a pity for you, sir,' said the Japanese in a matter-of-fact voice. 'We're bound to find out sooner or later anyway.'

While most of Singapore uneasily awaited a fate of which they could not be certain, the General Hospital was in a turmoil. On the Monday the Japanese announced that every single one of the thousands of patients had to be evacuated within twenty-four hours. They wanted the hospital for their own wounded by Tuesday afternoon. Over a thousand civilian patients who could walk had to leave for their homes almost immediately. More than seven hundred civilians were hastily sent in convoys of ambulances to the Singapore Asylum, from which mental patients had already been evacuated to an island in the harbour. The military, numbering about 1,300, were sent either to the Singapore Club in Fullerton Building, the Cricket Club or the Victoria Memorial Hall. It was chaos. By the Tuesday morning every single Chinese boy and amah had vanished. Freddy Bloom remembers that it was impossible to cook any lunch, though she did find a case of sardines and some bread which the nurses and patients shared. Freddy at least had one stroke of luck. Normally she might have expected to go to the Asylum with the civilians, but Philip Bloom, as a major in the RAMC, was able to arrange for her to accompany him to the Singapore Club to tend wounded troops rather than civilians. At least they would be together until the last moment.

There were others who longed desperately to be together for the few hours of liberty that remained, including two members of an unusual group gathered in the matron's office at the General. It included a young, good-looking lieutenant called Alastair MacKenzie of the Malay Regiment, who before the war had been an executive with the Singapore branch of the Commercial Union Assurance Company, and by his side, a pretty volunteer nurse called Sybil Osborn, dressed in hospital white spattered with blood, her dark brown hair covered in a white square, for she had come straight from an operating theatre. Facing them stood the frail figure of Archdeacon Graham-White of the Cathedral. And there, in the matron's office, he finally came to the magic words, 'I now pronounce you man and wife.'

Sybil and Alastair had been engaged for some time, but the war had divided their lives. Now that it was all over he had wanted to get married in the brief spell of liberty still left. It had taken him two hours to find Sybil in the confusion of the hospital. He had had no time to buy a ring, but at the last moment Sybil remembered a keepsake—too big for her—that she had kept in her pocket. He slipped it on her finger, after which the Archdeacon wrote out, from memory, the marriage certificate (which was witnessed by the matron) on a slip of hospital paper. Within a few minutes Alastair had left to rejoin his regiment. He managed to snatch a few more moments with Sybil before internment, but it was three and a half years before they saw each other again.

Life in the General Hospital had been hard, but it was nothing compared with the primitive conditions that awaited

Freddy Bloom and the ten other MAS women when they reached the Singapore Club Fullerton Building.

The large main club room, with its long bar at one side, was crowded with rows of wounded—hundreds of them, some on stretchers, some on beds, some on the floor. Freddy and the others were steered to the bar and offered a glass of lime juice. As she stood there sipping it, looking round the incongruous surroundings, the sober walls of the lofty room, the pretentious marble pillars, the plain mahogany bar— she could not help reflecting that this was probably the first time in the history of the club that women had penetrated this male holy of holies.

Going on duty, Freddy found that every corridor, every ante-room, was overflowing with wounded. Feeling helpless in these new, unfamiliar surroundings, Freddy stood talking to a soldier when a doctor bustled up and, seeing her nurse's uniform, said briskly, 'Prepare the patient for an operation. Give him a quarter of a grain of morphia and dress his arm.' Before Freddy had time to reply, the doctor had hurried on. Freddy had never given an injection in her life, but at least she felt she could make a start by dressing the arm of the soldier, who seemed to be little more than a boy. He was, however, very cheerful. 'Got a fag?' he asked with a grin. Freddy pulled out a pack. 'You'll have to light it for me,' he apologised, and as she knelt down, she saw that the 'arm' she had to dress was nothing more than a bloodied stump.

'Just a minute,' gasped Freddy before rushing into a corner and vomiting.

That was Freddy's introduction to a nightmare world which lasted two weeks—two weeks in which a handful of semi-trained women had to do everything—hauling buckets of water up flights of stairs, emptying lavatories by hand, giving injections, improvising bandages, plus most of the cooking. At night the only illumination in the big room—apart from the occasional in-and-out glow of a cigarette being puffed —came from the lighted electric clock. The nights were filled with cries of 'Sister' or 'Water!' The water shortage heightened her sense of despair almost as much as the sight of pain, for often there was not more than a single cup to share amongst a score of groaning men. The best she could hope to do was to pass the cup from man to man so that each one could at least wet his swollen cracked lips. More than one man went mad. Some tried hour after hour to get out

246

of bed, motivated by a wild hallucination that it was their duty to escape and fight again.

When the patients had been quietened, Freddy had to take her turn at cooking. Luckily there was plenty of food, though it was all tinned, but the kitchen was on the fourth floor and the only water was on the ground floor until an engineer found an ancient petrol engine and was able to pump water to the top of the building where it was mixed with tinned porridge and soup, the mainstays of the patients' diets.

Inevitably in makeshift surroundings, much of the careful training of the MAS women now frequently had to be forgotten or ignored. Nobody could adhere to a rigid set of rules in a world that had no rules of its own. Because they *were* volunteers, the MAS had been carefully trained to regard each patient with strict impersonality. They had, for instance, been warned that jobs like body washing had to be done 'with discretion'. They had also been warned about 'nakedness'. Now it passed unnoticed. Katherine de Moubray, the volunteer MAS wife of a high Government official, recorded how she went to help two orderlies washing blood-stained uniforms, 'and had a good two minutes conversation with one of them, scrubbing clothes on the floor, before I even noticed the second man was naked'.

Some of the orderlies kept a predatory eye open for possible last-minute affairs, as Katherine de Moubray discovered when in the darkness one man suddenly took her in his arms and kissed her. Katherine got rid of him without any trouble—by pointing out gently that they were almost standing on a row of corpses sewn in blankets.

Dr. Cicely Williams and her family of children were also facing more and more difficulties. Abruptly she had been told to evacuate them from the Dental Department to a maternity block behind the hospital. Somehow she and a few volunteers carried the babies to their new quarters, after which Cicely Williams discovered there was no water. She now set about carrying water herself the two hundred yards from the General until the hospital authorities were able to send over a water cart.

Then the next morning, 'just as I was beginning to get things straight', Cicely Williams was ordered to move again —this time to the Mental Hospital. As she noted despairingly in her diary, 'This shifting about from place to place is a sort of disease that people get in war-time, and is one of its worst horrors'. Dreading the move that lay ahead, Cicely Williams knew that she and her helpers could not carry on much longer. Her health was rapidly giving out. She had started a bout of dysentery, and due to the walking and lack of washing in the tropical heat, 'my feet were only kept together with Elastoplast'.

Haunted by the fear of what would happen to her tiny charges if she were taken to hospital, Cicely Williams hit on a brilliant idea—one that would at least give some of her babies a sporting chance in life. She began to give them away. It had started by chance, when Cicely Williams found herself facing more and more distraught parents who had arrived to see their wounded children, only to discover they had died. To weeping mothers she could not even give any records of what had happened for all had been lost in one of the moves. Nor could she hope to find the bodies in the mass grave pits. More to console one hysterical mother than for any other reason Cicely Williams suggested that she should take another baby in place of her own. The offer was accepted with such alacrity that Cicely Williams tried it on again. Soon delighted parents had told their neighbours, and a stream of Chinese who had heard that the white doctor 'was giving away children for nothing' arrived at the hospital. In many ways it was a heart-breaking business, for Cicely Williams could not know any details about the prospective parents, and had to trust her judgment and instinct. Yet 'I felt that almost any sort of home might be better than the treatment we were producing.' She gave ten away that morning.

On the floor below Cicely Williams in the Mental Hospital, a VIP had arrived from the General Hospital—'Dickie' Dickinson, who was so badly injured that he remained in a coma for three days. He woke up to find himself with hundreds of civilian patients on the floor of the asylum. His major operation had been successful, though he was still on the danger list and it would be three months before he was well enough to be transferred to Changi. Two things had helped to pull him through. For the first three or four days Bunny, his wife, was able to stay with him, before she was taken off to the women's camp. And though the Japanese had warned the British to leave every item of medical equipment and drugs behind when evacuating the General Hospital, Bunny had managed to slip a Dunlopillo mattress into his ambulance; more—she had secretly deflated it, and then stuffed it with all the drugs and medicines she could lay her hands on.

By ten o'clock on the Tuesday morning two thousand men, together with three hundred women and children, were lined up in the blazing sun on the Cricket Club padang. The men were at one end, the women and children at the other. It was one of the hottest days of the year. Not even the sea, which almost lapped its edge, could provide a breeze to temper the stifling heat that beat down relentlessly on this beautiful sports ground, with the blue water on one side and the Municipal Buildings, flanked by flame trees, on the other.

This was the first batch of internees—for some men like Buckeridge and women like Freddy Bloom, were still 'essential' and at liberty—and it was a heart-rending scene of chaos. Men stood miserably by their pathetic bundles of salvaged luggage. The women, their frocks already limp with sweat, were not allowed to talk to the men, but tried desperately to hold back their tears as they made sure the children, playing cheerfully, kept on their hats against the sun. Some women had brought prams in which to carry their belongings. A few dogs scampered about, unable to realise their mistresses would soon be leaving them. Inevitably a few of the 'heartier' women made it their business to try to cheer up the despondent ones, but there was little they could do. The confusion reminded one woman of a railway terminal on a Bank Holiday, with mothers losing children, mislaying packages, and occasionally fainting. And around the padang, framed in the flame trees, a crowd of Asians squatted, silent and sympathetic. If the Japanese had hoped for scenes which would humiliate the whites, they were disappointed.

In a knot slightly apart from the other men stood the senior government officials who had walked across Anderson Bridge from the Singapore Club. Sir Shenton Thomas was dressed in newly-pressed clean white ducks. Already he had come in contact with the enemy. Now on the padang, the Governor held his head high, for he felt (as he said later) that he was with his people, and he wanted to take his punishment as they did, without fear or favour. Already, however, he was to be singled out as 'a special case to be humiliated' for though the Japanese permitted several senior officials to drive to the first camp, they specifically insisted that the Governor should walk the whole distance.

Everybody had been told officially to bring clothes for ten days, but that food would be provided. After a wait of two hours a Japanese officer climbed on a wooden box and addressed the assembly. The Japanese would observe international law and protect all internees, he promised them. The civilians were to make for a point—which he didn't specify —near the Sea View Hotel at Katong. They would remain there for a few days before going to Changi. The Japanese would provide transport for women and children, and for baggage. The men would walk. And then he dropped a bombshell. 'Everybody,' he announced, 'must provide their own food.'

This was disastrous. The official order had categorically said food would be provided. Some, like Tim Hudson, had put a tin or two of food in their suitcases or rucksacks. Others, like Tommy Kitching, made a quick dash to the Cricket Club pavilion and found 'a very dry biscuit or two' and some water for the march.

Since nobody seemed to be moving off the padang, another thought now struck Kitching. He had noticed some government officials drive off. He also had a car and petrol. Why not drive out to the Sea View? It was 12.40 and already they had spent nearly three hours in the hot sun. So Kitching and four colleagues just walked off the padang—observed, but not restrained—got into Kitching's car and drove out along the coast road. Occasionally they were stopped by Japanese sentries 'who seemed to be more bewildered than us', before arriving at a big block of flats near the Sea View Hotel. This, they felt sure, must be their first internment camp.

Later, however, all hope of living in the block of luxury flats was rudely shattered by a Japanese officer who announced that, for the time being, the women would live in a group of houses a few hundred yards down the road, while the men were given the option of either staying in the local police station or in another group of four old houses. All who could made for the houses, for their large compound at least led to a strip of beach.

It was nightfall before the last of the long procession of civilians finally arrived at this, their first stop. It had been a grim march, with Sir Shenton bravely leading the straggling column through the heat of the day. One of his closest friends, who had been allowed to use his car, deliberately drove behind the column in case the Governor needed help, but he never faltered; he had been sustained, he said afterwards, by the sympathy of the Asians lining the route—weeping women, or men who rushed out with a handful of biscuits or a bottle of water.

Now the civilians had their first taste of filth and squalor. The houses had been stripped of every item of furniture. They were scrofulous. The mosquitoes never seemed to stop biting, though Kitching managed to snatch an hour or two of fitful sleep by wrapping himself completely in a sheet and covering his face with a handkerchief. His last thought as he drifted off was that his son Brian (safely in England) 'would had liked pancakes today—so would I.' For it was Shrove Tuesday.

(As the first civilians tried to sleep on the stone floors at Katong, the first troops were arriving at the military barracks at Changi, where they would be housed separately from the civilians, who would go to Changi jail. They had marched the nine miles in one day, in a column led by generals, four files of brigadiers and colonels, each man humping his kit bag and anything else he could manage to carry.)

During the first days at Katong the Japanese showed no signs of the bestiality that was later to smear forever their honourable code of Bushido. True, there was not enough food, and the condition of the children was already pitiful, but it seems that this was due more to maladministration than to deliberate cruelty and several men were surprisingly given permission to leave the 'camp' at Katong if they could produce a sufficiently valid reason.

Hugh Bryson, clerk to the courts (amongst other jobs), persuaded a Japanese sentry to let a small group borrow a lorry and drive to their houses to pick up anything that would be useful during internment. Bryson reached his home in Mount Pleasant, only to find it had been stripped of every item except a few old photographs which had been swept into a corner. So he went to the next-door bungalow. There nothing had been touched. He took what he felt would be useful, including an assortment of ladies' clothes which he handed over to the women's camp on his way back.

Christopher Dawson, the Secretary of Defence, was also allowed out on a foraging expedition. He was given a special sticker for his car, and warned to report to the Tanglin Club on his way back to camp, where a Japanese officer would examine everything he had collected. Dawson, prompted by a feeling that this would be a long, long internment, gathered together all the books he could find from the houses of friends, and towards evening presented himself at the Tanglin Club. The Japanese officer carefully scrutinised each book, finding nothing contraband, until his eye lit on one word in a suspicious title. Carefully he examined the book over and over again. He knew the implications of that secret service word on the title page—and flatly refused Dawson permission to take along P. G. Wodehouse's *The Code of the Woosters*.

One other item was of course banned from Katong—whisky. But even so one bottle went into camp—well, in a fashion—for Hugh Bryson remembers standing by the camp gate when a straggler arrived clutching a bottle of Scotch. It was almost full. Sternly the Japanese warned the man that on no account could he bring it in. 'Okay!' cried the man cheerfully, and pulling out the cork, put the bottle to his lips and drained it to the last drop before staggering into camp.

Across the dead calm seas south of the island a flotilla of small ships—Singapore's 'Dunkirk'—struggled vainly to reach the sanctuary of Sumatra or any of the hundreds of islands sitting astride the equator. Sampans, rowing boats, junks, yachts from the Singapore Yacht Club with idly flapping sails, launches with feeble, puttering outboard motors, tourist launches ('Round the Harbour $5') and the occasional ancient gunboat carried over three thousand men and women. To a Dutch reconnaissance pilot who saw the scene far below, the stream of slowly-moving boats amidst the tiny islets on the unrippled sea 'looked just like models on a sheet of glass'.

Every stratum of humanity crouched in the vessels. There were generals, an admiral, an air marshal. There were hundreds of women and children. There were deserters who had slipped away secretly under cover of dark. 'Some of the larger boats also carried deserters who had forced their way on board at the point of the pistol.'³ Though nearly fifty vessels were sailing under official evacuation schemes, not a soul aboard them had formed any real plans. Every man—from general to deserter—was bound by only one compelling

³ *The War Against Japan.*

252

human instinct: to put as many miles as possible between them and the nightmare through which they had somehow managed to live thus far.

At first all had seemed to be going well. Unseen currents of the north-east monsoon, now on the wane, guided them slowly in a south-westerly direction towards Sumatra; the bigger vessels (a comparative term) were routed for Java via the Banka Strait, a strip of water separating the east coast of Sumatra from Banka Island. With each hour that passed, with each mile of flat water that receded astern, fears began to dwindle, hopes began to rise. For not one of them had the faintest inkling that Admiral Ozawa of the Japanese Navy was already lying in wait for them with two eight-inch cruisers, a carrier and three destroyers. Tokyo radio had cried, 'There will be no Dunkirk at Singapore. The British are not going to be allowed to get away with it this time. All ships leaving will be destroyed.' Admiral Ozawa was there to make certain the threat was not an idle boast.

The people in the boats did not know another dreadful fact: almost before they had left the blazing harbour of Singapore, the Dutch in Sumatra had learned the whereabouts of Ozawa's fleet and had been frantically tapping out messages to the last remaining wireless set in Singapore, with a warning that Ozawa had spread his warships across the approaches to the Strait while aircraft from his carrier were scouring the waters to the north. Naturally the messages had been in code, but—irony of ironies—the man with the code book had been evacuated, and he had taken the only copy with him. The messages were received, but nobody could unravel the jargon of the ciphers.

Ozawa launched his first attack at dawn with cruisers, destroyers and aircraft, which blew the defenceless, over-crowded vessels out of the water. Out of the forty-four ships which had sailed under Admiral Spooner's official evacuation on Black Friday, forty were sunk by bombs or gunfire. Scores of other vessels, including an evacuation flotilla that had left on the Thursday, suffered a similar fate.

Those who escaped were wrecked on the small desert islands that dot the archipelago. Some starved to death, some died of thirst, some of tropical diseases. The tiny launch carrying Admiral Spooner, Air Vice-Marshal Pulford and a small party of officers and men was beached on a small mala-rial island barely twenty miles from Banka. For two months they suffered agonising privations. Eighteen died, including the Admiral and the Air Marshal, before the remnants managed to cross to Sumatra in a native boat and surrender.

No one has ever been able to compute accurately the number of boats and lives that were lost, for the simple reason that scores of deserters or private parties of civilians left unofficially, without any record having been kept. Yet one thing seems fairly certain. If only the fleeing vessels had been able to make some form of contact or understanding with the Japanese, many, many lives would have been saved, as the story of the *Giang Bee* shows.

This was the vessel on which Rob Scott had sailed, and it provides a typical example not only of the awful fate which overtook many vessels, but of the frustrations and errors caused by the language barrier, and we have to thank Scott for a detailed official report of exactly what occurred. Though damaged by repeated air attacks, the *Giang Bee* managed to survive until she was 170 miles south of Singapore, when Japanese warships appeared on the horizon. The captain ordered the white ensign to be lowered and told all the women to show themselves on deck. As two destroyers came towards them at high speed, the Japanese signalled the *Giang Bee* in incomprehensible Morse code, and the *Giang Bee* tried in vain to explain that she wished to surrender. Finally the Japanese appeared to understand the *Giang Bee*'s request to them to send a party on board, for a launch took off from one destroyer. It was within a hundred and fifty yards of the *Giang Bee* when an RAF bomber from Sumatra suddenly appeared and started circling overhead. The Japanese opened fire, the plane flew off, the enemy launch was recalled—and the British lost their only opportunity of making contact with the destroyers, of which two remained about half a mile away with their guns trained on the *Giang Bee*.

Now followed a period of eerie, uneasy waiting. Why didn't the destroyer sink them? What were they waiting for? Nobody knew. Nobody could find out. As the hot day cooled off, and the red sunset turned to dusk with tropical swiftness, the Japanese destroyers trained their searchlights on the *Giang Bee*. And still nothing happened. Finally, around 7.30, the captain decided to order all women and children to take to the boats. He was convinced his ship would be sunk at any moment. 'It was a heart-rending business,' Scott remembers. 'In the darkness, lit by the gleam of enemy searchlights, we packed about fifty into each boat. A heavy sea and a strong tide swept the lifeboats astern as soon as they cast off.' Distracted mothers searched for their children—there were eleven in one Eurasian family alone—'but all we could do was pack in as many as possible, lower the boat and let it go, regardless of missing children and friends'.

Earlier air-raid damage now came to light. The ropes supporting one lifeboat parted as she was being lowered, spilling her passengers into the darkness. A second lifeboat was successfully lowered, but she had been holed by splinters and 'as she drifted astern we could hear the passengers crying out that they were foundering'. When the last lifeboat had been cast off, there were still about a hundred on board and in a final despairing effort to make contact with the enemy, the captain decided that a party should try to row the ship's thirteen-foot harbour dinghy to the nearest destroyer and ask the Japanese to help the women and children and to make it clear that he wished to surrender. Somehow the dinghy was lowered into the heavy seas, and Rob Scott, together with three others, set off for the destroyers.

To their amazement, the Japanese destroyers refused to have anything to do with the tiny, unarmed cockleshell. For two hours in heavy seas, lit up by Japanese searchlights, 'we rowed in frantic but vain efforts to reach a destroyer.' In a bizarre and incredible game of ocean 'tag', played in the dark, the British boat would almost reach a destroyer, which would then adroitly move just out of range. Time after time the tiny dinghy was within a few yards of the enemy, but 'it was hopeless for a small unseaworthy dinghy in heavy seas to try and catch a destroyer which did not wish to be caught.'

They were still trying when, about 10.30 p.m. what they had, all expected happened. Without warning one of the destroyers fired six rounds at the *Giang Bee*. She glowed red from stem to stern and sank in a few minutes. The Japanese dimmed their searchlights, and the destroyers quickly made off.

To this day Rob Scott is convinced that the Japanese, when they first intercepted the *Giang Bee*, did not intend to sink her. 'Otherwise, why not have done it on sight?' he asked. 'I learnt later that a number of other ships caught in that area were ordered . . . to surrender. This involved no loss of life.

The enemy gained a ship. I think that if we had been able to understand the Japanese signals this is what they probably wanted us to do. About 200 lives might have been saved.'

In the darkness, Scott's dinghy managed to pick up a few survivors and after five days the exhausted party reached a fishing village on the coast of Sumatra, where at first Scott was hidden and looked after, but later denounced, when it was discovered that his name was on a 'wanted' blacklist. He was finally shipped back to Singapore. For Rob Scott the worst part of his war was just about to begin.

While Scott had been trying to catch the Japanese destroyers and offer to surrender, other strange fates were overtaking some of the characters whom we have come to know, and one at least became the central figure in a true saga that would tax the imagination of any fiction writer. Group Captain Nunn, head of the Public Works Department, had, in the words of the Governor, 'thoroughly blotted his copy book' by leaving with his wife on the *Kuala* when he knew perfectly well that he was under orders to remain at his post. When the *Kuala* was sunk, Nunn, his wife, and some of the PWD officials who had left with him were marooned on Pompong Island in the Java Sea, where Nunn, according to those who survived, quickly became 'King' of the island. He had of course held a senior position, but he also must have shown considerable resourcefulness, for in typical Robinson Crusoe fashion he managed to get a fair supply of food for his party off the *Kuala* before she went to the bottom, so that they had enough to eat until help arrived in the form of friendly natives from Sumatra. Other small parties had also reached Pompong, but Nunn had established his authority by the absurd announcement that he was carrying highly confidential documents from the Governor which he had to hand over to General Wavell,[4] and now when the unexpected fishing boats arrived he promptly commandeered the only vessel with an auxiliary engine for himself, his wife and his closest cronies, leaving behind key RAF personnel, many of whom fell into Japanese hands. Nunn reached Sumatra, bluffed his way to the head of the queue of escapers, and on February 26 sailed with his wife for Colombo on the SS *Rooseboome*.

[4] There was of course no truth in this. The Governor later held an official enquiry on the evacuation of Nunn and PWD officials, with legal affidavits from the survivors, which remain today in his private papers.

256

Among his fellow passengers was a young officer, Lieutenant G. G. Gibson. The long voyage across the Indian Ocean was uneventful, and when the *Rooseboome* was a bare thirty-six hours out of Colombo, the passengers, including Nunn, of course, met in the saloon to celebrate their impending arrival in a safe port. Spirits were high when, at ten minutes to midnight, a Japanese submarine surfaced. She fired only one torpedo, which hit the old Dutch steamer amidships. Three of the four lifeboats were smashed. The *Rooseboome* herself sank in four minutes, but Nunn's last action was to grab hold of his wife and push her through an opening in the torn side of the sinking vessel. He had no time to escape himself and went down with the ship.[5]

Not all who tried to escape died, though some who lived paid for the privilege. General Gordon Bennett reached Sumatra after an adventurous trip, and almost immediately flew to Australia. He called on General Sturdee, the Chief of the Australian General Staff, where 'to my dismay,' Bennett remembered, 'my reception was cold and hostile. No other member of the Military Board called in to see me. After a few minutes' formal conversation, Sturdee told me that my escape was ill-advised, or words to that effect. I was too shocked to say much. He then went on with his work, leaving me to stand aside in his room.'[6]

[5] The story does not end here. Mrs. Nunn, clutching a piece of wreckage, survived the night, and when dawn broke the few who had scrambled into the only lifeboat found there were 135 survivors, most of them in the sea. Eighty managed to, get into the lifeboat. The rest clung to the sides. Hoping for the best, for they were not very far from Colombo, they waited for a passing ship to see them. None appeared. Even worse, the boat, with its human beings clinging to the gunwales, started drifting remorselessly eastwards. For twenty-six days no ship appeared. Day after day under the tropical sun, more survivors died of thirst or sunstroke. Mrs. Nunn lasted some days but finally—according to a signed statement by Gibson in Sir Shenton Thomas's papers—'she died in the life boat where, before her death, her conduct was beyond praise. I personally put her body over the side. She said that Nunn himself had sacrificed his life to get her off the sinking ship.' By the time the lifeboat beached itself on a remote island sixty miles west of Sumatra, only four were left alive—a Chinese girl, two Malays, and Gibson, of whom Gibson was the only one to survive Japanese torture after capture.

[6] After the war General Percival wrote to the Australian Army Board about Bennett's conduct, and a judicial enquiry was held into his escape. The finding was that Gordon Bennett should have remained

One other important Australian managed to reach land. Henry Bowden, the Australian Commissioner who had at first been refused permission to escape, was ploughing through the Banka Strait in the *Mary Rose* when a searchlight from a Japanese patrol boat suddenly stabbed the darkness. There was nothing to do but surrender, and the captain seems to have realised the urgency of making the Japanese understand that they agreed, for though they had no white flag to hoist, one of the party took off his underpants and waved them. The Japanese understood, and the men were taken to Banka Island where, as their baggage was being examined, Bowden complained to a guard and brusquely demanded to see a Japanese officer so that he could furnish proof of his diplomatic status. Possibly Bowden, a tough Australian who did not pull his punches, was not quite as tactful as the situation demanded, for though he was elderly and white haired, he was first punched and threatened with the bayonet, and when he showed no signs of meek obedience, was taken out by two guards. 'Squaring his shoulders he was led from the hall. . . . About half an hour later two shots were heard, and the guards returned cleaning their rifles.' They had taken him outside, made him dig his own grave, and shot him at the edge of it.

All this, of course, was unknown in Singapore. Back in the bomb-scarred city the bewildered troops and the stunned civilians were preparing in their different ways for the grim years that lay ahead. Now, as before, the war caused inequalities. Some men and women went into internment, others were still left in comparative freedom to help the Japanese to get the city on its feet again.

Typical of these was 'Buck' Buckeridge, who of all the civilians who had fought throughout the siege experienced perhaps the least painful transition from war to 'peace'. It was not wholly painless, for as Buck wrote, 'one could never, never forget the feeling of humiliation'. But while thousands of civilians now suddenly found themselves with endless idle hours in which to think, Buckeridge was work-

---

with his troops 'until surrender was complete' but that his escape was 'inspired by high patriotism and by the belief that he was acting in Australia's best interests'. He was never again asked to serve in the field, and retired from the Army. He died of a heart attack in 1962, aged 65.

ing from dawn to dusk, trying to restore order, particularly in those parts which had suffered extensive fire damage. On the very first day the Japanese had asked him to help in putting the city back on its feet, and it was a colossal task. (In fact, it was to be six months before Buckeridge was interned in Changi.) His first problem was to control the dock fires, for at least twenty godowns were either blazing of smouldering. Mountains of coal were still on fire. A Blue Funnel liner was burning alongside the Empire Dock. On the shore opposite was the wrecked skeleton of a crashed Hurricane. Here and there in the adjoining streets were corpses—and also, Buck noticed, several dead cows, that must have belonged to the Dairy Farm herd. 'It gave the place a curiously Indian look.' A dozen fires still licked goods carriages in Singapore railway station. One platform was strewn with abandoned Army equipment—everything from official papers to a searchlight.

Buckeridge had been told to tour the few godowns that had not been bombed, to make certain they contained nothing inflammable. Some were filled with tinned food, others with bales of crude rubber. These were the sort of items he had half expected, but when he forced open the sliding doors of one particular godown, Buckeridge (who was not unfamiliar with colourful language) exploded into a string of oaths. For there in front of his eyes, was the one item of equipment for which he and the ARP chiefs had begged time and again, only to be told repeatedly that none existed in Singapore —neatly stacked rows of new helmets. They must have arrived even before the war started. 'While every civilian in Singapore had been begging for helmets, someone in authority had forgotten all about this little lot.'

Luckily for Buckeridge, the Japanese military officer in charge of the fire brigade was a Lieutenant Nakani, whom Buck found 'an exceptionally nice fellow who spoke excellent English, was well travelled, broadminded and full of consideration'. During the first few days Nakani asked Buckeridge to take him on a tour of the city. Most of the shops were still closed, the streets were deserted, and to Buckeridge it was like some unreal dream, sitting by the side of this intelligent, courteous man who seemed genuinely concerned, almost apologetic, for winning the war. He remembers that as their car swung round from Nassim Road into the wrecked, smashed-up Orchard Road, Nakani—almost as though to make polite conversation with a new acqaintance—turned to Buckeridge, and asked, 'What did you feel like when you heard we'd sunk the *Prince of Wales* and the *Repulse*?' For a moment Buckeridge could think of nothing in the way of a reply, until he blurted out the single word, 'Sad!' 'Naturally,' agreed the Japanese with genuine sympathy.

Buckeridge had a particular talent for making the best of any situation in which he found himself, and had made up his mind to 'stick it out with a grin', but once his determination faltered, and he could actually feel the blush of shame flooding his cheeks. He and Nakani were driving towards the East Coast road on their 'guided tour'. At the corner they had to stop, for nothing could enter the big, broad road, which was filled with a tired, straggling column of men, some carrying suitcases, others humping rucksacks or with paper parcels under each arm. All were marching east. They were the civilians—many of them his friends—on their way to Changi jail. He caught sight of Tim Hudson, straight-backed, beard jutting out. Buckeridge was in his fire brigade uniform, and 'I felt like a fifth columnist, sitting there in a big, comfortable car with a Japanese officer. I tried to smile cheerily at them but I had nothing to do it with. My face was out of commission.' Lt. Nakani, seeing his obvious anguish, gave a rapid order in Japanese to the driver, who backed the car swiftly away from the corner. 'I am very sorry,' murmured Nakani, with even more consideration than usual.

Not all the Japanese were as considerate, particularly on the occasions when Buckeridge was endeavouring to buy communal food supplies, for like other civilians in essential services, he went out twice a week to buy what he could in bulk. In theory it seemed a simple operation—but in fact all fresh meat, fish, bread and vegetables had by now disappeared. Occasionally Buckeridge would find a Chinese shop with a slender stock of tinned goods, but as he was completing his purchases a Japanese sentry would inevitably appear and arrest the Chinese 'for selling to the British'. Despite Buckeridge's protest—and his written slip of authority in Japanese—selling to the British was a heinous offence in the eyes of ordinary Japanese soldiers. On the other hand, while the fires still burned by the docks, Buckeridge had ample opportunity for 'a little quiet looting' from the stocks of food still remaining. He also received the occasional leg of pork

260

from an unexpected source—the Municipal Veterinary Surgeon, who for the time being had not been interned, and 'who appropriated certain pieces daily for examination purposes'. But perhaps the best meal of all arrived after one of Buckeridge's firemen ran across his old Malay driver, who offered to buy him a piece of beef. When the joint arrived, 'it turned out to be a refrigerated chunk of cowmeat, but in a casserole with tinned carrots, Simpsons in the Strand had nothing on it'.

While people like Buckeridge were still technically at liberty because the Japanese needed their help, 'Willie' Watt of McAlister's was finding it absolutely impossible to drive the eight miles from his house 'San Remo', near Changi, into Singapore for the express purpose of surrendering. On the Tuesday morning, as soon as the radio had announced that all civilians must parade on the padang, Watt and three friends who had been sharing his house set off for Singapore. They were allowed past several Japanese sentry posts along the East Coast road until they reached Kallang Bridge. Here the Japanese—who did not understand a word of English—were obdurate. They could not pass. Using sign-language, Watt tried to explain that he *wanted* to surrender, but the Japanese, wielding bayonets, 'demonstrated in no uncertain manner that our further approach would be our last'. There was nothing to do but return to 'San Remo' and pour out drinks from their whisky hidden in the lalang, while they discussed what their next step should be. Incredible though it may seem, there was no 'next step' for two weeks, for though the small party of Britishers did from time to time make contact with the Japanese, the enemy refused to do anything about their plight. And soon it did become a plight, for though they had enough money, and Watt had had the foresight to hide in the lalang a plentiful supply of his favourite 'Old Rarity' whisky (for which McAlister's fortuitously held the agency for Malaya) they had very little in the way of food. Some Japanese tried to be helpful, and went away with vague promises that never materialised. Others were aggressive—like the officer who hit Watt across the forehead with the scabbard of his sword, knocking him off his feet. Another officer arrived leading a party searching for a radio—at least Watt assumed he was, for his limited English seemed to consist entirely of the words 'Buzz, buzz!' Through an interpreter he warned Watt and the others to

261

remain just where they were without moving until the house had been thoroughly searched. Watt couldn't have been more delighted, for he was standing three inches from the back cushions of an old cane sofa under which the radio had been hidden.

One man still at liberty wondered what the future would hold for him. Leslie Hoffman was quietly keeping out of sight in his father's house at Serangoon, but he knew that somewhere the Japanese must have a file on him and the anti-Japanese articles he had written. There was nothing he could do at this stage but wait. His powerful new radio was working splendidly. On the morning after capitulation he had listened in to Churchill's sombre broadcast which had been relayed to the world. 'I speak to you all under the shadow of a far-reaching military defeat,' Churchill had said. 'It is a British and Imperial defeat. Singapore has fallen. All the Malay peninsula has been overrun.' At least, thought Hoffman, straining to catch every word from the whispering radio, Churchill had offered no lame excuses. Indeed he had cried, 'This is one of those moments when [the British Nation] can draw from the heart of misfortune the vital impulse of victory.'

As yet Hoffman's plans for helping in that victory were only vaguely defined. He had the radio. He could, he hoped, keep in touch with the world. He would have to find a way of passing that information on to those interned in Changi.

From the outset the nurses and doctors at the Singapore Club had realised their days of freedom were limited. Most of the civilian nurses at the Mental Hospital had been swept into internment within the first week, and now the Japanese gave notice that Fullerton Building had to be cleared by the end of the month. The next morning the doctors and nurses started the heartbreaking evacuation of desperately ill patients to the military prison at Changi. All extension splint cases were given a shot of morphia before being loaded up into the ambulances, but even so the most optimistic doctors admitted that not more than half would survive the rigours of the journey. Sick with the inhumanity of being forced to move them, Katherine de Moubray felt 'as though iron bands were compressing my chest, it was sheer physical pain.'

On the last day Freddy Bloom and the other MAS women went on a 'scrounging' expedition in the bedrooms of the Singapore Club, which were cluttered with suitcases and steamer trunks, left by members and their wives who had been hurriedly evacuated. Now the MAS women had their pick of everything they had left behind—not only dresses, shorts and blouses, but linen, towels and anything they could carry. Freddy Bloom 'hated the idea of opening somebody else's suitcases' but she consoled herself with the thought that if *she* didn't take the clothes, the Japanese most certainly would. She had almost finished her selection when a doctor rushed up to her and said, with an air of knowing, 'I've been told all the women are going to be repatriated. Take my tip, Freddy, and grab something warm for when you get to England.' On an impulse she seized a handsome fur coat— and doggedly kept it until she *did* arrive in England, nearly four years later.

On the final day at Fullerton Building, when the last patients had gone, the nurses and doctors had a special 'farewell lunch'—their last square meal for over three years. Despite the primitive nature of the 'hospital', the suffering had welded doctors, women volunteers, ambulance drivers, orderlies, into a warm-hearted community, more closely knit than they could ever have been in the antiseptic atmosphere of a real hospital. The ambulance drivers had gone out 'on the scrounge' to return with a case of pineapple chunks and—from some mysterious source they refused to reveal— more than enough beer to go round. It was a sad, but wonderful lunch, and after it was over and the time came for good-byes, Freddy turned to Philip, her husband of three weeks, and said, right from the heart, 'You know, darling, despite everything, I've never been so happy as I have been here.'

There were no opportunities for long farewells. The doctors were leaving in one set of lorries, the nurses in another, and they moved off immediately. Almost at the last moment a large soft object, expertly thrown, hurtled towards Freddy. It was a farewell gift from Philip, 'the most precious thing he could give me'—a mattress.

Almost at the same time as Freddy, clutching her mattress, was watching Philip's lorry take him away to internment, 'Willie' Watt was standing, a tommy-gun digging into his back, watching his own grave being dug. For two weeks he and his friends had been living 'off the land'. They had virtually given up trying to surrender, for each time they had made contact with another Japanese patrol nobody had seemed interested in helping them—until suddenly a new patrol arrived at the bungalow which was 'obviously not so friendly'. The four Britishers were marched for a couple of miles along the East Coast road to a big Japanese camp near Siglap. 'Several officers were approached,' Watt remembers, 'but would have nothing to do with us until eventually we struck one who appeared to know the answer.'

The four men were marched to an open space on the side of a hill. Out of the crowd of Chinese and Indians which had inevitably appeared, the Japanese soldiers plucked half a dozen men at random, gave them spades, and ordered them to start digging four graves for the Britishers. An Anglo-Indian with a tommy-gun was in charge, and Watt remembers that his entire Malayan vocabulary seemed to consist of 'Lekas! Lekas!' ('Hurry up! Hurry up!') In the broiling heat of noon, the gravediggers reached a depth of four feet. Watt's friend muttered under his breath, 'I don't like the look of this!'—a remark which Watt regarded as 'a mild understatement of the situation as I saw it'. He remembers that, despite the hot sun, 'I felt quite cold. I only prayed that we would have a quick despatch and not get knocked about in the process.'

The Britishers were surrounded by Japanese with bayonets and tommy-guns. The officer in charge held 'a sword nearly as big as himself' and it was painfully obvious to Watt that he was about to be beheaded. As the minutes ticked by, the gravediggers hurled out the last of the earth, and looked up expectantly at the Anglo-Indian guard and the Japanese officer.

And then suddenly, in an unbelievable finale, a senior Japanese officer burst through the guards. Furiously he shouted to the officer in charge of executions. As the arguing was all in Japanese, Watt never had the faintest idea what had happened. To this day he does not know. He remembers that at first he wondered whether perhaps the senior Japanese was only angry because of the large crowd of witnesses. But then it began to dawn on Watt that the execution officer was looking crestfallen and he was being roundly abused. The first wild hope of a reprieve began to make Watt's heart beat quickly.

With an agonising slowness the minutes ticked away in violent argument. Then Watt knew that—for the moment, anyway—he was saved. Abruptly the execution officer turned
264

on his heel and the senior officer, with polite gestures, ordered the four Britishers to march away from the graves. In the Japanese camp they were presented with passes to return to 'San Remo', together with a firm promise that arrangements would be made shortly for them to be interned. The four men 'celebrated our escape with half a bottle of "Old Rarity" whisky recovered from the lalang.'

The officer who had for some mysterious reason so dramatically intervened to save their lives was as good as his word. Within a week they were given passes to enter Changi jail. Indeed, they were even allowed to drive to the jail in Watt's car.

Only one thing had changed since the awful moment a few days previously when Willie Watt had stood waiting to be beheaded. His fine head of thick fair hair had turned snow white.

About this time—the beginning of March—the men were moved from their temporary quarters near the Sea View Hotel into Changi jail. A week later the second great march of the women and children covered the seven miles on foot from their temporary camp at Katong to Changi, where they were to be lodged separately. By now the numbers of women and children had swollen to four hundred with latecomers —including Dr. Cicely Williams, who had been forced through dysentery to give up her family of children. She had given away as many as possible, and had left the few who remained with a Chinese nurse and two amahs. The Bishop of Singapore, who was not being interned, had promised to look after them.

Only the old, infirm and ten pregnant women were allowed transport. The rest had to walk in a procession that straggled for miles. Some of the women pushed old prams or rickshaws filled with pots and pans, towels, even newspapers. All were dressed in whatever clothes they had been able to salvage. A woman near Freddy Bloom wore a lampshade to protect her head. Freddy remembers how she was dressed for comfort—in khaki trousers, a long-sleeved white evening blouse (as a protection against mosquitoes) her nurse's veil tied like a turban, and a big, black umbrella.

The march took almost a day, with rests each mile or so, often in the shade of rubber trees, or close to a Malay kampong or village half hidden by waving coconut palms or the deep green leaves of papaya trees. Sometimes the villagers shyly emerged with offerings of fruit. Others offered bottles of water which the thirsty women did not dare to drink.

It was four o'clock as the bedraggled procession, carrying its hand luggage and pushing its perambulators and rickshaws, finally reached its destination. Fifty yards or so from the prison gates the column stopped for a moment, as though to brace its collective shoulders for the march-in. At the head of the procession was one of the civilian matrons. She was tiny—just under five feet tall—but she was a human dynamo of immense courage. 'Come on now,' she cried, 'let's sing our way in.'

Someone started the 'Sea View' tune and, as they reached the prison walls, nearly four hundred tired cracked voices —as though given new strength and impetus for this one moment—were singing the tune so many of them had sung on that last sunny Sunday of peace. With the tiny matron leading the way, the women marched through the prison gates singing 'There'll always be an England'.

They must have sung lustily, for the sound of their voices penetrated to husbands, lovers, life-time friends on the other side of the high wall that divided Changi jail in two. A great burst of cheering from behind the wall drowned the noise of the gates being closed, and then the sound of men's voices, deeper, gruffer, more resonant, joined in the tune that belonged to them all, a tune that was a way of life put to words and music:

> 'There'll always be an England,
> And England will be free.'

CHAPTER TWELVE

THE YEARS OF AGONY

For three and a half years thousands of men, women and a handful of children were interned on the island of Singapore. None of the civilians had the remotest chance of making a dash for freedom from a speck in the ocean as escape-proof —and as evil as Devil's Island. And though it was hope and faith that sustained the majority, it was hard even to have any hope in those first months when it seemed that nothing on land, in the skies and on the oceans could arrest the all-victorious Japanese. 'We never *really* lost hope,' Tim Hudson remembered later, 'but it was damned difficult when you tried to analyse the reasons for hoping.'

Life was wretched. Malnutrition caused many deaths. So did the peculiar Japanese indifference to illness, so that, for example, chronic diabetics died simply because the Japanese refused to issue the insulin which existed in Singapore. Others died as the added privations advanced old age. The frail Mrs. Graham-White, who had introduced the half-naked survivors of the *Empress of Asia* at Freddy Bloom's wedding 'reception', quietly faded away because she did not have any hidden reserves of stamina to sustain her. Tommy Kitching died of a malignant disease which he had probably contracted before internment. Yet Lady Thomas—who was afforded no privileges of any sort—managed to survive despite the severe dysentery from which she had been suffering.

In the soldiers' camp at Changi military barracks (as distinct from the civilians in Changi jail) the long and terrible trek to the Siamese railway of death soon began. The lucky ones stayed in Changi, for those who were sent to the work camps died in their thousands. Yet both soldiers and civilians managed to keep their sense of humour—and, occasionally, so did the Japanese. When Captain H. L. Greener, an education officer, was interrogated by Lt. Yamaguchi, the following light-hearted conversation (of which Greener made a note immediately afterwards) took place.

Yamaguchi: Is it wise, do you think, to appoint a man with only one eye [Wavell] to watch over all India?

Greener: India can be fixed firmly with the glass eye. With the other he will watch the Japanese. (Japanese laughter.)

Yamaguchi: Are the Australians not worried that there are so many Americans in Australia, making advances to their women while they are away at the war?

Greener: They do not seem to worry. You see, we have great confidence in our women. (Laughter.)

Y: It is said that they are marrying many of your girls. There will be perhaps none left when you get back. Is that not bad?

G: Oh no. Those Americans will stay in Australia and we wish to increase our population.

Y: And who will your young men marry?

G: We shall send for some girls from America. It is only fair. (Laughter.)

Y: We are told the Americans in India have better conditions than the British, and they are stuck up.

G: People are often stuck up when they have more money.

Y: But will not such jealousy impair your war effort?

G: In the last war there was much jealousy. American and British troops used to fight in the estaminets in France. Yet we won the war together.

Y: I cannot believe there is affinity of spirit between the Allied Nations sufficient to win the war.

G: Do you believe that there is much affinity of spirit between the Germans and the Italians? (Loud and prolonged mirth.)[1]

Everybody made the best of a bad job, not only to bolster morale, but in a practical manner. Gardens started sprouting. Plays and concerts were produced. A school was started for the children in the civilian camp. Cicely Williams had never worked so hard doctoring the sick. Freddy Bloom became editor of the women's camp paper, while beyond the wall that separated men from women, clandestine short-wave radio sets went into operation, giving the camp a daily bulletin of what was happening in the rest of the world. The radios were miraculously contrived out of bits and pieces often smuggled into the camp with the help of the Chinese in Singapore who rallied magnificently to the aid of the internees. Many of the Chinese were discovered and tortured. Scores paid for their loyalty with their lives. Yet there always seemed to be another man eager to help, ready to step into the shoes of the one who had mysteriously disappeared.

Contact between the city and the camp was not difficult if one had nerve and courage. At first many Europeans were at liberty. But even when men like Buckeridge were interned after six months (to join Tim Hudson in a cell with flaking walls bearing the roughly painted sign 'Hudson's Bay') the Japanese needed to send small but regular parties of Europeans into Singapore for a variety of reasons, and though they always went under guard, sometimes the soldiers could be bribed, while others were so lazy it was easy to deceive them.

One man who had to make frequent trips to the city was

[1] Quoted in *The Japanese Thrust*.

Norman Coulson, a PWD water engineer who had flatly refused to leave with the ill-fated Nunn party. The water system at the Changi was constantly in need of repairs and replacements—no doubt helped by a little sabotage—and Coulson, as the only expert, was detailed to buy the spare parts in Singapore. Before long he was in touch with the Chinese underground, and—through go-betweens—with Leslie Hoffman, who was daily operating the short-wave radio he had concealed from the Japanese. In the hope that the news would seep into Changi, the British in India were broadcasting hours of morale-boosting personal items from wives, relatives, and friends of those in camp. Hoffman faithfully wrote down the simple, poignant messages—many telling a man in prison the one item of news he most wanted to know—that the wife he had evacuated was safe. The problem now arose of how to smuggle the news into camp, and Hoffman had to act with the utmost discretion, for almost immediately after capitulation he had been interrogated and beaten up by the Kempetei; and though he had been released after some weeks, he was still under suspicion. However, he and Coulson contrived an ingenious plan. Hoffman wrote the notes on rice paper. These were then delivered to a Chinese plumber, and each time Coulson visited Singapore he was able to hide the precious messages in the pipes and joints he bought from the plumber for the ancient pumps at Changi. In all Hoffman sent several thousand messages into Changi. It was then a simple matter (comparatively simple, that is) to relay the messages from the men's to the women's camp. (So efficient was the camp smuggling that, though Freddy Bloom was only allowed to see Philip once for a few minutes in three and a half years, they kept in touch with smuggled messages, and even managed to exchange Christmas gifts.)

For some the black deeds of the Kempetei started early. While most civilians were settling down in camp as best they could, Rob Scott was taken from Sumatra to Singapore in handcuffs and kept in solitary confinement for eight and a half months in a cell with no light or running water. Each day he was taken to the Kempetei headquarters in the YMCA building for cross-examination. At first sessions lasted fourteen hours a day, but as Scott laconically noted, 'later the interpreter got tired'. The Japanese demanded to know the most incredible details—everything from the name of Scott's grandfather to a list of Shakespeare's plays—this last wildly irrelevant topic because the Japanese had discovered a slip of paper on which Scott had written the quotation, 'Seeking the bubble reputation even in the cannon's mouth', and seized upon it as a code. During these months the Japanese used bluster, threats—'even beer on some occasions'—but no actual physical violence. And then in February 1943, 'I was suddenly released to the comparative paradise of ordinary internment'.

The indefatigable Scott was not idle for long. Soon he was playing a leading role in the secret camp news organisation—a committee of five which co-ordinated the operation of the increasing number of hidden short-wave receivers. The identities of the committee of control and of the camp operators, scouts, messengers, were known to only a few, and even inside the organisation many did not know the identities of their colleagues. It worked with astonishing efficiency for many months—until the fatal day of October 10, 1943.

On this day—known in Singapore as the 'Double Tenth'—a large force of Kempetei and Japanese troops without warning raided the camp. Scott remembers that 'I had the dubious honour of being the first to be arrested'. Every inch of the camp was searched and inevitably the Japanese discovered several indiscreet diaries of war news and camp activities. These were not fatal, but then, in the cell of one of the key men in the committee—a man who had operated a radio set—the Japanese discovered notes of a BBC news bulletin. The man was arrested. At first he feigned ignorance, but after weeks of torture he revealed the names of his colleagues —including Scott, Coulson and Hoffman. It was a disaster of the first magnitude to the camp, for about fifty internees, including two women—Freddy Bloom and Cicely Williams— were rounded up, together with a similar number of Asians in Singapore.

Some were released after a few days of questions; others were incarcerated for more than a year, and in this terrible period thirteen men died in the Kempetei cells of disease after torture. One was tortured to death. One man committed suicide rather than face the prospect of more torture. A man in Scott's cell cut his tongue out in front of Scott so that he could never betray his colleagues. Many who suffered diabolical torture were innocent of any 'crime'. One man was arrested, never once questioned, and kept for five months until he died of dysentery and medical neglect. As the torture proceeded, the waves of suffering spread to the entire camp. Rations were cut, even for children. Games, concerts, plays, lectures, school lessons were forbidden for months.

Soon after the Double Tenth the Kempetei swooped on the old house on stilts in Serangoon where Leslie Hoffman was living. As luck would have it, Leslie was not listening in that night and he had concealed the radio so well that the Japanese were never able to find it. Nonetheless he had been betrayed, and the Kampetei were convinced the set existed. For months Hoffman was brutally tortured—he was accused of being 'a Rob Scott spy'—but as with Scott, all the sadistic tortures the Kempetei could invent never broke him. Despite months in the cages, often starved for days at a time, beaten daily for weeks at a time, he never divulged the name of a single accomplice.

Freddy Bloom and Cicely Williams spent several months in one tiny cage which they shared with several men. They had no beds. Indeed, the sole item of 'furniture' consisted of a toilet—in full view of the men and the guard who watched them unceasingly through the bars. They had no protection against lice and mosquitoes. The only way to get any water for drinking or washing was to flush the lavatory. Night after night they were grilled, refused sleep, denied food. For several weeks Norman Coulson shared their cage. Day after day the man who had smuggled the news into camp was flogged with such severity that, in Freddy's words, 'his back and legs were as raw as liver in a butcher's shop'. After each beating, when the guards threw his limp body back into the cage, Freddy and Cicely cleaned his mangled flesh with the aid of one small handkerchief they had secreted, dipping it into the lavatory water to make some sort of cold compress.

Coulson must have been a man of extraordinary courage for Freddy remembers that one morning, just as he was about to be taken out for grilling, he said to her with a grin, 'You don't look your usual cheery self this morning!' Freddy told him not to worry—but she had suddenly got a raging toothache. Hours later, when a bleeding Coulson was dumped back in the cage, and the women tried to wash his wounds, he held out a tightly-clenched fist to Freddy. It contained one tablet of aspirin which a Japanese had given him, but instead of crunching it to ease his intolerable pain, Coulson had kept it for Freddy's toothache.

The most vicious torture of all, however, appears to have

been reserved for Rob Scott, and his punishment included one week in which he was never allowed to sleep, lie down or relax, and during which he was on half rations for the first four days, and given no food for the rest of the time. When not being questioned he had to squat, Japanese fashion, in front of the sentry, who could see at a glance everything inside the cage. During questions he was usually forced to kneel on a rack, sometimes tied by a wrist to a window, with his arm fully extended. Japanese sentries doubled his legs under him and jumped on the soles of his feet until the open wounds exposed the ligaments and bones. He was flogged repeatedly. He would be called out of his cell about 11 p.m. —'my interrogator preferred working at night'—put on a rack for a couple of hours in silence, then questioned for twenty minutes and beaten up for an hour. At last it would be over, and by 2.30 in the morning, Scott would be sent back to his cell. Then would come the worst torture of all. Tottering with fatigue and pain, he would be called out again only half an hour later—to go through the entire procedure once more. At the end of 'one hectic session' he was told he had been sentenced to death and compelled to write a farewell letter to his wife. 'I was then in such a state that the sentence left me unmoved, even when he announced the date and place, and brought in the sword with which I was to be beheaded, making me run my finger along the blade to test its keenness. In a way I welcomed the prospect, and regretted the reprieve twenty-four hours later, because it meant that the examination would be continued.'

Some died after torture—including Coulson and Hugh Fraser, the acting Colonial Secretary, who had driven out to Bukit Timah to make the first arrangements for surrender. Yet the fact remains that though Rob Scott had been singled out as the archcriminal, the Kempetei were never able to break either his spirit or his body. It was not only a question of bravery; a man needed reasoning; an understanding of the way the Japanese mind worked; and Rob Scott, with his lucid brain, was one of the few men able to analyse afterwards just how he had been able to keep on living, and indeed how he had been able to outwit the Kempetei in the physical and mental battle that lasted for over twelve months.

Scott realised immediately that behind the Double Tenth arrests lay a Japanese suspicion that the civilian camp harboured a big spy, sabotage and counter-propaganda organisation in radio contact with India. Early on this absurd suspicion became almost a certainty in their minds, and because of his background Scott was cast in the role of master spy. 'I was the super criminal.' They firmly believed this. From time to time they even flattered Scott. He was, said the Kempetei, 'more dangerous than a division of the British Army'. His name 'was known to every schoolboy in Japan'.

Scott, however, knew the mentality of the Kempetei. He likened them, in his brilliant unpublished report, to 'spoilt boys of fourteen, headstrong, selfish, brutal'. They had 'the schoolboy's imagination. As his mind teems with images of fighter pilots, Red Indians round the corner, spies, hidden treasures, so the Kempetei seemed to live in a world of melodrama where everyone and everything was suspect, all foreigners were spies, and the wilder the story the more fascinatingly probable it became.' Nothing was too outrageous. At one time Scott was accused of running a secret radio station in a tomb in a Chinese cemetery during the very time he had been locked up in solitary confinement miles from the spot. And he discovered another trait which was to prove invaluable. 'Like children they are sensitive to criticism', so that in the wary battle of wits that followed day after day, night after night—a battle in which Scott, despite his suffering, had to be constantly on the alert to avoid traps—he found one sure line of defence. Whenever he was flattered, he would insist that he was unworthy of the honour of being 'the man who had turned the people of South East Asia against the Japanese'. Inevitably he would then be asked who *was* responsible. And if the interrogation then took a dangerous turn, if Scott felt the Kempetei were setting a trap for him, he always had one further line of defence: The Japanese themselves, he would say, were to blame. Time and again he made this point—which, of course was true—and it never failed to infuriate them. As he wryly noted later, 'Anti-Japanese criticism of this type was most useful in distracting them when questions began to get embarrassing. The immediate results for me were usually painful, so I used this device as a last resort. It never failed to work.'

As the months dragged on, Scott, despite his suffering, was able to realise that his tormentors were getting less and less sure of their ground. Many internees had been tortured into giving conflicting stories. They would say anything to avoid torture, and as Scott puts it, 'The Japanese had collected too much evidence and did not know what was true and what was false. I began to sense a lack of certainty and assurance, however much they blustered and shouted. It became, in my mind, a race with time; could I by denials convince them that they were after a mare's nest, or at any rate so discredit the evidence collected as to shake their faith in it before I collapsed? I won, but only by a short head.'

With typical modesty, Scott in his report glossed over the terrible suffering he endured. But it is a fact that by keeping a tight hold on his reason Scott was able to beat the Kempetei, even though after months of torture and neglect he was suffering from bacillary dysentery, oedema, scabies and many minor ailments. And in the end the Kempetei gave up. They sent him back to the civilian camp, convinced he was about to die. Scott, who at the capitulation had weighed fourteen stone six pounds, had shrunk to seven stone ten pounds, and even with all the care the British doctors in camp could lavish on him, it was months before he could walk. In camp, however, he was at least able to get some extra food to supplement the miserable rations doled out by the Japanese. A flourishing black market had sprung up, and internees could buy goods on credit, signing chits to be paid at the end of the war. The prices were fantastic—butter cost $430 a pound, jam $280 a jar, while a tin of powdered milk cost $700. Scott signed the chits cheerfully—and is convinced to this day that without that extra nourishment he would have died.

Slowly the years of agony rolled on until men and women, who could hardly remember anything other than the stifling atmosphere of the camp, suddenly began to sniff a new and heady scent—the scent of victory, of liberation. V.E.-day came and went. On the secret radios—now operating again —news filtered through of the massive American naval victories in the Pacific, to be followed by the details of Hiroshima, so that almost before the prisoners realised what was happening, Cicely Williams, on one of her occasional medical visits to the men's camp, was startled to see a cheerful British soldier pat his Japanese guard on the back, whereupon the guard offered him a bar of chocolate.

Were the rumours of Japanese surrender true? asked Cicely Williams, whereupon the Tommy gave a reply that only a soldier could give.

'Don't worry, lady,' he grinned. 'The Emperor's signing on the dotted line next week.'

One more scene of internment must be recorded. Two men, talking earnestly, walked slowly round the perimeter of the camp. One was tall, thin and gangling, the other of more athletic build. One was a general, the other a brigadier. One was Percival, the other was Ivan Simson. Despite their differences during the war, despite that dramatic midnight meeting, despite even Percival's last-minute refusal to give Simson the opportunity to escape, a strange kind of friendship seems to have grown up between the two men. Perhaps it was because Simson was, after all, a loyal soldier to whom the Army meant more than life. And it was during one of these long walks together that Percival, as though unburdening himself of a secret he could no longer keep to himself, finally admitted to Simson that he had been wrong in refusing to build up the defences of the island. 'He was the only one of all the senior men to admit that his decision on defences had been wrong,' wrote Simson later, adding with characteristic charity, 'That goes a very long way in my opinion to expiate his first error.'

When freedom came on September 5, 1945, one of the first men to greet Rob Scott was Ian Morrison of *The Times*, who had arrived with the advance troops. Morrison had made no secret of his admiration for Scott, but in a curious way Scott could sense that his old friend was ill at ease. He seemed embarrassed. At last Morrison blurted out the truth. He had written a book about the fall of Singapore and it contained 'a sort of obituary notice' of Scott. For Morrison (in common with the Foreign Office) had for years assumed he had perished on the *Giang Bee*.

Scott managed a grin and said to Morrison, 'Don't worry —I'll write your obit for you!'[2]

To others, release came in different ways, but perhaps nothing was so typical of Chinese loyalty—and Chinese memory—as the moment when Tim Hudson stepped from internment to freedom.

Hudson had kept in fairly good health—though he had

[2] Scott did. When Morrison was killed in the Korean war, Scott happened to be in London, and went straight to *The Times* and wrote Morrison's obituary notice.

lost a great deal of weight—and he walked sturdily to the camp gates to savour the greatest moment of his life—a breath of fresh, free air. And he had barely moved outside before a small figure clutching a parcel elbowed her way out of the dense waiting crowd. She looked a little older—and she looked as though she, too, had suffered—but it was Mei Ling, carrying—just as she had done the night before Tim went into camp—a parcel of freshly-laundered clothes. 'They were still warm with the beautiful smell of a hot iron,' Tim remembers.

Rob Scott was involved in one last macabre incident that followed liberation, when Lt.-Colonel Sumida, chief of the Kempetei, was tried in Singapore. Scott was called to give evidence, which 'I gave reluctantly because I did not hold with war crimes' trials'. In fact Scott—as impartial and dispassionate as ever—went out of his way to show that the man responsible for so much torture had only been behaving in 'his own Japanese way'. Sumida was, however, sentenced to be hanged, whereupon he sent Scott a message 'thanking me for the fairness of my evidence'.

Rob Scott now did an extraordinary thing, which is best described in his own inimitable way. 'I thought that the least I could do, to close that chapter, was to go out and see him hanged. Which I did—rather closer than I meant to, as it began to pour with rain, and the only covered, sheltered spot in the prison yard was the scaffold, so I mounted it with the executioner, and stood to one side, an inch or so from the trapdoor, whilst it was sprung with Sumida on it.'

Considering the years of rigorous confinement and torture, it is astonishing how many of those who lived through that time are still extremely fit. One would have thought that the starvation diet, the sapping effect on morale, would have lopped a few years off the later years of their lives. But it seems to have made no difference. If any unconsciously needed time to adjust themselves, if any found it difficult to start normal lives again, they solved their problems in their own ways.

Brigadier Ivan Simson, who had hidden his secret report from the Japanese for three and a half years, decided that the best way to rid his system of the nightmare would be to expand the report into a longer work. It was not written so much for publication (in fact it was never published)

276

but for himself and his friends and to erase painful memories. It took him many years. Today Brigadier Simson, in his seventies, lives in an old rambling house of oak beams at Witney, the market town famous for its blankets. An old walled garden, with pear trees flattened against the dull bricks, gives him privacy. Perhaps Simson's back is not as straight as it was the night he bearded Percival in Flagstaff House, but he still has an alert, quick mind, and though his hair is now white, his moustache is still trim. He is an indefatigible correspondent, he drives a car, and in the summer of 1967 blithely set off on a motor tour of Austria.

The imperturbable 'Dickie' Dickinson, who had been so horrified at Duff Cooper's unseemly conduct, is another who has grown gracefully into old age. Still handsome—with a faint trace of spit and polish subtly transferred to his well-cut suits—Dickinson, in his seventies, lives a few yards from the Thames at Maidenhead. He bears no trace of the grenade that hit him as he stood on the balcony watching the first moments of peace. He too set off in the summer of 1967, to Italy and Greece, followed by a visit to Canada.

Of all people who might have been expected to require a long period of readjustment, Rob Scott comes high on the list, and there were some who doubted if he would ever be able to resume his brilliant career in the Foreign Service. Not at all. For some months Scott lay in a hospital in India. Though little more than a bag of bones, he began to fret so much for work to do—above all wanted to get his impressions on paper while they were still fresh in his mind —that he persuaded the Foreign Office to send him a typist. When she arrived, Scott firmly grabbed the typewriter and told the young lady to go away and enjoy herself. He preferred to do his own typing; and it was in hospital that he wrote his two lucid reports—one on the sinking of the *Giang Bee*, the other on his torture—that summed up so brilliantly the problems involved between the different races.

Predictably, Rob Scott had a meteoric rise in the Foreign Service, becoming Minister at the British Embassy in Washington, followed by spells of duty as British Commissioner-General in South East Asia, Commandant of the Imperial Defence College, and finally Permanent Secretary at the Ministry of Defence until he retired in 1963—retired being a comparative term, for he still serves on countless committees. He received a knighthood and a string of letters after his name. Now Sir Robert lives in an old disused railway station near Peebles in Scotland, which he has transformed into a delightful split-level house set amidst the rolling countryside he loves so much.

Leslie Hoffman also had a remarkable rise in his profession. After the war he moved from the *Tribune* to the *Straits Times*, and he recently received the Malayan equivalent of Rob Scott's knighthood. Today he enjoys the title of Dato Leslie Hoffman, and is now editor-in-chief of the influential *Straits Times* group.

Others took up less predictable careers. Who would have guessed that Jimmy Glover, who had so often crossed swords with authority and government, would eventually work *for* the British government in London? After his escape from Singapore Jimmy was reunited with Julienne in India, where he worked on propaganda until Singapore was liberated. When he returned to the city where he had made his career, he found it difficult to settle down, and after some years he and Julienne moved to England.

Tim and Marjorie Hudson are two others who have had a full and rewarding life. Though he had not been tortured, Tim was in poor shape when he arrived back in England on one of the first evacuation ships. Marjorie was waiting to greet him at the docks, and whisked him away to a small village in Devonshire. And there she kept him for a year until he was fit again—despite pleas from Dunlop's that they badly needed his services in Singapore. Tim *would* have gone—only Marorie never let him see the letters until she was satisfied he was well. Besides, there was something else. Tim and Marjorie had never had any children, and so while they were in Devonshire they adopted a baby girl called Bridget. A year or so later the three Hudsons returned to Singapore where Tim worked until 1954, when he returned to England. Both he and Marjorie felt that it was time Bridget had a brother or sister, even though it did not seem that they would ever have any children of their own.

They now took an extraordinary, courageous step. They were offered, in exceptional circumstances, an unborn child. They contracted to take it. It turned out to be another little girl whom they named Melanie. And exactly three weeks after welcoming Melanie to the Hudson household, Marjorie became pregnant for the first time in fourteen years of marriage. Before the end of the year Heather arrived, and today the Hudsons are one of the happiest, closely-knit families it is possible to imagine. They live near Ashford in Kent, in a house facing the rolling countryside, with apple blossom in the spring, and fields of tawny corn in the autumn; and where Marjorie Hudson has, of all things, become one of Britain's leading breeders of Siamese cats.

Fame has come to Dr. Cicely Williams, who at the age of 73 lives an active life that would be the envy of many women half her age. Though she is based in London, she still roams the world, mostly on lecture tours. In June 1967 she flew to Atlantic City to be awarded the Joseph Goldberger medal for her original work on nutrition. It was the first time in history that the award—made by the American Medical Association in conjunction with the Nutrition Foundation—had ever been made to a foreigner. A few months later Cicely Williams had a farewell dinner with Philip and Freddy Bloom, then set off on a year's world tour, lecturing and advising in places as far apart as Australia and Jamaica.

Oddly enough, while Cicely Williams, an Englishwoman, received an American award, Freddy Bloom, the American who shared her Kempetei cage, received a British award— the OBE—for her untiring efforts over twenty-five years to help deaf and handicapped children. Her marriage to Philip Bloom has never looked back and today they have two fine grown-up children and live in London, near Philip's consulting rooms in Harley Street. Though Philip was not the sort of man who needed time to readjust himself to civilian life, the war in Malaya and the years in captivity were directly responsible for him becoming one of the pioneers in Britain in a field of medicine which had previously received only scant attention. Before the war Philip had been a gynaecologist, but—as Freddy puts it—'He didn't have much opportunity to practise his profession in camp.' Philip had, however, always been attracted by the problems of sexual maladjustment, and his interest in this field was heightened during captivity. As soon as possible after the war he became a consultant on sexual and marital problems, and has now reached the peak of his profession with a practice in London's West End. On February 6, 1967, they held a party to celebrate the twenty-fifth anniversary of that strange wedding ceremony in Fullerton Building during an air raid. Freddy was still wearing the sapphire ring Philip had bought from a street trader on the way to the registrar's office.

Some have died, of course. Though Lady Thomas is still alive, Sir Shenton Thomas, who fought to the end of his life to vindicate the slurs cast on 'whisky-swilling planters', died in 1962 aged 83. Duff Cooper, who became Ambassador to France and later Lord Norwich, died at sea in 1954, a few days before his sixty-fourth birthday. General Percival was 79 when he died a broken man in 1966. And though the events of Singapore speak for themselves, one cannot help a feeling of sympathy for the general who was expected to fight to the last man without any air or sea power.

And some, of course, could not bear to leave their beloved Singapore. 'Willie' Watt, who watched his own grave being dug, is now in his seventies, and retired in 1965 after forty-three years with McAlister & Co., the last twelve years as chairman. He is passionately addicted to racing. The walls of his flat in Rochalie Drive are lined with photographs of his winners—and he still keeps ample stocks of 'Old Rarity', the brand of whisky he hid in the lalang during the crazy days when the Japanese refused to allow him to surrender. George Hammonds has not only stayed in Singapore (he, too, worked in India till Singapore was liberated and then joined the *Straits Times*) but has taken up Singaporean nationality. He looks upon the city as his real home, and he felt that the only right thing to do was to become a citizen of the city and country he had chosen.

Two more will never leave Singapore—'Buck' and Lucy Buckeridge. Buck is in his sixties, Lucy ten years younger, and when Buck retired from the fire brigade in 1957 he and Lucy took a trip round the world for the express purpose of choosing the ideal country in which to retire. They never found a country they liked better than Malaya, so they returned, and will stay in Singapore for the rest of their lives. Lucy Buckeridge, who had helped so many penniless evacuees with cash loans, left Robinson's when Buck retired, but in 1960 the firm's chief accountant died suddenly, and Robinson's begged her to help out for three months until they could find a replacement. Lucy said she would—and has remained at Robinson's ever since.

It was the sameness of Singapore that had first astonished the internees when they were freed from their prison camps after three and a half years. Somehow they had vaguely expected the Japanese to have left their own imprint on the
280

great city and port, to have changed it visually and physically. Instead they found it very much as they had left it, and though there have been vast changes in Asia since those far-off days twenty-six years ago—changes involving the independence of Malaya and Singapore—there is still in a curious, haunting way a sameness about the city to remind the wanderers returned of the grim days of 1941 and 1942.

Perhaps it is the weather—the pitiless sun or the pelting rains of the monsoon thrashing against the rattan blinds. Or perhaps it is because Singapore is an island port, so that as one's ship steams in towards Keppel Harbour, past the hot, shimmering, outlying islands, one's first sight is as it always was: an overwhelming sensation of green after days at sea, the lines of waving palms, the unchanging apparatus of dockland, the same pewter-coloured petrol tanks. Fullerton Building is still a landmark on Collyer Quay, and Battery Road, linking it with Raffles Place, is still as narrow as ever, though Maynards the chemists, where Mrs. Jackson used to superintend the facials, has disappeared, and Gian Singh, the nearby food store where Europeans brawled for a few tins of cigarettes just before the capitulation, is now a bank. But the shape of the streets in the centre of the city, the squares, the sports grounds of those days are totally unchanged, Robinson's still dominates Raffles Place. Kelly and Walsh, where Tim Hudson was given two books to take into camp, has been replaced by an airline booking office, but behind it the narrow bustling Change Alley is still thronged with tourists in search of bargains or sailors in search of girls.

But it is in Chinatown that one experiences the greatest sense of sameness, and if one takes a taxi—larger now than the old yellow Fords, and air-conditioned too—and drives through Chinatown with its families squatting over their rice bowls beneath the flags of washing, one will eventually land up near the Pulo Saigon Bridge, still looking like an outsized Meccano model, and unchanged since the day when its steel girders were blazing from end to end. Below it the Singapore River is still covered with a patchwork quilt of sampans. Raucous voices cry their wares as the waterboats and food hawkers make their daily rounds. Agile, skinny Chinese leap from one floating family to another, past women cooking rice and fish in the same kind of coalpots that Cicely Williams used to save the lives of the children she later gave away. And above all, the sweet and sour stink of the river, an odour no old Singaporean can ever fail to recognise, permeates the air.

It gives one an almost uncomfortable feeling of never having been away, even after all these years, and the sensation persists as one drives back towards 'white' Singapore, for though this is now an Asian country, nothing seems to have changed physically. The civic centre—the Municipal Buildings, the Supreme Court, the Memorial Theatre—still functions as it did under previous masters. The cathedral, surrounded by its green sward, has not been changed by so much as a stone or a new flower-bed since the days when 'The Rev.' hurriedly cleared the nave to make room for the wounded. Raffles Hotel is still there, though its barn-like lounge, where Leslie Hoffman served steaks during a raid, is now enclosed and air-conditioned. The Central Fire Station in Hill Street still looks the same—and there is still the old balcony where Hudson and Buckeridge sat drinking a stengah as they watched the rockets to the north announce the Japanese landings on the island. In South Bridge Road the balcony where Dickie Dickinson was hit by a grenade is unchanged. And along Bukit Timah Road, down which the Japanese tanks thundered in their last advance, orchids still blossom on the banks of the canal. With independence there are new schools, enormous housing projects, new buildings, so that the city has spread, of course; but even so, the outskirts still hold a fascinating mixture of city and jungle, with one moment the roar of cars, the next the croak of bullfrogs; in the old-fashioned bungalows Tamils still scythe the coarse lalang, and the glimpses of attap huts, bright green banana trees, the heavier leaves of papaya, produce a nostalgia that is almost overpowering.

In Stevens Road, where Tim and Marjorie Hudson used to live, hardly a house has changed, and their bungalow is just as it was, with the bank of lawn leading down from the verandah to the garden and the hedge of hibiscus still screening the garage where Tim used to keep his sturdy little Hillman. Orchard Road, where Tim dug frantically with his hands after Marjorie had been buried by a bomb, boasts a few more tall buildings, a few more bars, a new magnificent hotel, but otherwise it is the Orchard Road of yesterday, with the fruit and vegetable market still at the corner of Cuppage Road near the splendid white building of the Cold Storage where Julienne Glover was caught in the gas bomb scare.

One might have thought that with independence at least Government House would have gone, if only to appease those to whom it was a symbol of centuries of Colonial government. But no, Singapore has a rare tolerance (and for that matter a rare sense of gratitude) and today nothing has changed to the eye. The hundred acres of green grass are as immaculately kept as on that fateful evening when Shenton Thomas paced the lawns after Percival had told him of the first Japanese landings. But no one lives any longer in the white elephant of Government House, and the vast dining-room where Lady Thomas sheltered under the table is denuded of furniture. One corner of the rambling, ornate building is used for government offices, and another wing has been refurbished to offer hospitality to important guests.

As the day's work ends, as the heat begins to wane, Singaporeans still foregather on the broad balcony of the Cricket Club facing the padang for an evening stengah. Here, with the sea on one side and a line of flame trees on the other, one is certain to stumble into an old friend as one watches Asians and Europeans happily playing tennis or football together in this club where once only whites were allowed. And it is then that a last bizarre thought comes to end this tale of blunders, of vacillation, of the greatest debacle in the history of British arms, in which thousands of men and women of all races and creeds died in the mythical fortress which no one would, or could, help in its death throes.

It is the trite observation that out of all evil some good can come; that the Asians, whose country Singapore now is, have ironically to thank the Japanese in some measure, for it was the Japanese victories in battle that destroyed forever the legend of the white man's supremacy, and so set in motion a train of events throughout Asia which led to eventual independence. And though it is true that the Allies returned to liberate the countries, it was never quite the same again. The awe, the *mystique* surrounding the *tuan bazar* had gone forever, and in Singapore it was only a question of time before the frenetic, humid, opulent port that is unlike any other in the world ceased to be known as Europe's gateway to the east, but rather as Asia's gateway to the west.

BOOKS CONSULTED

An asterisk marks those from which quotations have been used.

ABEND, HALLET, *Ramparts of the Pacific* (John Lane, The Bodley Head, 1942)

ALLBURY, A. G., *Bamboo and Bushido* (Robert Hale, 1955)

*ATTIWILL, K., *The Singapore Story* (Muller, 1959)

*BENNETT, LT.-GEN. H. GORDON, *Why Singapore Fell* (Thacker, Bombay, 1945)

BHARGAVA, K. D. and SASTRI, K. N. V., *Indian Armed Forces in the Second World War, S.E. Asia 1941-42* (Combined Inter-Services, Historical Section, India, 1960)

BRADDON, RUSSELL, *The Naked Island* (Werner Laurie, 1952)

BROAD, LEWIS, *The War that Churchill Waged* (Hutchinson, 1960)

BUGGY, HUGH, *Pacific Victory* (Robertson & Mullens, Melbourne, 1947)

BULCOCK, ROY, *Of Death but Once* (F. W. Cheshire, Melbourne, 1947)

CHAPMAN, F. SPENCER, *The Jungle is Neutral* (Chatto & Windus, 1949)

*CHURCHILL, WINSTON S., *War Memoirs* (Six Volumes, Cassell, 1948-54)

CLARKE, BLAKE, *Pearl Harbour* (The Bodley Head, 1942)

*COOPER, DUFF, *Old Men Forget* (Hart Davis, 1953)

CREW, F. A., *The Army Medical Services*, Vol. II (H.M.S.O., 1957)

*DONAHUE, A. G., *Last Flight from Singapore* (Macmillan, 1944)

EHRMAN, JOHN, *Grand Strategy*, Volumes II, V, VI (H.M.S.O., 1956)

ESPOSITO, BRIG.-GEN. VINCENT J., *A Concise History of World War II* (Pall Mall Press, 1964)

GALLAGHER, O. D., *Retreat in the East* (Harrap, 1942)

GILMOUR, O. W., *Singapore to Freedom* (Burrows, 1943)

*GLOVER, E. M., *In Seventy Days* (Muller, 1946)

GRAVES, PHILIP, *Record of the War, The Tenth Quarter* (Hutchinson, 1942)

GRENFELL, CAPT. RUSSELL, *Main Fleet to Singapore* (Faber, 1951)

HARRISON, KENNETH, *The Brave Japanese* (Angus & Robertson, 1967)

HOUGH, RICHARD, *The Hunting of Force Z* (Collins, 1963)

KASE, TOSHIKAZU, *The Eclipse of the Rising Sun* (Cape, 1951)

KERR, GEORGE F., *Business in Great Waters* (Faber, 1951)

*KIRKBY, MAJOR-GEN. S. WOODBURN, *The War Against Japan*, Vol. I, *The Loss of Singapore* (H.M.S.O., 1957)

LOCKHART, BRUCE, *The Marines Were There* (Putnam, 1950)

MCCARTHY, DUDLEY, *Australia in the War 1939-45*, *S.W. Pacific Area* (Army) (Australia War Memorial, Melbourne, 1959)

MACKENZIE, COMPTON, *Eastern Epic* (Chatto & Windus, 1951)

MACMILLAN, NORMAN, *The R.A.F. in the World War* (Harrap, 1950)

MAXWELL, SIR GEORGE, *The Civil Defence of Malaya* (Hutchinson, 1944)

*MORRISON, IAN, *Malayan Postscript* (Faber, 1942)

MOUNTBATTEN, VICE ADMIRAL EARL, *Report to the Combined Chiefs of Staffs* (H.M.S.O., 1957)

ODGERS, GEORGE, *Australia in the War 1939-45*, *War Against Japan* (Air) (Australia War Memorial, Melbourne, 1957)

ONN, CHIN KEE, *Malaya Upside Down* (Jitts & Co., Singapore, 1946)

OWEN, FRANK, *The Fall of Singapore* (Michael Joseph, 1960)

PERCIVAL, LT.-GEN. A. E., *The War in Malaya* (Eyre & Spottiswoode, 1949)

*PLAYFAIR, GILES, *Singapore Goes off the Air* (Jarrolds, 1944)

RICHARDS, DENIS & SAUNDERS, HILARY ST. GEORGE, *The Fight Avails* (H.M.S.O., 1952)

RIVETT, ROHAN, *Behind Bamboo* (Angus & Robertson, 1950)

ROBERTS, DENIS RUSSELL, *Spotlight on Singapore* (Anthony Gibbs and Phillips, 1965)

ROSE, ANGUS, *Who Dies Fighting* (Cape, 1944)

ROSKILL, CAPT. S. W., *The War at Sea*, Vol. II (H.M.S.O., 1956)

ROSKILL, CAPT. S. W., *The Navy at War* (Collins, 1960)

SLEEMAN, COLIN & SILKIN, S. C., *The Double Tenth Trial* (Wm. Hodge, 1951)

STEWART, BRIG, I. MCA., *History of the Second Argyll & Sutherland Highlanders* (Nelson, 1947)

SLIM, SIR WILLIAM, *Defeat into Victory* (Cassell, 1956)

STRABOLGI, LORD, *Singapore and After* (Hutchinson, 1942)

*TSUJI, MASANOBU, *Singapore—The Japanese Version* (Constable, 1960)

WALKER, ALLAN S., *Australia in the War 1939-45*, *Middle East and Far East* (Medical) (Australia War Memorial, Melbourne, 1953)

WAVELL, GEN. SIR ARCHIBALD, *ABDA Command* (H.M.S.O., 1948)

WAVELL, FIELD MARSHAL, *Speaking Generally* (Macmillan, 1946)

*WIGMORE, LIOÑEL, *Australia in the War, the Japanese Thrust* (Angus & Robertson, 1958)

*WINANT, JOHN G., *A Letter from Grosvenor Square* (Hodder & Stoughton, 1947)

DOCUMENTS CONSULTED

ANONYMOUS, The Alexandra Hospital Outrage, The Imperial War Museum.

BROOKE-POPHAM, AIR CHIEF MARSHAL SIR ROBERT, Official Dispatch (*London Gazette* 22.1.48)

Fuehrer Conferences on Naval Affairs (Berlin, 1942)

LAYTON, VICE-ADMIRAL SIR GEOFFREY, Official Dispatch (*London Gazette* 26.2.48)

MALTBY, AIR VICE-MARSHAL SIR PAUL, Official Dispatch (*London Gazette* 26.2.48)

PERCIVAL, LT.-GEN. A. E., Official Dispatch (*London Gazette* 22.6.48)